CITIES, POVERTY, AND DEVELOPMENT
Urbanization in the Third World

To Jacqueline,
Daniel and Susanna

To Janine,
Saskia and Rachel

CITIES, POVERTY, AND DEVELOPMENT

Urbanization in the Third World

by
ALAN GILBERT
and
JOSEF GUGLER

OXFORD UNIVERSITY PRESS

Oxford University Press, Walton Street, Oxford OX2 6DP
Oxford New York Toronto
Delhi Bombay Calcutta Madras Karachi
Petaling Jaya Singapore Hong Kong Tokyo
Nairobi Dar es Salaam Cape Town
Melbourne Auckland
and associated companies in
Berlin Ibadan

Oxford is a trade mark of Oxford University Press

Published in the United States
by Oxford University Press, New York

© Alan Gilbert and Josef Gugler 1981

First published 1982
Reprinted with corrections 1983, 1984, 1987
Reprinted 1989, 1990

British Library Cataloguing in Publication Data
Gilbert, Alan
Cities, poverty, and development,
1. Cities and towns—Underdeveloped areas
—Growth
I. Title II. Gugler, Josef
307.7'6'091724 (expanded) HT119
ISBN 0-19-874084-0 ✓

Library of Congress Cataloging in Publication Data
Gilbert, Alan, 1944–
Cities, poverty, and development.
Bibliography: p.
Includes index.
1. Underdeveloped areas—Urbanization. 2. Under-
developed areas—Cities and towns—Case studies.
3. Underdeveloped areas—Housing. 4. Underdeveloped
areas—Poor. 5. Sociology, Urban. I. Gugler,
Josef. II. Title.
HT169.5.G53 307.7'6'091724 82–6297
AACR2
ISBN 0-19-874084-0

Printed in Great Britain by
Billing & Sons Limited,
London and Worcester

PREFACE

The twentieth century may come to be seen as the age of urbanization. Urban settlements were first established more than five thousand years ago, but as recently as 1900 only one in eight people lived in urban areas. Before this century is out half of mankind, three billion people, will live in urban settlements and two thirds of that number will live in the Third World.

In this book we are attempting to provide a comprehensive account of Third World urbanization, spanning three continents and several academic disciplines. Our collaboration brought together backgrounds in economics, geography and sociology, extensive experience in Latin America and in Africa, and lengthy periods of interest in urban issues. We were aided by a body of research and writing on Third World urbanization that has expanded at a fast pace over the last decade. Along the way we were assisted by friends and colleagues. Most easily traced are the contributions made by Floyd Dotson, David Drakakis-Smith, Susan Eckstein, William G. Flanagan, Howard Handelman, Peter Kilby, Tony O'Connor, Henry Rempel, and Peter Ward, all of whom made useful comments on individual chapters. Josef Gugler would also like to acknowledge the support of the American Institute of Indian Studies for a stay in India that allowed him to become familiar with urbanization research in the subcontinent, to express his appreciation to colleagues and students at the Population Studies Center, University of Pennsylvania, who provided a stimulating environment for final revisions during a visiting appointment, and to thank Betty G. Seaver, editor extraordinary. We thank Yvonne Gavon and Claudette John for their typing of numerous drafts and Christine Daniels who prepared the figures.

We recognize that despite these people's efforts all too many shortcomings remain. One issue in particular merits comment. We have drawn on a heterogeneous body of research and writing; across the regions the quality of information available, the disciplinary emphasis of such information and its ideological perspective vary strikingly. We have attempted to provide a comprehensive account of this information and have sought broad generalizations. But the task has proved daunting and important aspects of the urban development process have been treated inadequately. We hope the reader will recognize the inevitability of such gaps and will find merit in our survey of the urban transition taking place in three diverse continents.

London and Storrs, ALAN GILBERT
February 1982 JOSEF GUGLER

CONTENTS

TABLES

FIGURES

INTRODUCTION

The literature on urban development is vast and growing daily. The very volume of this literature, added to its often specialized nature, makes much of the writing inaccessible even to the expert. Much useful work in sociology is unknown to economists, political scientists, planners, or geographers; much interesting Latin American work is unknown to Asian specialists. To help overcome this problem is one of our principal reasons for writing this book. Our main objective is to review current theoretical ideas about urbanization and poverty and to apply those ideas to the diverse conditions found in the Third World. To date, interesting ideas have often been developed and tested only within a particular country or region. For example, 'dependency' theory was developed largely in the context of Latin America, the role and influence of urban ethnic associations tested mainly in Peru and West Africa, and the concept of circular migration examined only in the Pacific region and in Southern Africa. Few ideas or phenomena have been considered comparatively across different areas of the Third World. Our aim, therefore, is to explain the more interesting theoretical concepts and to examine their relevance to Latin American, Asian, and African experience.

Clearly, this is not an unambitious task. For a start, the process of urban development is part of the comprehensive phenomenon of societal change. The main objects of our study, the city, the poor, and the Third World, all form part of a complex reality which requires some consideration of factors which, at first sight, seem to be divorced from our main theme. Since urban growth in poor countries is linked integrally to rural change and since the development or underdevelopment of the Third World is linked to the process of development in the First World, we are forced to discuss, at least superficially, giant issues such as the broad sweep of world history over the past five centuries, the current world economic situation, and the meaning and nature of 'development'. In this respect, recent changes in the social sciences have strongly influenced the form of this book. During the seventies, studies of the less developed world, and indeed of urbanization generally, have increasingly shifted their attention towards what is commonly known as a 'political economy' approach. It is a move towards a more holistic and class-based view of society, away from a functionalist, positivist, and consensual view. In the field of development studies the rise of 'dependency' and 'neo-Marxist' schools of thought have shifted the scale of analysis away from the individual. Instead of considering how individual peasants respond to rural–urban income differentials, current work focuses more on the causes of those differentials. Poverty and its manifestations are no longer perceived as something attributable to an individual person, city, or country, or remediable by national governments using technical planning processes. Rather, poverty, or more accurately the state of relative poverty, is seen to be a consequence of a historical process of incorporation into the world capitalist system. To use Dos Santos's (1970) much quoted term, the economies and societies of poor countries have been 'conditioned' by their relationship with colonial and neo-colonial powers.

In urban studies a parallel shift towards a radical approach has occurred; Castells (1977a) and others have reformulated the urban question. They have attacked the belief that urban form emerges through a neutral process of individual decision making. For Castells and Harvey (1973), urban areas can be understood only in terms of the conflicts between classes which are a direct outcome of the operation of the capitalist mode of production; urban form, urban issues, urban government, urban ideology can be understood only in terms of the dynamic of the capitalist system. Space is socially determined: the outcome of conflicts between different social classes. Urban 'problems' have arisen not by chance or through mismanagement but because the interests of one or other social class fraction have been served by the emergence of such problems. Squalid back-to-back terraced housing in British cities was built for low-paid workers; it was not in the interest of dominant groups to replace it. 'Urban disorder was not in fact disorder at all; it represented the spatial organization created by the market, and derived from the absence of social control of the industrial activity' (Castells, 1977a: 14-15). State planning can reduce such disorder but cannot remove it, for resources are allocated on the basis of a struggle between competing groups. Ideally, the process of planning allocates these resources fairly among all groups and integrates society through its decisions; in reality, it does not operate that way. Those who wield political power influence planning decisions against the interests of the powerless. Planning does not serve the public interest because there is no such interest (Simmie, 1974; Saunders, 1980).

Of course, some analysis of these issues has always been included in urban and development studies, but the paradigm shift has raised them from the second or third rank of importance to top place. This book has been strongly influenced by that paradigm shift. Rather than pose the issue of what governments should do to remedy the obvious problems facing the Third World urban poor and how individuals should act in a particular urban situation, we ask why particular phemonena have occurred in the first place and indeed why specific governmental reactions have evolved in the way they have? To a much greater extent than many previous writers concerned with Third World urbanization, we are concerned with the issue of power and the subsequent allocation of resources between nations and between classes. Why are decisions made in the way they are, who benefits and who suffers from those decisions, and what is the relationship between urban development, society, and the State?

We follow the approach of the new paradigm in so far as we accept that conflicts between social groups have an important bearing on the structure of Third World societies and therefore on the process of urbanization. We agree with much Marxist writing about the ideological nature of many of the earlier studies of urban development and planning (Castells, 1977a) and in much of the book we follow a <u>political-economy approach</u> to the analysis of urban issues. At the same time, we differ from some of the writing of the far left in accepting the possibility that the living conditions of the urban poor may actually improve without socialism. Running through the book, therefore, is a normative component which offers some hope for reorganizing society without revolution. This is not to deny that in many Third World societies some form of revolution is necessary. Our position is to suggest that since the Third World contains such a diverse range of societies, generalization of the order that social revolution is, inevitable and essential may be too embracing. Where revolutions have occurred it is by no means obvious that socialism has overcome the worst economic and social difficulties. The worst forms of inequality have been eliminated, but not always to the accompaniment of rising living standards. To an extent, we agree with Lefebvre (1970, 220) that 'the same problems (of urbanism) may be found under socialism and under capitalism with the same absence of response.'

But if we are less optimistic of the outcome of revolution to recommend it as a general strategy, we have no doubt that the <u>world economy is organized to the detriment of the great majority of mankind</u>. <u>To a large extent, the poor in the Third World are poor because the rich in the First World are rich.</u> Few indigenous Third World societies were Utopian before Europeans set sail to reach them, but there can be no doubt that the arrival of Cortés, Cook, Vasco da Gama, and much later, of Henry Ford's machines and Rockefeller's oil rigs, <u>had a traumatic effect on most of those societies</u>. If the idea conveyed in Haley's *Roots* of merrie indigenous Africa (and by implication of merrie Asia, Latin America, and Melanesia) is erroneous, the superimposition of colonialism and capitalism has hardly created the cheerful, cosmopolitan world of the Coca Cola advertisements. <u>The most that can be said is that poor, unequal, somewhat isolated Africa eventually became somewhat less poor, much more unequal, distinctly more populous, and decidedly more integrated into the world economy.</u> Change there was, but little progress. <u>We would not deny that economic growth occurred in many parts of the Third World, and that inequalities were reduced in some instances, but there can be no doubt that such developmental opportunities as arose were only very partially realized.</u> Third World countries are characterized by underdevelopment, by patterns of economic growth and income distribution that are little geared to increasing the welfare of the masses. If we are not sanguine about the prospects, we still foresee a measure of economic growth for Third World countries, and we perceive increasingly powerful pressures towards some reduction of the more blatant inequalities among nations and within nations. We are tempted to speculate that the idol of economic growth is losing adherents in the industrialized world and that the rich will agree to reduce the yawning gap that separates them from much of humanity. If we are not prepared to abandon hope for the future, there is certainly every reason for alarm at the slow pace of such improvements as can be discerned at this time. The Brandt

Report may have reached the media headlines, but it is not long since the Pearson Report did the same. The first Development Decades have come and gone, the world has changed, but the poor are more numerous than ever.

We are raising these issues because the process of urbanization cannot be understood in isolation from social differentiation, political conflict, the operation of governments, and the nature of the dominant economic system. The future of the Third World city cannot be understood without questioning the basis of the world division of labour and the interests of governments ostensibly managing cities. Part of the reason that much of the academic discussion of urbanization and planning in the Third World has been so anaemic is that it has avoided such issues.

Within this broad perspective we compare the processes of urban change in different Third World countries. We are seeking to generalize, but are aware that the differences in the ways in which poor countries were integrated into the world economy has created many distinctive urban features. More women migrate to cities in Latin America, but more men migrate in most Asian and African countries; many families invade land in Latin American cities, but organized squatting is less common in most African and Asian cities; urban areas house most Argentines and Mexicans, but a minority of Indians and Ghanaians. Why have these differences emerged and to what extent are they tending to disappear as the international economy ever widens its embrace? How far can we generalize meaningfully about urban conditions and about the prospects for change? By comparing the literature on African, Asian, and Latin American cities and societies, we hope to demonstrate both the strengths and the weaknesses of recent generalizations emerging from the new social science paradigm. In writing this book, we are seeking to unravel some of the main issues that will determine our future. Understanding may not bring change, but change rarely occurs without it.

The Third World

Throughout the book we use the much abused phrase the 'Third World' to refer to the world's poor countries. We are well aware of the deficiencies of this term. It may be that there are now more accurately six worlds (O'Connor, 1976) or four worlds (Wolf-Phillips, 1979), it may be that the older terms, such as less developed countries, developing nations, poor countries, etc., are equally appropriate descriptions, it may be that there is no meaningful distinction between the First, Second, and Third Worlds. Our use of the term 'Third World' merely reflects current usage: it is the most frequently employed general term to describe poor countries. Included in the Third World in this book are those countries whose populations had a per capita income below 3,000 dollars in 1978 or a life expectancy of less than seventy years (World Bank, 1980: 148-9). This arbitrary, if still meaningful, dividing line means that all the nations of Asia,

Africa, Latin America, and the Caribbean are included with the exceptions of Israel, Japan, Hong Kong, and Singapore. Unlike some authors, therefore, we include several poor countries often described as part of the Second World; socialist, centrally planned economies such as Cuba, the People's Republic of China, Vietnam, Laos, Kampuchea, and the Democratic Republic of Korea. We have included them because of their poverty and because of their still recent colonial experiences. Perhaps more debatably, we exclude the nations of under-developed Europe (Seers, 1979); nations that in terms of per capita income and life expectancy are little different from the poor nations we have included. While Portugal, Yugoslavia, Albania, and Romania all fall below our statistical dividing line and might justifiably be included in the Third World, we have excluded them largely on the grounds of convention.

Current Patterns of Urbanization

Even if Berry (1976) has noted signs of counter-urbanization in the United States and other highly developed nations, the world's population is becoming increasingly urban. In the Third World the pace of urban growth has over the past thirty years been truly dramatic. Since 1950 the proportion of the Third World's population living in cities has roughly doubled from its initial 16 per cent (Abu Lughod and Hay, 1977: 90). Fuelled by high rates of natural increase, rapid in-migration, and changes in rural society, urban areas have grown immensely in most parts of the Third World. Major cities have been expanding at rates of 5 per cent or more, so that most of the world's major metropolises are now found in the less developed countries.

Table 1.1
Urban Population Share by Major World Regions, 1920–1975 [a]

World Region	1920	1940	1960	1975
Europe	34.7	39.5	44.2	48.2
United States and Canada	41.4	46.2	58.0	65.4
Soviet Union	10.3	24.1	36.4	46.4
Oceania	36.5	40.9	52.9	57.1
East Asia	7.2	11.6	18.5	23.7
South Asia	5.7	8.3	13.7	17.4
Latin America	14.4	19.6	32.8	40.5
Africa	4.8	7.2	13.4	18.1
Developed nations[b]	29.8	36.7	45.6	52.1
Less developed nations[c]	6.9	10.4	17.3	22.2
The world	14.3	18.8	25.4	29.7

[a] Urban places are those with more than 20,000 inhabitants.
[b] Includes Europe, the United States and Canada, the Soviet Union, and Oceania.
[c] Includes Asia, Latin America, and Africa.
Sources: Frisbie (1976: table 4); UN (1969: table 31).

Table 1.2
Urban Population Growth and Development Indicators for Selected Third World Nations

Country[a]	Urban population as per cent of total population[b]		Annual rate of urban growth[b]		Per capita income[c] (US dollars)	Annual growth in p.c. income[c]	Life expectancy at birth[c]	Total population[c] (millions)
	1980	1960	1960–70	1970–80	1978	1960–78	1978	1978
Mozambique	9	4	6.6	6.8	140	0.4	46	9.9
Upper Volta	9	5	5.3	4.1	160	1.3	42	5.6
Malawi	9	4	6.6	6.2	180	2.9	46	5.7
Tanzania	12	5	6.3	8.3	230	2.7	51	16.9
Uganda	12	5	6.3	7.0	280	0.7	53	12.4
Kenya	14	7	6.6	6.8	330	2.2	53	14.7
Ethiopia	15	6	6.1	6.9	120	1.5	39	31.0
Madagascar	18	11	5.1	5.2	250	-0.3	46	8.3
Guinea	19	10	6.2	6.1	210	0.6	43	5.1
Mali	20	11	5.4	5.5	120	1.0	42	6.3
Nigeria	20	13	4.7	4.9	560	3.6	48	80.6
Angola	21	10	5.1	5.8	300	1.2	41	6.7
Zimbabwe	23	13	6.8	6.4	480	1.2	54	6.9
Sudan	25	10	6.9	6.8	320	0.1	46	17.4
Senegal	25	23	2.9	3.3	340	-0.4	42	5.4
Zaire	34	22	5.2	7.2	210	1.1	46	26.8
Cameroon	35	14	5.6	7.5	460	2.9	46	8.1
Ghana	36	23	4.6	5.2	390	-0.5	48	11.0
Ivory Coast	38	19	7.3	8.2	840	2.5	46	7.8
Zambia	38	23	5.4	5.4	480	1.2	48	5.3
South Africa	50	47	2.8	3.1	1,480	2.5	60	27.7
Sub-Saharan Africa[d]	23	14	5.6	5.9	375	1.3	47	319.6
Nepal	5	3	4.3	4.7	120	0.8	43	13.6
Bangladesh	11	5	6.7	6.6	90	-0.4	47	84.7
Thailand	14	12	3.6	3.5	490	4.6	61	44.5
Afghanistan	15	8	5.4	5.6	240	0.4	42	14.6
Indonesia	20	15	3.7	3.6	360	4.1	47	136.0
India	22	18	3.3	3.3	180	1.4	51	643.9
Vietnam	23	15	5.3	5.1	170	–	62	51.7

China, People's Republic	25	19	3.1	3.4	230e	3.7	70	952.2
Sri Lanka	27	18	3.7	4.3	190	2.0	69	14.3
Burma	27	19	4.0	3.9	150	1.0	53	32.2
Pakistan	28	22	4.3	4.0	230	2.8	52	77.3
Malaysia	29	25	3.5	3.5	1,090	3.9	67	13.3
Philippines	36	30	3.6	3.8	510	2.6	60	45.6
Korea, Republic	55	28	4.8	6.4	1,160	6.9	63	36.6
China, Republic	77	36	4.1	3.3	1,400	6.6	72	17.1
Korea, Democratic Republic	60	40	4.3	5.0	730	4.5	63	17.1
*Low-income Asia*d	30	19	4.2	4.3	459	3.0	58	2,194.7
Yemen Arab Republic	10	3	7.3	7.5	520	—	39	5.6
Morocco	41	27	4.5	4.3	670	2.5	55	18.9
Egypt	45	38	3.0	3.4	390	3.3	54	39.9
Turkey	47	30	4.6	5.1	1,200f	4.0	61	43.1
Iran	50	34	4.9	4.7	2,160f	7.9f	52	35.8
Syrian Arab Republic	50	37	4.7	4.8	930	3.8	57	8.1
Tunisia	52	36	3.8	3.8	950	4.8	57	6.0
Algeria	61	30	6.4	6.1	1,260	2.3	56	17.6
Saudi Arabia	67	30	6.5	7.5	7,690	9.7	53	9.2
Iraq	72	43	5.4	6.2	1,860	4.1	55	12.2
*Middle East and North Africa*d	50	31	5.1	5.3	1,763	4.7	54	195.4
Bolivia	33	24	4.3	4.1	510	2.2	52	5.3
Guatemala	39	33	3.7	3.6	910	2.9	57	6.6
Ecuador	45	34	4.5	4.4	880	4.3	60	7.8
Dominican Republic	51	30	5.3	5.8	910	3.5	60	5.1
Brazil	65	46	4.3	4.8	1,570	4.9	62	119.5
Cuba	65	55	2.4	2.9	810	-1.2	72	9.7
Peru	67	46	4.4	5.0	740	2.0	56	16.8
Mexico	67	51	4.5	4.8	1,290	2.7	65	65.4
Colombia	70	48	3.9	5.2	850	3.0	62	25.6
Chile	81	68	2.4	3.1	1,410	1.0	67	10.7
Argentina	82	74	1.8	2.0	1,910	2.6	71	26.4
Venezuela	83	67	4.2	4.7	2,910	2.7	66	14.0
*Latin America*d	62	48	3.8	4.2	1,225	2.5	63	312.9

a Countries with populations of more than 5 millions are included.
b World Bank (1980: 148–9).
c World Bank (1980: 110–11)
d Unweighted averages.
e Estimate.
f 1977.

Of course, rates of urban growth differ widely throughout the Third World. Latin America has long been the most urban of the continents and it is not surprising that after three or more decades of rapid cityward migration, the pace of urban growth has begun to slow there. Currently, it is the least urbanized nations that are experiencing the highest rates of urban growth, notably tropical Africa, Melanesia, and parts of the Middle East. The broad patterns can be seen in tables 1.1 and 1.2 and in figure 1.1. Throughout the world there is a broad correlation between levels of urbanization and levels of economic development. Lofman (1979) has calculated that among Third World nations there is a correlation coefficient of 0.75 between GNP per capita and the percentage of population living in urban areas. Clearly, some areas, such as North Africa and the Middle East, diverge from this pattern since they have a long history of urban development, and others, such as the Persian Gulf states which, although they now have high levels of per capita income, are still essentially rural. But the broad picture conveyed by figure 1.1 is still one in which most developed countries are highly urbanized and the countries of the Third World contain major areas of rural population. There is of course a spectrum of urban development, with Africa the least urban, then Asia, then Latin America, then Europe and North America.

These facts are by now well known and there seems little point in describing in detail the statistics of Third World urbanization. We have included only basic information and refer those interested in more specific data to consult basic reference works such as Davis (1969) and the United Nations Demographic Yearbooks. The only points we wish to underline are that while the world is becoming rapidly more urban, there are major variations between regions, and that the forms of this urbanization vary considerably between the developed and the less developed nations and indeed within the Third World itself.

Patterns of Inequality

The patterns and processes of urban development that we describe in this book are those of an unequal world. There is no way in which the process of urban development can be understood in isolation from the processes that generate that inequality. We have already referred to the inequalities that exist at the world level but there are also important inequalities within Third World countries. Table 1.3 indicates the extent of this inequality. The poorest quintile of households received as little as 1.9 per cent of total household income in Peru and a maximum of 8.7 per cent in Taiwan, compared to the top decile of households, which received from 24.7 per cent of total household income in Taiwan to 50.6 per cent in Brazil. Unweighted averages of these figures demonstrate that Third World countries as a group are less equal than industrialized countries, the top decile receiving 35.0 and 26.3 per cent of total household income respectively. At the other end of the scale the difference was less marked, whether calculated

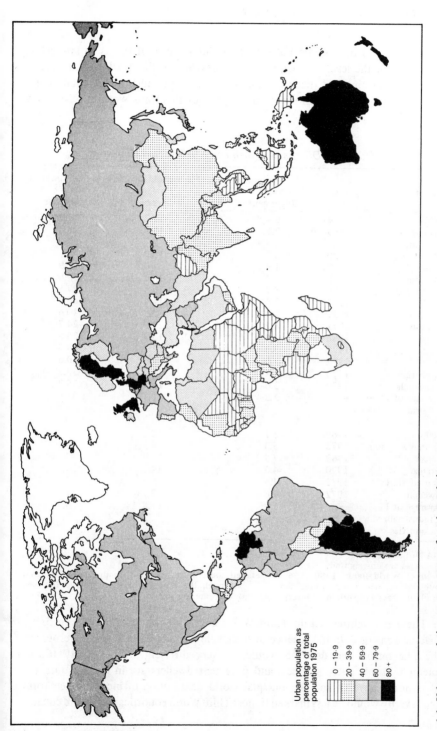

Urban population as
percentage of total
population 1975

	0 – 19.9
	20 – 39.9
	40 – 59.9
	60 – 79.9
	80 +

1.1 Urban population as percentage of total population

for the bottom one or the bottom two quintiles. Even if this is an interesting comment on the levels of inequality still prevalent in the developed nations, it should be remembered that these are low shares of a much higher total household income. Poor households in most parts of the Third World receive a low share of a very small total.

Table 1.3

Household Distribution of Income in Selected Countries

Country	Year	Percentage share of household income by household group		
		Lowest 20 per cent	Lowest 40 per cent	Top 10 per cent
India	1964–5	6.7	17.2	35.2
Sri Lanka	1969–70	7.5	19.2	28.2
Honduras	1967	2.3	7.3	50.0
Philippines	1970–1	3.7	11.9	NA
Peru	1972	1.9	7.0	42.9
Malaysia	1970	3.3	10.6	39.6
Korea, Republic	1976	5.7	16.9	27.5
Turkey	1973	3.4	11.4	40.7
Mexico	1977	2.9	9.9	40.6
Taiwan	1971	8.7	21.9	24.7
Chile	1968	4.4	13.4	34.8
Costa Rica	1971	3.3	12.0	39.5
Brazil	1972	2.0	7.0	50.6
Argentina	1970	4.4	14.1	35.2
Venezuela	1970	3.0	10.3	35.7
Average of Third World Countries	—	4.2	12.7	35.0
Italy	1969	5.1	15.6	30.9
United Kingdom	1973	6.3	18.9	23.5
Japan	1969	7.9	21.0	27.2
France	1970	4.3	14.1	30.4
United States	1972	4.5	15.2	26.6
Sweden	1972	6.6	19.7	21.3
Average of 12 Industrialized Countries	—	6.0	17.8	26.3

NA Not available
Averages are unweighted
Source: World Bank, 1980: 156–7. Detailed sources are provided on pp. 164–5 of that publication, which also notes that '. . . although the estimates are considered the best available, they . . . should be interpreted with extreme caution.'

These inequalities within Third World countries condition the urban forms that have emerged. In the absence of such wide inequalities in access to resources, the phenomena we describe would be very different. While shanty towns, unemployment, petty services, and pavement dwellers are in part an outcome of national poverty and the unequal world distribution of income, their form and severity would be less marked if most Third World countries were more equal.

URBAN DEVELOPMENT IN A WORLD SYSTEM

Urban form is a direct outcome of the ways in which different societies are organized. In an unequal world, therefore, it is not surprising that cities should also be unequal. Indeed, it has been argued that cities have served élite groups throughout history and that it is only in élitist societies that cities can actually develop. Wholly egalitarian societies based on what Polanyi calls 'balanced reciprocity' cannot produce cities. Without a central power and a mechanism to generate a surplus over consumption and to concentrate it into urban areas, cities cannot grow. It is only in societies based on 'redistribution', where a surplus over consumption can be appropriated by a particular group, that urbanization is possible. But, the fact that urbanization depends upon some mechanism to concentrate wealth does not lead us very far. Through time, the world has contained a wide range of urban societies with fundamental differences between them. The theocratic societies of ancient Mexico or China, for example, supported urban areas very different from most contemporary cities. The ancient cities contained administrative and religious élites who were supported by the agricultural surplus extracted through a combination of military force and moral pressure. In so far as the élites in these societies posed as the representatives of God and even as gods themselves, their rural subjects had little choice but to offer tribute. By contrast, modern industrial societies rely less upon force, although European colonialism and contemporary military dictatorships suggest that force is scarcely alien to capitalism, and more upon a complicated web of interlinked interests. Capitalist societies contain élites as powerful as those of theocratic societies, but the mechanisms for generating and accumulating a surplus are clearly very distinctive. Rather than justifying tribute in terms of religious or magical functions, the ideology of capitalism legitimizes urbanization in terms of its contribution to the growth of the gross national product. Whether all capitalist cities perform that role is a debatable issue. Certainly, a case can be made that urban areas in developed countries are 'generative' in Hoselitz's (1957) sense; the services of the banks and finance houses of London have long generated income for the rest of Britain, as have the factories of Birmingham and Manchester and the ports of Liverpool and Southampton. But they are also as 'parasitic' as the cities of the Third World with respect to the natural resources and the primary products emerging from the less developed countries. Throughout the world cities extract surplus, whether it be from local agricultural areas or from half-way across the globe. Today large areas of the world are integrated into a single economy. Rural areas and mining centres produce for distant populations and consume products manufactured far away. Within this world economy, individual cities perform specialized functions and their individual prosperity depends greatly upon their position in this economic system. Indeed, it is one of the major arguments of this book that the size, role, and characteristics of individual cities reflect the world roles of the societies of which they form a part. Thus the evolution of a city in the American Middle West or in southern India cannot be understood solely in terms of its local or even its national functions; its development is dependent on the way it is linked into the wider system. Needless to say, the strength of the linkages between different cities and the world system vary greatly. Nevertheless, in so far as the development of the world economy has created an interlinked economic system, different cities perform the roles allocated to them within that system.

In this respect, the modern world is different only in degree from the ancient world. In the past, regions were allocated roles by an imperial power and the cities within those regions reflected those roles. In the Roman Empire major communication centres, such as Alexandria, and cities that controlled rich agricultural regions, such as Damascus, acted as administrative centres of the empire and grew in size and prosperity; at the apex of the urban hierarchy was the imperial capital. The magnificence of Rome was generated by the tribute or surplus available to it. In this sense, it would seem to support Sjoberg's (1963: 220) proposition about urban growth in the pre-industrial world: 'at any given stage of technological development, the grander the empire, the grander the size and number of its cities.'

But should this proposition be confined to the ancient or pre-industrial worlds? Perhaps its value is nowhere better demonstrated than in the development of British cities up to 1900. London, for example, has always had national importance, but its growth since 1500 has been stimulated by its position as one of the centres of world power. Spanish silver and gold stolen by pirates such as Drake, Hawkins, and Vernon sustained sixteenth-century and seventeenth-century England. The slave trade and other forms of international commerce maintained momentum in the seventeenth and eighteenth centuries along with the expansion of colonies in the Americas. The activities of the East India Company extracted huge revenues for Britain during the eighteenth century in India (Chamberlain, 1974; Dutt, 1968). Rapid urban expansion, however, awaited the industrial revolution of the eighteenth century. During the nineteenth century the growth of the textile, steel, and engineering industries led to the unparalleled expansion of Manchester, Glasgow, Liverpool, Birmingham, and the mill towns of Lancashire and Yorkshire. Such industrial and urban expansion, of course, did not benefit all of Britain's trading partners; not every nation accepted the principles of liberal political economy. And when other less enlightened nations objected to the logic of free trade, or other European powers attempted to limit British penetration through political means, Africa, Asia, and the Caribbean were formally enlisted into the British Empire. Latin America was not incorporated into the formal empire, but British capital built railways, extracted nitrates, stimulated the expansion of cattle and cereal production, and generally accelerated export-based growth. A combination of military force, advanced industrial technology, and improved communications created and sustained both a formal and an informal empire. The great Crystal Palace Exhibition of 1852 is apt enough comment on Britain's reliance on the rest of the world. Victorian Britain's wealth and self-confidence, and therefore the greatness of its cities, were based on its foreign 'empire'. British cities expanded and the British urban system evolved on the basis of this new world division of labour.

Britain was exceptional but not atypical. Most of the great cities of Europe evolved and prospered on the basis of foreign empires: Paris, Madrid, Amsterdam, Vienna are notable examples. The grandeur of European, and indeed North American, cities at the turn of this century can only be explained in terms of the international division of labour and the evolution of a world urban system.

Urban Expansion in the Third World

The cities of Europe and the United States would have emerged in less grandiose form without the benefits of empire but urbanization in the Third World would have been very different. Karl Marx once described modern history as the 'urbanization of the countryside'; it is a peculiarly accurate aphorism for most parts of the Third World. Indeed, it is possible to argue that without the intrusion of industrial capitalism and imperialism some Third World societies would still lack major cities. In major parts of America and Africa urban development was superimposed by capitalism on essentially rural societies. In Peru, Mexico, India the Middle East, and China, where indigenous urban civilizations had already developed, urban forms were radically altered. The impact of European expansion from the sixteenth century onwards transformed urban structures in the Third World. The functions and forms of contemporary Third World cities cannot be understood without a consideration of this process. As Hoselitz (1953: 204) has pointed out 'the cities of contemporary underdeveloped countries are hybrid institutions, formed in part as a response of the indigenously developing division of social labour and in part as a response to the impacts made upon less advanced countries by their integration into the world economy.' The next few pages will describe this process of European capitalist penetration and its effects on Third World urbanization.

The most obvious effects of European and later United States expansion in the Third World were the creation of new cities, the generation of new urban forms, and sometimes the destruction of existing urban cultures. In Latin America the Spanish removed most signs of the conquered civilizations. The great cities of the Incas and the Aztecs were demolished and replaced by new Iberian architectural forms. Thus Tenochtitlán, the Aztec capital, was destroyed and Mexico City erected on the same site: the sacrificial temples of Moctezuma and his conquered civilization were replaced by a Catholic cathedral and the new city's main square, the Zócalo. Similarly in Peru, Cuzco, the 'city of the sun', was obliterated as the Spanish superimposed their own urban forms on Inca society. During the next three centuries the Spanish created a wholly new urban form and settlement system in the Americas. Small towns based on a central square, a church, and a gridiron street pattern were established throughout the Spanish realm (Hardoy, 1975; Morse, 1971). Many cities were constructed in previously non-urban areas; most of today's major cities were built by the Spanish: Lima, Buenos Aires, Bogotá, Caracas, Veracruz, and La Paz were all founded by the new Spanish masters. Elsewhere in South America, the Portuguese assumed a similar role and established most of Brazil's contemporary major cities including Rio de Janeiro, São Paulo, and Salvador de Bahia.

The process of urban growth came earlier and was more marked in the Spanish and Portuguese empires than elsewhere, but in other parts of the 'traditional' world the arrival of Europeans was eventually to lead to the foundation of cities which were to dominate the emerging settlement systems. Some of the fort settlements established by the British, French, and Portuguese along the shores of West Africa were to become the 'primate' cities of the twentieth century; only where urban patterns were long established, in the Sudanic belt and among the Yoruba, were European cities less influential. In the rest of Subsaharan Africa, the story was similar: Johannesburg, Cape Town, Nairobi, and Salisbury were all established by Europeans.[1] Similarly, in Asia Europeans built new urban forms which complemented the existing interior cities of the Indian and Chinese civilizations. Europe built coastal cities to act as foci for trade, cities which were to become future metropolitan centres. Thus in India, while the ancient cities of Delhi and Hyderabad survived in modified form, the British founded Calcutta, Bombay, and Madras. Only in China, North Africa, and parts of the Middle East do the indigenous centres still dominate the urban systems, albeit with certain foreign additions and considerable modifications.

Throughout the 'traditional world' Europeans destroyed, transformed, or distorted indigenous civilizations. The newly founded cities reflected the new power structures and exercised functions relevant to the interests of Europe. They were beginning to become part of a world economic and social system. They were moving towards an equivalent, international position to that Sjoberg (1963: 223) describes for the cities of traditional empires.

The lower ranks of the ruling élite have often resided in the lesser cities scattered about the realm so that the hierarchy of cities has reflected, albeit crudely, the status system in the society as a whole. These lesser cities have been situated astride the principal communication routes; thus the local or provincial rulers could maintain contact with the control centre — the capital — and the key political function.

The new cities clearly reflected the aims of European expansion and the social system being superimposed on the new territories. The Spanish aimed at the conquest and subjugation of the indigenous populations in America and the Philippines. New territories were to provide wealth for the crown and their populations were to be 'civilized' and converted to Catholicism. The city was the instrument of conquest. New cities were established throughout the empire and each urban area granted jurisdiction over a large tract of land and its dependent population. The first of the newcomers tended to pre-empt land surrounding a new town and to incorporate municipal commons into private ownership. These newcomers

maintained discipline, accorded civil and criminal justice, and distributed the dividends of enterprise-as-conquest: the assignment of native labor in encomienda for estates, mines and public works, the disposition of tribute and services owed by the new Amerindian vassals incorporated or in process of incorporation into the new order. At the local level, the colonial conquerors, transformed rapidly into mine operators, large-scale agricultural proprietors, and cattle ranchers, consolidated their position in the town councils whose members they chose. They were the local aristocracy no matter what their metropolitan social origins. (Stein and Stein, 1970: 70–1)

City and country became inextricably linked with most of the conquerors living in the city and most of the conquered in the countryside. The city became the centre of the local aristocracy and the main link in the chain of political control held by Spain.

In South-East Asia cities were also the vanguards of the new colonial and trading empires. At first, the modest trading aims of the Westerners were represented in small maritime towns which were scarcely rivals of the great inland metropolitan capitals. They competed only with the towns of the coastal Asian traders. But, as Western technology exerted its superiority and Europeans began to dominate regional patterns of trade, the towns came to reflect this dominance. By the nineteenth century the European cities were the main centres of power.

European cities prospered throughout the Third World. In Latin America they benefited from control over land and labour. Elsewhere cities grew more on the basis of trade, although most gained from their location between the imperial capital and the outer edges of the empire. But such a position also limited their autonomy; their roles were limited by the nature of their relationship with the 'mother country'. In the Caribbean, and indeed in colonial America generally, the functions of cities reflected the limited freedom given to the colonies by the colonizing power. As Clarke (1974: 224) points out, 'historically, Caribbean towns were ports, administrative centres, retail outlets but never locations for manufacturers. They were pre-industrial by predilection and prescription.' When the colonies became politically independent there was little change in their position in the world system. Most Latin American societies had gained their independence by 1830, but by then they were already strongly integrated into the world trading system, and they were to become still more enmeshed over the next fifty years.[2] In Asia and Africa political independence came much later and therefore gave the cities in these societies still less scope for an independent existence. In many cases the only change independence brought in Asian and African cities was to substitute local citizens for European administrators and élites.

Dependent Urbanization

There are close parallels between our present argument and the school of thought that emerged in Latin America known loosely as 'dependency' theory. The critical argument in this approach is that Latin American development has been 'conditioned' by the region's incorporation into the capitalist mode of production (Dos Santos, 1970). The social and economic structures that have emerged in the region represent the outcome of a historical process of interaction with Iberian, then British, and later North American expansion. This interaction explains the economic and social-class formations that have emerged in Latin America, the urban structures contingent on those formations, and indeed the structure of trade, technology, and investment between the developed world and Latin America. Later authors (Wallerstein, 1974; Amin, 1974; Emmanuel, 1972) have applied this argument to other parts of the Third World.

Dependency formulations gained wide circulation largely as a result of the work of André Gunder Frank (1967: 1969). Given the popularity of Frank's work, it is perhaps necessary to qualify some of the ideas presented in his early writings. Frank argued that Iberian conquest absorbed pre-Columbian America into the world system of capitalism. As a result of this incorporation, economic surplus was extracted by Spain (mainly in the form of silver) and Portugal (mainly through cotton, sugar, and gold) and later, when Spain and Portugal became economic dependencies of newly industrialized Britain, the surplus found its way to Britain. Latin America was therefore linked into a chain of surplus extraction which both 'developed' Britain and 'underdeveloped' Latin America; development and underdevelopment were not to be viewed as separate processes but as different outcomes of the same process. The chain of surplus extraction created centres and peripheries both on a world scale and within Latin America. At a world scale, Latin America came to supply the developed countries with raw materials and in return imported manufactured products. At a regional level the major cities acted as the centres, with the provinces and rural areas relegated to peripheral status. The Latin American city acted as a crucial link in the chain of surplus extraction. Within the city local élites benefited from foreign domination and from the periphery's underdevelopment. Once political independence had been won, the interests of those dominant national élites were to perpetuate the process of dependent development and to impede structural change. Rural underdevelopment and poverty for the masses were the inevitable outcomes of this historical process.

Today, this is seen to be a crude and somewhat inaccurate account (Palma, 1978; Oxaal, Barnett, and Booth (eds.), 1975; Roxborough, 1979). First, Frank was clearly wrong in asserting that the arrival of Cortés and Pizarro led to the immediate incorporation of Latin America into the capitalist system. As Laclau (1971) indicates, a distinction must be made between capitalism as a mode of exchange and capitalism as a mode of production. The exchange of products on a market basis is a necessary, but not a sufficient, condition of capitalism. What is required is a shift in the ownership of the means of production and the emergence of classes; a bourgeoisie and a proletariat. Even today some parts of Latin America remain to be fully incorporated into the capitalist mode of production.

Second, the aftermath of the Iberian conquest modified existing productive systems in a multitude of ways. In some places subsistence agriculturalists farmed much as they had always done, merely giving the surplus to the Spanish rather than to the Aztecs or the Incas. Elsewhere, *haciendas* emerged whereby the Indian communities were forced to work on the land of the *hacendado* in return for the right to work their own plot of land. In still other places plantations were established as the mechanism of surplus extraction. Clearly the process was similar in the sense that surplus was generated for the benefit of local and foreign élites. On the other hand, recognition of the fact that pre-capitalist forms of enterprise survived and in some cases were re-created by the new élites introduces a whole new level of sophistication into the argument (Pearse, 1975).

Third, it was implicit in the Frankian argument that the process of surplus extraction had impoverished Latin America, even though the facts suggested a different interpretation. For example, the investment of British capital in Argentina and Uruguay had created railways, urban infrastructure, and the basis of cattle, wool, mutton, and cereal production. The incorporation of many areas into the capitalist mode of production had generated wealth. It was first pointed out by Cardoso (1972) and Warren (1973) that a necessary distinction should be made between 'dependent' development and impoverishment. While impoverishment might be the outcome of capitalist expansion in certain areas, in others it might increase material prosperity. In such areas, surplus would be extracted by dominant class interests but from a larger product. Poor groups would not become poorer, the process was one of relative, not absolute, exploitation.

Fourth, the local impact of export generation differed considerably. According to the nature of the export product, regions might prosper or decline. As Furtado (1971) has argued, the size and the form of the multiplier linkages were critical factors in determining the regional effect. Bolivian tin, employing few miners and offering little opportunity for local processing, created few multiplier effects. By contrast, Colombian coffee and Argentinian wheat established large numbers of producers, stimulated the construction of railway networks, and encouraged industrial development, thereby offering an opportunity for local expansion (McGreevey, 1971b; Balán, 1976).

Current interpretations of dependency theory all accept these arguments, but differ widely on many issues (Palma, 1978). Indeed, differing strands of Marxist and neo-Marxist thought have created a position where there is no such thing as dependency theory, probably no longer a single dependency approach, and conceivably not even a recognizable dependency school. While this debate is critical at the theoretical level and for political prescription, it is less important for the current theme. What is critical here is to underline that the developed and the underdeveloped countries did not emerge independently; the development of the one was integrally related to that of the other. The dominant social formations and productive systems of the Third World have emerged in response to colonial and capitalist development. If social and economic formations in the Third World have been 'conditioned' by the expansion of capitalism, urban forms have clearly been affected by a similar process. It is this argument that has led to Castells' (1977a) invention of the term 'dependent urbanization' and to Harvey's (1973: 232) statement that 'global metropolitanism is embedded in the circulation patterns of a global economy ... different city forms are contained within that economy.'

The following discussion stems from this argument. The present forms of urban development in the Third World can be understood only as an outcome of the historical process of expansion by capitalist powers. At the same time, the effect of that expansion cannot be understood except in terms of the nature of raw-material production and the forms of the indigenous societies that were incorporated. In the next few pages I shall consider the process of urbanization in the light of these two different sets of factors. I shall first examine the nature of indigenous societies, their urban institutions, their economic and military strength, and their response to European contact; and second the timing and form of European contact: to what extent did Spanish, Dutch, Portuguese, British, Turkish, Belgian or US colonialism establish different forms of urban structure and to what extent did different forms of export product establish different kinds of social and economic structure and thereby influence the form of urban society that eventually evolved in the Third World?

Society and Urban Tradition before European Contact

Europe encountered a diverse range of societies in its expansion after 1500; primitive hunters and gatherers, agricultural societies, theocratic military societies, industrial economies. The India of the eighteenth century was a great manufacturing as well as a great agricultural country; 'Indian methods of production and of industrial and commercial organization could stand comparison with those in vogue in any other part of the world' (Anstey, 1936: 5). By contrast, European observers of some African peoples were anything but impressed. Elements of the 'noble savage' come across in some accounts, but many evoke the image of Darkest Africa, full of cannibals. Burton (1856: 65), for example, observed a Danikil caravan in Eastern Africa and commented that the 'men were wild as orang-outangs and the women only fit to flog cattle.' Such accounts are as much a comment on the observers as on the observed and there can be little doubt that the vanguard of European expansion did not constitute the cream of European society. As Kiernan (1972: 25) points out, 'these Europeans were pirates, traders, grabbers and settlers by turn . . . and it gave the world a picture of Western civilization very much like the picture of Islam that the Arab slave dealers gave.' This vanguard did anything but persuade the great Eastern civilizations that they had anything to learn from Europe. Proud China despised Western culture and its agrarian Confucian ideology conservatively refused to adopt Western ideas or ideals. The reaction in the Islamic kingdoms of the Middle East and India was much the same.

The diversity of the newly discovered world was due more to its vast geographical area than a function of isolation. Certain regions had remained relatively autonomous for many centuries, particularly in the Americas. But in most places conquest by other peoples was a recurrent fact of life. In what is now contemporary Mexico the Aztecs had come to dominate many other civilizations compelling them to provide the human sacrificial offerings that fed the gods. In most parts of Asia, Europeans encountered societies which were under the domination of foreign or semi-foreign élites; large areas of India had been invaded over the centuries by Aryans, Arabs, and Monguls; China was controlled by the Manchu dynasty. In Africa major population movements frequently led to conflict. In the West Islamic traders and teachers from across the Sahara had superimposed a new religion and urban form on existing societies and forced some peoples towards the coast. In Southern Africa Europe came into contact with African civilizations at the time of the *Mfecane* (great smashing); the series of conflicts among indigenous societies which 'scattered African chieftains in fragments across half the continent of Africa' (Davenport, 1977: 10). The conflicts between peoples was not only characteristic of the world Europe 'discovered' but also a great aid in its incorporation and subjugation. Thus, slavery in West Africa was facilitated by inter-group antipathy and the existing slaving tradition. The Spanish conquest of Mexico was eased by the way Cortés could enlist the support of Indian peoples previously conquered by the Aztecs. In India the East India Company made alliances with one kingdom while in conflict with others.

The diverse, and in certain places rapidly changing, societies encountered by Europeans clearly possessed widely differing urban traditions. In the Pacific and in major parts of Africa urbanization was non-existent, however loosely the term is defined. By contrast, urbanization in the Americas, the Middle East, India, and China often made European cities look infants in comparison. Indeed, what Wheatley (1970) has described as the areas of 'primary urban generation' were confined to what is now the Third World.[3] The great urban achievements of the 'traditional' world greatly impressed the European who encountered them. Cortés found himself unable to describe the beauty and greatness of the buildings he found in Moctezuma's capital. Further south, the Spaniards marvelled at the magnificence of the Inca cities (Burland, 1967). In other parts of the world it was the size of the cities as much as their architecture that impressed the Europeans. In China before 1900 there were more large cities than in Europe, not only in absolute numbers, but even in proportionate terms. In the Middle East ancient Alexandria and Baghdad are both estimated to have had 1 million inhabitants. In 1803 Delhi's palace, fort, great mosque, and most of its population were encircled by a wall 9 kilometres long. In Subsaharan Africa similar urban magnificence was absent and a strong urban tradition had evolved only in a few regions. Major towns existed in the area under Islamic influence, both in the Sudanic belt and on the East African coast. In the Yoruba territories it was common for agricultural peoples to live in towns for social, religious, and defensive reasons; and after the nineteenth-century wars the traditional Yoruba towns, as well as new cities, became swollen with refugees (Mabogunje, 1962).

Undeniably great though many of these cities were, they were not the cities of modern Europe. They were more akin to what Sjoberg (1960) has described as the pre-industrial city. These cities were reliant on simple inanimate forms of technology and dependent on religion. In Inca Peru power derived ultimately from Inti, the sun god; the construction of the city was the highest expression of Inca art and organization of the state. Its culmination occurred in Cuzco, 'the navel of the universe and the seat of the sun's earthly descendent, the Sapa Inca' (Burland, 1967: 40). In traditional Asia cities 'were intended as cosmic creations, substantive and symbolic pinnacles of, and resplendent thrones for, the great tradition, enshriners as well as administrators of the relatively homogeneous and particularistic culture, to which the market towns and the peasant villages of the little tradition also belonged' (Murphey, 1969: 68). The sacred determined their form and their very existence. Throughout the 'traditional' world, in fact, Wheatley (1967: 9) has suggested that this 'cosmo-magical symbolism . . . informed the ideal type traditional city in both the old and the new worlds . . . brought it into being, sustained it and was imprinted on its physiognomy.'

These great cities were supported by, and dictated orders to, the rest of society. In ancient China each city received its orders from Pekin and passed them down the urban hierarchy. In Inca Peru town officials formed part of an efficient civil service hierarchy. Such cities engaged in commerce and manufacturing but these functions were subordinate to religious and state needs. Even in the Yoruba cities, inhabited by agriculturalists and traders, the main function was as the seat of an *oba* – 'the visible symbol of the deity . . . the High Priest of his kingdom' (Ojo, 1966: 75).

These urban civilizations were to affect profoundly the form of modern cities. In both their locations and their morphology, 'traditional' cities were to help to mould European urban influence. And, in so far as these urban civilizations differed from one another, they made different kinds of contribution to the evolution of modern cities.

European Contact: Colonialism and Neo-Colonialism

Diversity was not confined to the colonized cultures; it was just as characteristic of the colonizing powers. Indeed, European expansion into the Third World assumed a marked variety of forms. Such variety was partly the outcome of the range of European nations engaged in colonial and commercial expansion; Spanish, Portuguese, Dutch, British, French, German, Belgian, and Italian styles of expansion were in many respects very different. The nature of European contact was also influenced by the kind of territory and civilization discovered. Thus the effects of the British in Australia and North America were very different from those in Africa. European influence also changed through time: the styles of the British in India changed markedly from the days of the East India Company to the Viceroyalty; the effect of Spanish colonialism in the sixteenth century was very different from that in the early nineteenth. Indeed, the form of capitalism had changed from mercantile capitalism to industrial capitalism and later to monopoly capitalism (Baran, 1957; Barratt-Brown, 1974). In addition, while many Third World countries had experienced contact with one European nation, others had come into contact with several. In the Caribbean, islands were constantly changing hands; Cuba was at different times under the rule of Britain, Spain, and the United States.

Different colonial experiences obviously had diverse economic and social consequences throughout the colonized world. In North America, Australia, New Zealand, and Argentina the unfettered expansion of capitalist agriculture in temperate latitudes eventually led to high levels of per capita income. In areas where an indigenous population was numerically superior, the local economic and social consequences were more variable. European expansion rarely helped indigenous commerce and agriculture but nor were indigenous institutions and enterprise automatically destroyed. Frequently Europeans did not even try to transform precapitalist agriculture and commerce into capitalism. As Foster-Carter (1978: 51) has pointed out, 'capitalism neither evolves mechanically from what precedes it, nor does it necessarily dissolve it. Indeed so far from banishing precapitalist forms, it not only co-exists with them but buttresses them, and even on occasion conjures them up *ex nihilo.*' Local variation conditioned by the European presence is the only adequate description of the economic impact of colonialism. Similarly, its effect on the demographic structure was equally variable. In North America, Argentina, and Australia extensive European settlement allied with the extermination of the indigenes created a new population structure; in the Caribbean the local population was destroyed and replaced with African slaves and indentured labour; in Spanish America both extermination of the indigenous population and racial mixing occurred; in most of Asia and Africa Europeans came and went with little effect; in Southern Africa Europeans coexisted uneasily with African populations. The urban consequences were similarly diverse.

It is probable, however, that the variations in European impact became less marked in the nineteenth and twentieth centuries. During the stage of mercantile capitalism Europe was interested mainly in trade and its effect on Africa and Asia was more limited. Under the phase of industrial capitalism Europe's effect on the rest of the world was greater. Whether Karl Marx was right in arguing that colonialism and imperialism were ordained by the expansionist logic of capital accumulation and the falling rate of profit remains a matter for debate, but industrial and monopoly capital certainly opened up the world (Barratt-Brown, 1974: 184). European powers colonized and/or established production facilities in most Third World countries. British and, later, French, Belgian, Dutch, and US capital developed mines and plantations, railways and ports, factories and cities. Through direct political control, through investment and with the ever present threat of the gunboat, the world came to be dominated by Europe and the United States. From this time on, the world began to look more similar. The cities associated with these developments, which began to expand in the late nineteenth century, resembled one another. The tram and the railway, the suburban house, and the occasional dash of town planning created passable imitations of European cities. The so-called modern cities contained all the advantages and extravagances of European urbanization together with the additional disadvantages of general poverty. The new cities were frequently insanitary, badly located, and tasteless. As Fisher (1976: 112) has noted,

both in Europe and in the United States, the industrial revolution rapidly bred an immense self-confidence and arrogance. Nature, it was automatically assumed, had been conquered and man was in full control. Such men felt no need to harmonize their activities with those of nature and, so far from being symbols of reconciliation, the upstart industrial cities of Victorian Britain were built in flagrant contempt of the natural order: this flagrant contempt of the natural order carried over into the Third World.

Urban functions and settlement systems naturally reflected the general orientation of the economy: cities were concerned with international trade. What Murphey (1969: 72) has said of Asia is valid for most parts of the Third World. By the time of independence 'national life had come to centre on Western-developed ports to an irreversible degree . . . As each Asian country had responded to Western stimuli and altered its own outlook, its world had been refocused on its seaward gates, originally the funnels for export and the vestibules for Western manipulators, but ultimately also the breeding grounds and the apexes of a new Asia.' These apexes were to develop into the primate cities which would dominate national settlement patterns. Into these cities would eventually move large numbers of rural migrants: their land alienated by the intrusion of capitalist enterprise, their numbers swollen by lower mortality rates. The cities we recognize today as being of the Third World had begun to emerge. Urbanization characterized by

an urban population unrelated to the productive level of the system; an absence of a direct relation between industrial employment and urbanization, but a link between industrial production and urban growth; a strong imbalance in the urban network in favour of one predominating area; increasing acceleration of the process of urbanization; a lack of jobs and services for the new urban masses and, consequently, a reinforcement of the ecological segregation of the social classes and a polarization of the system of stratification as far as consumption is concerned. (Castells, 1977: 57)

Recurrent Patterns

Social scientists seek to generalize and urbanization has long been the object of such generalization. Pirenne (1925), Sjoberg (1960), Mumford (1975), Friedmann (1961), Schnore (1965), Castells (1977a), and Harvey (1973) have all in their distinctive ways sought to generalize about urban change in different parts of the world. One of the enduring elements in these efforts has been the proposition that cities have assumed a more homogenous form through time. Whether one accepts the validity of Schnore's (1965) argument about urban form in Latin America converging towards the North American model, or Davis and Hertz's (1954) hypotheses about urbanization increasing lineally with levels of development, or Castells's (1977a) theory of the capitalist logic underlying urban development, the assumption underlying all these arguments is that urban form and development have become more universal. Not infrequently, normative statements have been implicit in this assumption. Underlying the approach of the 'modernization school' is the belief that the emergence of the modern cities and log-linear city-size systems improves conditions for the populations of poor countries.[4] It is divergence from this pattern in the form of *favelas*, primate cities, or inflated service sectors that slows the process of economic development and lowers the welfare of Third World populations.[5] A contrary view is presented by the Marxist literature, where generalization has attempted to show that conditions of poverty and inequality are not confined to the Third World but are entrenched even in the most affluent of capitalist cities; what planners designate as 'problems' are in fact the inevitable urban outcomes of capitalist development. One of the objectives of this book is to examine in what respects urban forms are becoming more universal and to discuss the implications for urban development of that tendency.

At first sight the suggestion of a common universal pattern of urban development seems absurd. It is true that Paris has recently had its *bidonvilles*, but there is no way that poverty in Paris can be compared with poverty in Calcutta or Jakarta, either in the severity of that poverty or in the relative and absolute numbers of people involved. Urban poverty in the Third World is on a scale quite different to that in the developed countries; it is a poverty, moreover, which is likely to persist for many years to come. In other respects, however, more credence can be given to the notion of universality.

Technology has always imposed certain similarities on city form. It is Sjoberg's (1960) contention, of course, that technology is the common factor which determined the form of the pre-industrial city. Technology created the social order comprising a small élite and much larger lower-class and outcast groups. The élite dominated the feudal city by controlling the main religious, political, administrative, and social functions. The spatial manifestation of this control was the wealthy, exclusive central core surrounded by an extensive area of poor settlement. Similarly, ideology and beliefs have always influenced urban form. Wheatley's (1969) concept of 'cosmo-magical symbolism' offers a means by which the structures of Inca, Yoruba, ancient Cambodian, Indian, and Chinese cities can be related. But pre-industrial cities, for all their similarities, were very diverse. The absence of inanimate energy may have limited communications in the cities of both the Incas and the ancient Chinese, but at least the Chinese had the horse and the wheel. Ancient cities may have shared a belief in God which articulated their societies and legitimized their élites, but in some societies this gave rise to human sacrifice, in others to slavery, and in others to harmonious social relationships.

By comparison, technology in the modern world is more universally available, at least to the élites. Ancient cities were similar because their inhabitants lacked the ability to travel rapidly or to build tall buildings cheaply. The modern city is similar because the know-how to construct large residential complexes and mass transit systems is international; sky-scrapers, underground railways, municipal fountains, and post office towers are becoming universal. International cities have become the norm ever since Le Corbusier, Doxiades, and others joined the world's jet set and Ebenezer Howard's image of a garden city became public property. Similarly, the logic underlying modern city growth is universal at least in the capitalist world. The price mechanism together with capitalist finance and real-estate institutions creates a distinctive pattern of land use with population densities and land-price gradients, central business districts, high-class suburban residential areas, and inner-city slums. This pattern is replicated with modifications throughout the capitalist world. The socialist city, of course, differs in several respects. In the main, urban areas in communist nations do not have population-density or land-value gradients and they lack the same clear segregation of social classes and specialized functions by area (French and Hamilton, 1979: 15–20, 101–2). But they share the same belief in 'progress' that dominates capitalist countries; with effective planning and economic growth cities can be made into better and more humane places. It is the hope conveyed by Mumford (1975: 651) that 'the oppressive conditions that limited the development of cities throughout history have begun to disappear.'

But is that hope justified? Are there good grounds for believing that the growing integration of cities with the internationalized economy is reducing inequality and improving living conditions? Unfortunately, even if a case can be made for the cities of developed countries, it is only too easy to argue that the Third World city occupies an underprivileged position in an unequal world economy. Admittedly, the city is not the most underprivileged part of the system; almost invariably it is the rural areas that occupy that position, but underprivileged it undoubtedly is. My proposition is similar to that of Kubler (1964) when he argues that the greater international exposure of Latin American cities after independence made them more provincial not more metropolitan: the 'physical equipment . . . of the provinces is imitative, derivative, and merely typical' (p. 59) and the ultimate outcome is 'a diminution in the cultural diversity of Latin American life, and in the range of choices freely made'.

Today the essential decisions about technology, employment, and economic growth are made in the metropolitan centres of Europe and the United States, and Third World urban functions and form have come to reflect their provincial status. The Third World city forms part of the world economy but its population does not share equal access to the world's resources. For this reason, and despite the countervailing power of government, inequality is being perpetuated today within the Third World city. Harvey's (1973) descriptions of the logic of capitalist expansion in Baltimore, with the parallel development of slum ghettos and affluent suburbs are applicable, to a greater or lesser extent, throughout the world. In the Third World city the relative poverty of the black Baltimore slum-dweller is accentuated by absolute material deprivation. Some poor people in the United States suffer from malnutrition, most of the poor in Indian cities fall into this category. Overcrowded tenement slums and too few jobs are abhorrent, but the lack of fresh water, medical services, drainage, and unemployment compensation adds to this problem in most Third World cities. Without wishing to paint Dickensian pictures of squalor, poverty, and crime, it is far too easy to sketch the outline of a basically unfair and degrading situation.

At the same time, it is doubtful whether urban inequality in any meaningful sense of the word is becoming more generalized or more pronounced with capitalist development. It is true that more poor people are living in Third World cities than ever before, but this is a simple outcome of demographic growth; there are very many more rich people in those cities too. Similarly, while levels of unemployment and relative numbers of shanty dwellers have risen in practically all Third World cities, this represents as much a transfer of rural poverty to the urban areas as the creation of a new group of poor (Gilbert and Ward, 1978). The vulgar statement that inequality and poverty are worsening is a reaction of the heart, not of the head. The capitalist Third World city is undeniably unequal but it is erroneous to accuse it of ineluctably accentuating those conditions. Any comparison of the modern capitalist city and the ancient city is unlikely to heap more criticism upon the former than on the latter; better a Calcutta street dweller, a Rio *favelado*, or an exploited domestic than a slave or a sacrifice to the Aztec sun god.

But if the advocates of future Third World doom are too strident, the techno-crats and the politicians are too complacent. Too often it is assumed that a unilineal pattern of urban development is characteristic of modern economic growth. That the London of Dickens, the Chicago of Upton Sinclair, the northern British cities of Orwell or Greenwood have substantially disappeared is not prescription, merely a welcome statement of fact. There is no obvious reason, given the current world distribution of capital, why contemporary descriptions of Third World cities will seem to belong to a different world when our successors look at urban conditions in the year 2050. When Mumford (1975) applauds the historical decay of oppressive urban conditions and argues that 'the history of the last 800 years is the progressive equalization of classes', he is wrong. He more nearly approaches the truth of the Third World city when he argues that 'the evil institutions that accompanied the rise of the ancient city have been reactified and magnified in our own time: so the ultimate issue is in doubt' (p. 651). While his definition of the evil institutions (Communism, Fascism, war) are highly subjective, the ultimate issue is undeniably in doubt. What is the future of Third World cities? Are the poor to escape their penury and marginal status or will peripheral capitalism accentuate their current situation? Do Third World cities have a 'generative' capacity or will they remain the 'parasitic' agents of Hoselitz's imagination? The rest of the book is concerned with this doubt.

URBAN AGGLOMERATION AND REGIONAL DISPARITIES

Economic development tends to favour certain geographic areas. Certain regions and cities attract economic activity and population more than others. Of course this tendency is more marked in some economic systems; dependent capitalist countries exhibit wider regional disparities than do poor socialist nations, certain governments take more determined action to redress such inequalities than do others. Nevertheless throughout the Third World there is a clear tendency for industry, commerce, agriculture, and other economic sectors to concentrate in particular regions. Certain areas are dynamic whilst the economies of others are growing slowly or even declining. Associated with this tendency is a marked trend for the population of Third World countries to become more spatially concentrated; migrants move from declining to dynamic regions, from rural to urban areas, from small cities to large.

Linked to the process of spatial concentration and to the shift from a rural to an urban/industrial economy is the accentuation of regional differentials in income and welfare. Most Third World nations exhibit wide disparities not only in personal incomes but also in the regional distribution of income. Of course we must be careful to distinguish between the different manifestations of regional and personal inequality. There is a long-recognized distinction to be upheld between 'place' welfare and 'personal' welfare: the fact that a region or city is rich does not preclude its containing many poor people; many poor agricultural regions have numerous affluent landlords. We must also guard against the automatic assumption that an area dynamic in terms of population growth is necessarily improving its per capita income or vice versa. As I shall demonstrate in chapter 8, much confusion surrounds the issue of personal and regional inequality and the appropriate means to reduce or modify such disparities.

My objective here is to describe and explain how major concentrations of population and economic activity have come about. In the first section I note some of the general patterns and tendencies found throughout the Third World. In the second I consider two theoretical models which purport to explain the processes of spatial concentration. Finally I examine the historical development of Third World space economies in search of common patterns and processes. Any normative conclusions are held back to chapter 8.

Contemporary Spatial Disparities

Economic and social change has been associated with the emergence of wide geographical disparities throughout the Third World. These disparities are linked to the nature of the economic model that underpins development in most of these countries and to the acute personal income disparities that have emerged. In this section it is sufficient to detail three broad patterns of spatial concentration and inequality: economic and social differences between urban and rural areas; economic and social disparities between different regions of a country; the degree to which one city dominates the national urban structure (urban 'primacy').

(a) Rural-urban disparities

Major differences are apparent in the standard of living in urban and rural areas. With the exception of certain socialist nations, where an effort has been made to reduce differentials, the rural areas of the Third World contain a high proportion of very poor people, are provided with a minimum of social services and infrastructure and offer little in the way of well-remunerated work. Per capita incomes are consistently lower than those in urban areas. In Thailand rural incomes in 1970 were only 41 per cent those of urban areas, in West Malaysia in 1970 33 per cent, in Indonesia in 1967 62 per cent, in Venezuela in 1961 40 per cent, and in Mexico in the early sixties 43 per cent (Friedmann and Douglass, 1976: 352; UNECLA, 1971: 105).

Similar disparities can be seen in terms of medical provision. In the late sixties there was one doctor for every 200,000 Ethiopians living in rural areas compared to one for every 3,000 urban dwellers; in India one doctor for every 40,000 rural dwellers compared to one for every 500 city inhabitants; in Nigeria the figures were 1:59,000 and 1:2,000 respectively; and in Indonesia 1:6 millions and 1:2,800 (OHE, 1972: 26).[1] These kinds of differential can be replicated for most kinds of health provision throughout the Third World (Gish, 1971; Gilbert, 1974c; Sharpston, 1972; Bryant, 1969).

(b) Regional disparities

However measured, regional disparities in Third World countries are extreme. In terms of medical provision, schooling, industrial activity, financial transactions, or the location of high-income groups, certain regions demonstrate a marked superiority over the rest of the country. In Senegal nearly 80 per cent of industrial enterprises, 66 per cent of all salaried employees, and 80 per cent of all doctors are concentrated in the Dakar region compared to a mere 16 per cent of the population (Gugler and Flanagan, 1978a: 189). In Pakistan Karachi generates 42 per cent of industrial value added and accommodates 50 per cent of all bank deposits compared to its 6 per cent of the national population (UNCRD, 1976: 145). In Mexico the capital contained, in 1975, 46 per cent of all commercial sales, 55 per cent of service activities, and 52 per cent of industrial production compared to 24 per cent of the total national population (Unikel, 1976: 68).

In general, regional disparities in less developed nations are far wider than those in developed countries. Williamson (1965) shows that the average differential in per capita income, as measured by the coefficient of variation, was only 0.19 for eleven developed countries in the fifties compared to 0.42 for the poorest nine countries in his survey. More recent data for a number of poor countries support the idea of major spatial imbalances (table 2.1). In Indonesia there was a twelvefold difference between the per capita incomes of the richest and the poorest regions in 1972 and in Brazil a ninefold difference in 1966. The average of the coefficients of variation for the eighteen countries in table 2.1 is 0.49.

Table 2.1
Regional Inequality in Selected Less Developed Nations

Nation	GNP per capita 1967[a]	V_W	V_{uw}	Date	Number of regions
Venezuela	880	.66	.74	1969	9
Argentina	800	.66	.59	1969	9
Spain	680	.30	.28	1971	50
Mexico	490	.65	.53	1965	32
Chile	470	.35	.60	1967	7
Peru	350	.53	.42	1961	23
Colombia	300	.24[b]	.29[b]	1964	15
Brazil	250	.60	.58	1969	21
Ghana	200	.55	.72	1960	7
Philippines	180	.64	.75	1966	11
Bolivia	170	.57	.64	1967	9
Thailand	130	.55	.50	1969	4
Kenya	120	.85[c]	.81[c]	1962	6
India	90	.17	.17	1964/5	14
Tanzania	80	.63[d]	.32[d]	1967	17

[a] IBRD World Bank Atlas of per capita production and population, 1969.
[b] Using the data of Daza Roa (1967), V_W = .59 and V_{uw} = 61.
[c] Separating Nairobi from Central Province, V_W = 2.20 and V_{uw} = 4.23.
[d] Separating Dar es Salaam from the Coastal Region V_W = 1.30 and V_{uw} = 2.08.
Source: Gilbert and Goodman (1976: 118).
Note: Williamson (1965) uses two main measures of inequality (V_W and V_{uw}), both based on the coefficient of variation.

$$V_W = \sqrt{\frac{\sum_i (y_i - \bar{y})^2 \cdot (n_i/n)}{\bar{y}}}$$

where n_i = population in region i, n = national population, y_i = income per capita of region i, and $\bar{y}$ = national income per capita

$$V_{uw} = \sqrt{\frac{\sum_i (y_i - \bar{y})^2/N}{\bar{y}}}$$

where N = number of regions.

Regional income disparities have two other major characteristics. The first is that there is no tendency towards greater equality in most Third World countries; for every nation in which regional income convergence has occurred there is another in which divergence has been the pattern (Gilbert and Goodman, 1976: 119).

The second is that there is no relationship between per capita income among low- and medium-income countries and the level of regional disparities. The level of disparities is more a function of national economic organization than of per capita national income.

(c) Urban primacy

In many Third World countries, most large-scale modern activities, most forms of social infrastructure, and most decision-makers are found in one major city. This concentration is mirrored in the urban-size distribution by the way one city dominates all others. Thus Lima-Callao has ten times the population of Arequipa, Peru's next-largest city; Kingston, Jamaica, twelve times the population of Montego Bay; Guatemala City, eighteen times the population of Quezaltenango; and Bangkok forty times that of the second Thai city, Chiengmai.

The 'four-city index' is a useful general indicator of the degree of urban primacy. It is calculated as a ratio of the population of the largest city to the sum of the populations of the four largest cities. For ease of description we have classified differing levels of urban dominance into four groups which we label high-primate, primate, non-primate, and low-primate distributions.[2] Table 2.2 shows how common primacy is in Third World countries. Of the seventy-five countries with a per capita income lower than 1,800 dollars in 1973, fifty-five exhibited primacy or high primacy. It is important to note, however, that twenty poor countries do not have primate urban-size distributions; for example, India, the Yemen Arab Republic, Zambia, and the Republic of South Africa. In addition there are countries in which a situation of dual primacy exists; two cities dominate the urban-size distributions of Brazil (Rio de Janeiro and São Paulo), Ecuador (Quito and Guayaquil), Syria (Damascus and Aleppo), and Pakistan (Karachi and Lahore).

Table 2.2
Degrees of Primacy and Levels of Per Capita Income

Gross National Product Per Capita 1973	Numbers of countries with: Low and non-primate distributions*	Primate and high-primate distributions*
More than US $1,800	17	11
US $601–1,800	5	17
US $0–600	15	38
Total	37	66

*For definitions see note 2, p. 198 below.
Source: World Bank Atlas, 1977.

Table 2.2 also shows that while primacy is more prevalent in Third World nations it is by no means confined to them. Rather, eleven of the twenty-eight high-income countries were primate or high-primate, with the dominance of Paris, Vienna, or Copenhagen serving to remind us that high primacy is not exclusively a Third World phenomenon. Indeed, various efforts to relate the degree of primacy to levels of urban development or per capita income have proved inconclusive (Berry, 1961; Mills, 1972; Mehta, 1964). If a relationship exists it is of a much more complex form.

In sum, therefore, while primacy is not limited to Third World nations, it is highly characteristic of them. And if high primacy is not limited to countries with any single characteristic, it is especially common in those that are small, highly centralized, and of medium income.[3] Whether such a phenomenon constitutes the social and economic problem that so many claim, is a theme I explore in chapter 8.

Models of Regional Change

Two broad theoretical approaches offer useful insights into the process of urban and spatial concentration and the related phenomena of regional welfare and income disparities. The first is John Friedmann's 'Centre-periphery' model; the second the work emerging from neo-Marxist writing.

The centre-periphery model

Friedmann's (1966) work had the major virtue of drawing together a wide range of ideas to create an evolutionary model of economic development and spatial change. It incorporated the ideas of Myrdal (1957) and Hirchmann (1958) about how market forces accentuated regional inequalities, general models of economic development (Rostow, 1960; Prebisch 1950), and regional planning strategies (Isard, 1960; Rodwin, 1973), to produce a simple, normative model of spatial development in less developed countries. The author himself no longer accepts many of the assumptions he made (Friedmann and Weaver, 1979; Friedmann and Douglass, 1976), but it is interesting to study his model because it incorporates many of the dominant ideas about spatial and economic development held in the 1960s and still held by many today. By explaining and criticizing the model we shall understand better some of the processes that have led to the emergence of urban primacy and regional disparities in so many Third World nations.

The model consists of four stages which trace the evolution of a spatial system from a sparsely populated and newly colonized nation to a fully integrated urban and regional system in a developed country (figure 2.1). The first stage conceives of an unexploited region with scattered rural settlement which is populated by a colonial power. The settlers establish mining and agricultural activities and urban centres evolve to service and administer these enterprises. Those cities that handle foreign trade or are located in rich agricultural regions prosper, but the urban system generally consists of regional centres with little interdependence.

The second stage is marked by the beginnings of industrialization and the growing concentration of investment into one or two main cities. Regional

1. Independent local centres, no hierarchy

2. A single strong centre

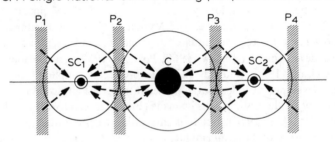

3. A single national centre strong peripheral subcentres

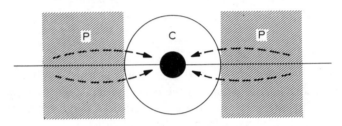

4. A functionally interdependent system of cities

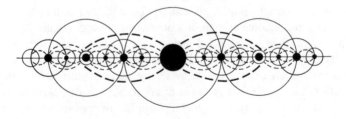

(After Friedmann)

2.1 A sequence of stages in spatial organization (from Friedmann, 1972)

disparities increase as resources continue to flow to the more productive regions away from those which are now 'locationally obsolete'. Gradually, a dualistic spatial structure emerges '. . . comprising a "centre" of rapid, intensive development and a "periphery" whose economy, imperfectly related to this centre, is either stagnant or declining' (p. 9). The major urban outcome is the emergence of a 'primate' city.

The third stage is marked by increasing industrial maturity and by rising political consciousness in the periphery opposed to the spatial concentration of wealth. Such opposition evokes a response from the national government in the form of a regional development policy. Such a policy is essential because 'on the whole, the unrestrained forces of a dynamic market economy appear to be working against a convergence of centre and periphery' (p. 18). Eventually the combination of national government intervention, provincial initiative, and the effects of rising national income reduce regional disparities and bring about greater spatial balance. Provincial cities now contain dynamic economic activities and help to stimulate agriculture in the surrounding regions. Poverty is not abolished, but is now confined to limited areas rather than being endemic in the whole periphery.

During the final stage a fully integrated space economy emerges which combines 'national integration, efficiency in the location of individual firms, maximum potential for further growth, and minimum essential interregional imbalances' (p. 37). In these conditions a balanced urban-size distribution emerges with regional centres competing effectively for resources with the national capital.

Friedmann's model is both descriptive and normative; it sketches the evolution of the space economy in less developed countries as well as prescribing the form that future regional policies should take. This model is the basis of a series of regional development strategies focusing on the concept of the 'growth centre' which are still being employed today (UNCRD, 1976; Apalraju and Safier, 1976; Kuklinski, 1972; Rondinelli and Ruddle, 1976). It is important, therefore, to consider the weaknesses of the model both as a description of the past and as a guide to government policy.

First, the model was made less relevant to most Third World societies by the assumption that original European colonization took place in a sparsely populated region. While Australia, North America, South-West Africa, and lowland South America conform in good measure to this assumption, most parts of the Third World do not fit at all. In most places European contact came face to face with large established populations (Horvath, 1972). Friedmann's model implies that the colonizing population settled and developed the area's resources and best lands without conflict and with the spirit and goodwill of a Daniel Boone. In fact colonial settlement was much more varied and warlike; European settlement in Asia was confined to the coasts for many years by the power of the existing civilizations; the Spanish conquistadores of Latin America located their settlements close to the main mines and cities of the conquered indigenous populations; Captain Cook did not just settle Australia but stole Aboriginal land. The lack of a *tabula rasa* created conflict and unequal societies, not merely an unintegrated urban and regional system.

Second, Friedmann considerably underplays the role of foreign influence. While external demand is seen to be an important stimulus to export production and foreign technology a major source of innovation, it is assumed throughout that most important political decisions are taken within the country and that foreign influence is favourable to high rates of economic growth. The historical circumstances facing most less developed countries hardly accord with this conception. Major economic decisions were always influenced by colonial or neo-colonial powers and sometimes resolved directly through political control or military threat. Similarly, the decisions of the élites who emerged in most independent Third World countries were conditioned by, and linked to, the interests of major foreign business groups. Industrial activity was owned and controlled by foreign corporations, exports were channelled through foreign-dominated cartels, and political decisions were subject to pressure from London, Paris, and Washington. The model errs in so far as it 'assumed that the problems of the dependent countries could be understood by analysing phenomena occurring within their geographical borders' (Stuckey, 1975: 97).

The third criticism is that the model is largely apolitical. It assumes that national governments introduce regional policies because it is in the public interest to do so. Beyond stating that regional politicians press for favourable treatment to compensate for past neglect, it fails to examine the nature of political influence and its spatial repercussions.[4] Clearly, different political forces evoke different kinds of national response. The kind of regional policy demanded by provincial élites politically aligned to national parties controlled from the centre will be very different from the response evoked through popular protest in the periphery. Because he believes government to be based on consensus rather than on conflict, Friedmann ignores the political feuds and rivalries that go to make up most government policies. Most importantly, he neglects the possibility that the political will to help the poor regions emerges less out of a sense of public spirit than as a response to political pressure generated by social protests (Castells, 1977).

Fourth, the phenomenon of poverty is treated as a regional rather than as a social phenomenon. This bias underlies the argument that the introduction of regional programmes to raise agricultural productivity and to improve transportation will eliminate poverty in the periphery outside certain isolated pockets. Higher per capita income will lead to the integration of centre and periphery and remove poverty. In reality, of course, poverty is maintained both in the periphery and increasingly in the centre as rural and small-town migrants move in search of better work opportunities. The model fails to treat the issue of poverty in the cities or indeed the personal disparities in income which exist in most Third World societies. Because poverty is treated in purely spatial terms, it is easy for Friedmann to slip into the belief that regional development will eliminate its worst manifestations.

Finally the model assumes that most poor countries will eventually become developed. In this assumption, Friedmann tends to follow the treatise of Rostow (1960: 166) and his belief that the 'tricks of growth are not difficult'. Unfortunately, even if high rates of economic growth can be achieved in the Third World, there is little evidence to suggest that most of these nations are developing highly educated, well-housed, and more equitable societies. The assumption that was so common in the 1950s, that there was a unilineal development path along which most countries would someday pass, is today much less widely accepted. Greater awareness of the relationships between developed and less developed nations and of the social-class interests which dominate political decision making in so many poor nations strongly point to the rejection of a unilineal development path. As such, the pattern of regional and urban change posited in Friedmann's model is unlikely to be replicated in most less developed countries.

These criticisms are not meant to remove all faith in the model, for there are numerous elements which still repay attention. The description of how the centre grows at the expense of the periphery and the critique of the spatial equilibrium model are masterpieces of clear exposition. In addition, some policy recommendations still offer good advice to the regional planner. However, what the model lacks is sufficient scepticism of the benefits offered by economic growth and of the social consciences of most Third World governments. Both these ingredients are offered, in good measure, by the following alternative model of regional development.

A Neo-Marxist Interpretation

A fully developed neo-Marxist theory of spatial evolution and underdevelopment has not yet emerged. Nevertheless, the work of Rofman (1974), Corraggio (1977), Wilson (1975), Stuckey (1975), Santos (1979), and others gives strong hints as to the eventual form of such a theory. The essential elements are the extraction of surplus value, the concept of dominant and dependent modes of production, the changing form of the capitalist mode of production, and the role of the state. The principal difference with the Friedmann model is the incorporation of social-class analysis and the resultant emphasis placed on control over the surplus generated by the productive process. According to Friedmann (1966), profits and capital are transferred from the periphery to the national centre but there is no explicit recognition that national resources are controlled by foreign groups and by capitalist interests in the centre.

The neo-Marxist models view the internal spatial structure of Third World countries as part of the world system of production and consumption (Wallerstein, 1974). The establishment of agricultural and mining activities by capitalist enterprises in the periphery gradually incorporates manpower into wage-labour relationships and thereby generates surplus value. The surplus value generated is transferred abroad either through the operations of foreign corporations or through unequal trade relationships. In either case, the extracted surplus is unavailable for investment in the regions of production. The surplus value that remains in the Third World nations is extracted by élite groups, mainly concentrated in the major cities, and therefore rarely benefits the periphery.

This simple model must be modified in several ways in order to explain the differing spatial and social structures of different Third World countries. The mechanism of capital accumulation varies according to the form of capitalism, the dominant mode of production, and its relationship with other modes of production within individual Third World countries. The articulation of dominant and subordinate modes of production determines social formations in the Third World society and the amount of surplus extracted. In turn, the degree of social-class conflict and the needs of the dominant mode of production determine the relationships between the main actors in the capitalist Third World economy: the foreign or multinational corporations, national entrepreneurial groups, the state, and the poor. Most decisions are made by one or more of the first three sets of actors. The specific interests of these fractions of the dominant class may well diverge, but their basic concern, to maintain the capitalist system which benefits them all, is shared. The critical role of the state is to arbitrate between these conflicting class fractions and to legitimize the system to the poor. While the state will frequently favour the dominant-class fractions through the instru-mentalist mechanisms described by Miliband (1969, 1977), still more essential is its maintenance of stability in the system (Poulantzas, 1969, 1973, 1976).

The relationships between different fractions of the dominant class and between that class, the proletariat, the peasantry, and pre-capitalist populations depend upon the stage of capitalism developed in the periphery. Neo-Marxist writers have distinguished a series of stages of peripheral capitalism, but a commonly cited typology is that described by Castells (1977). World capitalism has been characterized first by colonialism, then by capitalist commercial domination and finally by monopoly capitalism; these stages at times having overlapped. The essential difference between the stages is that the dominant mode of production changes its form through time so that the method of surplus extraction and the consequent social formation change also. Thus, under colonialism, surplus is extracted through foreign political control over trade, investment, and domestic economic policy. Under capitalist commercial domin-ation the Third World nation will be politically independent, but the surplus will be extracted through unequal trade arrangements. In the stage of monopoly industrial and financial domination, the peripheral country will have developed its own manufacturing and agribusiness sectors, but multinational corporations will control these sectors through subsidiary or finance-holding companies. Surplus will then be extracted through profit repatriation, royalty, and patentcy arrangements, and through accounting mechanisms within the corporation.

The expansion of peripheral capitalism generates a strong process of urbaniz-ation. First, cityward migration increases as precapitalist forms of agriculture are disrupted by the penetration of commercial agriculture or by the introduction of monetary taxes on the rural population. Similarly urban migrants are created as the viability of craft industry in the periphery is undermined by cheap imports and later by the products of national manufacturers. Second, surplus generated in the periphery is extracted by national bourgeois groups and representatives of foreign capitalist interests based in the main urban centres. The process of extraction leads to the expansion of the main transportation and market centres and to the rapid growth of the national capital and main ports. Third, the growth of manufacturing within the Third World economy concentrates produc-tion still further in the largest cities, stimulates the growth of a national state bureaucracy to encourage the process of industrialization, and leads to the concentration of higher-income groups in the major centres where surplus is accumulated. Fourth, labour moves to the largest cities to look for work and produces surplus in the national centres both through wage labour and through petty-commodity production which supports the expansion of the capitalist sector. Fifth, the state acts to support industrial expansion by providing infra-structure in the main urban centres and by legitimizing the continued functioning of the system through the provision of social services to selected groups. The capitalist system requires a strong state, both to subsidize the process of surplus accumulation in the private sector (through the development of communications and the provision of education and health services etc.) and to maintain the system thereby ensuring both the state's and the system's reproduction. Sixth, as metropolitan development accelerates, private capital begins to deconcentrate to areas within the metropolitan region but outside the main city in order to avoid rising land prices, labour costs, and traffic congestion (Rofman, 1974). The state may encourage the process of deconcentration or introduce measures to encourage decentralization.

The essential element in the process is the need for the capitalist system to accumulate capital. The spatial formation is an outcome of the particular needs of the capitalist system at any historical conjuncture and of the conflicting interests between the distinct social classes to control the surplus. Normally, dominant class interests, both directly and through their control of the state apparatus, accumulate surplus which is recirculated within the largest urban areas at the expense of the periphery. The spatial effect is to increase regional disparities and to undermine the autonomy of the subordinate regions. The system may impoverish the poorest regions by a very high rate of surplus extrac-tion (absolute exploitation) but equally it may lead to higher income levels as well as a high rate of surplus extraction through the raising of labour productivity (relative exploitation). The latter process is more typical during the stage of monopoly capitalism.

To a considerable extent the neo-Marxian view is a straight historical description of the evolution of capitalism, it is therefore a generally accurate if sometimes distorted view of reality. But one of its principal strengths, flexibility, is increasingly its greatest weakness. For although non-Marxian analysis is often accused by its opponents of being inflexible, current interpretations such as those of Cardoso (1972; 1977), which accommodate new developments in the capitalist system, serve to make the theory less concise. For example, since that theory accepts that the state must assume a measure of autonomy from dominant class interests, that the interests of the capitalist mode of production may be satisfied under different circumstances by either spatial concentration or decentralization, and that the mechanisms and extent of surplus extraction depend on the particular stage of class conflict, the social and spatial implications of the theory become more diffuse. Recent debates about the role of the state (Poulantzas, 1973; Miliband, 1977; 1969) and about the meaning of the mode of production reflect this difficulty (Hindess and Hirst, 1975). Like any theory, the closer neo-Marxian analysis approximates reality, the more complex it becomes and the less able it is to predict the future. Indeed, recent neo-Marxian analyses of spatial development, while very different in terms of the role given to class conflict and to the final outcomes of current state policies, are not dissimilar from those of many neo-Marxian writers (Pahl, 1977; Gilbert, 1978; Stöhr and Fraser, 1981).

The Process of Urban and Regional Concentration

In the absence of any single satisfactory model of spatial evolution I shall resort here to a more descriptive account of urban and regional development in Third World countries. This account takes ideas from both the Marxian and the non-Marxian literature and is premissed on the perception that both intellectual and ideological traditions demonstrate many similarities of interpretation about spatial change. Essentially, I am seeking to explain why urban 'primacy' has emerged in so many Third World nations together with its corollary, constraints on the development of provincial centres and the emergence of major regional disparities. I see these patterns as 'distorted', not simply in the sense that they are in themselves an undesirable manifestation, but more that they reflect a distorted and undesirable pattern of development. Whatever the policy implications to be drawn, which are discussed at length in chapter 8, few now doubt that Third World urban and regional systems are a reflection of basically distorted patterns of development.

The emergence of these urban and regional patterns can be divided into two phases; the spatial changes associated with the export orientation phase of the economy (including both the colonial and the post-colonial phases); and, the spatial changes associated with the inward-oriented industrialization and modernization phase — a phase, of course, which some Third World countries have scarcely begun.

The Export-Orientation Phase

Throughout the Third World the growth of major cities was linked to the growth of international trade; São Paulo grew on the basis of coffee, Singapore on tin and rubber, Calcutta on jute, cotton, and textiles, and Buenos Aires on mutton, wool, and cereals. Whether or not export-linked metropolitan development led to urban primacy was dependent upon the degree to which one or several centres controlled the flow of international trade. In those few cases in which control over the production, transportation, and profits was spread among a variety of centres, non-primacy was the result. More typically, the national capital controlled the flow of exports, the revenues deriving from those exports, and the importation of goods financed by the export flow. Primacy in Third World countries, therefore, can be explained in terms of the geographical location of export production, the transport networks which emerged to ship those exports and, most fundamental of all, the location of the main beneficiaries of the profits generated by international trade.

It is no coincidence that so many primate cities are major ports. The coastal cities generally benefited because they were located close to the centres of export production or commanded the main channels of trade.

The great port cities in Asia, as elsewhere, arose where navigable water and productive land met and where internal lines of access were concentrated. The major river mouths were obvious places of this sort; in the island countries, strategically located coastal sites could develop similar access to the most productive areas by coastal shipping . . . Given this sea-oriented pattern, Singapore could easily serve the whole of the tin and rubber belt along the west coast of Malaya, as Colombo could for the quite compact plantation areas of Ceylon, Manila for the Philippines as a whole, and Batavia for Indonesia, where commercial production was heavily concentrated in Java and along the east coast of Sumatra. (Murphey, 1969: 79)

In Latin America and Africa rivers were less often the main export channels and railways were built by British, French, and US capital to serve this role. Some railways did serve other functions: in India the British built lines to sensitive frontier areas and linked the major cities for strategic reasons, but their prime function was to move exports to the main ports. Even today the orientation of the main railway systems of Africa and Latin America reflects that dominant pattern. The mass of lines in Argentina spreading out from Buenos Aires like the spokes of a wheel and the isolated tracks of the Ecuadorian, Peruvian, Angolan, Kenyan, or Tanzanian systems all link the mineral and agricultural export areas with the main ports.

The major ports often developed into primate cities as a consequence of their control over international trade. But primacy was not always linked to port locations. In Latin America several major capitals emerged in areas physically separate from the main production areas and export routes. In Venezuela petroleum is produced in, and shipped from, areas hundreds of kilometres away from the national capital, Caracas; in Chile most of the copper is produced in the far north of the country. But these paradoxical situations serve only to emphasize the point made earlier that the critical issue in the evolution of primacy is control over the surplus of profits generated by international trade. In Venezuela the foreign revenues derived from petroleum poured into the government exchequer after 1935 and served to swell the government bureaucracy in the national capital (Lieuwen, 1961). This flow of funds led to the concentration of high-income groups in the city and to the development of a lucrative import business. In Peru, almost a century earlier, the growth of the guano trade had led to Lima's rapid expansion. Within a few years a whole-sale market and slaughterhouse had been built, a new water system constructed, and a telegraph system opened. New avenues, squares, and parks were opened, the population and geographical area of the city expanded, and a luxurious life-style established for the rich of the city (Romero, 1949). In Peru, as else-where, control by the state bureaucracy and private interests, located in the national capital, over the surplus generated by international trade was the critical factor in the domination of the primate city over the provincial cities.

Clearly, however, the degree of control exercised by the élites in the capital city varied greatly between countries. In several Third World nations the benefits of export expansion contributed to the growth of more than one large city. More balanced regional development was normally associated either with a division of functions between cities or with control over different export products. Thus, in Colombia the national capital was neither a port nor the main centre of export production. While Bogotá was a major centre of international commerce and political power, control over the coffee sector lay also in the cities of Medellín, Manizales, and Pereira to the west. Similarly, the lack of a dominant port led to competition among four main centres for the nation's international trade. With mountainous terrain limiting further the control exercised by any one city over the domestic economy a rank-size distribution emerged. Bogotá undoubtedly benefited from export expansion, but so did a whole series of provincial cities. In countries with a more recent colonial past, local agents of Empire controlled the surplus less than they channelled it to the Imperial capital. Thus, in India surplus extraction benefited London more than it did the main Indian cities. Nevertheless major urban centres developed precisely because they were the channels of the export trade; jute, tea, and indigo went through Calcutta, tobacco and cotton through Madras, textiles from Bombay, and cotton and tobacco through Karachi. The combination of geographical size and the development of non-contiguous export areas led to the emergence of several major port cities. Delhi, the interior viceregal capital, played little part in the export traffic and consequently failed to dominate the urban system.

By contrast, the overwhelming primacy that developed in Argentina was linked to the monopoly of one city over most administrative, commercial, and industrial functions. Buenos Aires combined physical proximity to the export areas of the Pampas, a stranglehold over imports, the ability to attract many of the massive flow of foreign immigrants, and most critically, a monopoly over political decision-making. In 1880 Buenos Aires was voted the capital of a new federal nation. But

[if] symbolically, the provinces gained a capital, in reality, Buenos Aires, seconded by other urban centres, continued to draw upon the resources, talents, and ambitions of the country and left the other provinces and rural areas drained and depressed. Politicians might come from the interior or the countryside, but in Buenos Aires they quickly forgot their origins and adopted the life and attitudes of the porteño city. (Scobie, 1964: 105)

The political status of the nation seems to have had little influence beyond affecting the rate and form of surplus extraction. Under foreign rule most administration was concentrated in the colonial capital; after independence new forces occupied the same positions and maintained control of the primate centres. Of course there are exceptions. In nineteenth-century Latin America, independence was often achieved by rural power groups whose concern was to limit the dominance of the national capital over their regional fiefdoms. Such a political situation led to a decline in urban primacy in the first few years of independence in a number of countries (Morse, 1971). In Africa and Asia, on the other hand, freedom from colonial rule tended to accentuate primacy as new functions and institutions were created in the new national capital. Frequently independence led to tighter control over the export surplus and to the bureau-cratization of government. Nor infrequently it also led to the espousal of an inward-oriented development strategy, the consequences of which we examine in the next section.

Urban primacy and the emergence of major cities was an outcome of export expansion and the channelling of the benefits arising from international trade. In this sense the urban-regional structure was a result of the superimposition of a foreign trading system onto an indigenous system. In turn the size and prosperity of the major city or cities was related to the revenues created by export production and to the proportion of that income which remained in the country of origin. Similarly, urban development in the periphery of Third World nations was linked to the process of export expansion. According to the form of this expansion, urban development was either dynamic or truncated.

At the local level the urban effects of foreign-owned plantations or mines differed greatly from those of small-scale peasant production. In fact one can posit that while certain forms of export production stimulated balanced regional growth and the evolution of active market towns, other forces limited such developments. Thus plantation systems tended to restrict urban growth by paying workers low wages, by reducing outside opportunities for small-scale agriculture through the control of land, and by monopolizing the services normally provided through small towns (Cross, 1979; Morse, 1975). Specialized export production generated little in the way of multiplier effects since the harvest was shipped directly to the ports and the profits from the plantations flowed to national urban centres or out of the country altogether. Admittedly, São Paulo's coffee plantations represent an exception to this generalization, but even there fifty years' expansion was necessary before urban development really got under way. Urban growth after 1900 can be explained by the fact that most coffee planters lived in the state and began to diversify their investments. Encouraged by the availability of a cheap and literate immigrant workforce, and helped by federal government provision of infrastructure, they created a major industrial metropolis. With this one exception, and noting differences in local plantation systems, the effect of plantation agriculture on local urban development was generally depressive. Whether we consider the tea plantations of India or Sri Lanka, the banana and sugar estates of the Caribbean, or the rubber, tobacco, and tea estates of Sumatra and Java, the urban effects were similar.

Mining enterprises were more likely to generate local urban development even though most mining centres were also enclaves within a national economy. Roberts (1978: 59), for example, notes that even 'where enclave production was strong, as in the mining towns of the central region of Peru, miners' incomes and revenues from contracts for food supplies, transport and construction for the mining company substantially raised regional income levels ... [which] made possible the diversification of village economies and the expansion of crafts.' Nevertheless, local processing of the raw material was limited to basic sorting and loading, and refining was often carried out in some foreign port. The mining town would attract migrants, either on a permanent or on a semi-permanent basis, but would generate little in the way of rural–urban linkages. Money would be transferred from mines to rural community, but supplies for the town would originate mainly in extra-regional, even foreign, regions. According to the wealth of the mines, the ownership, and the social system operating, mining might create metropolitan cities, for example Johannesburg, or small depressed centres such as the tin towns of Bolivia. In either case mining activity would be linked more closely to the international than to the local economy.

By contrast, small-scale peasant production tended to stimulate local urban growth. The production of coffee in western Colombia, of cocoa and palm oil in West Africa, and of rice in South-East Asia created relatively large and prosperous agricultural groups. A surplus over subsistence stimulated demand for consumer products and for agricultural inputs such as fertilizers, seeds and tools. This demand was channelled through local markets rather than through the mine or plantation store. Continuing growth of the export economy led to the gradual evolution of a diversified, integrated urban system, and in areas of exceptional prosperity, gave rise to an indigenous process of industrial and commercial expansion.

Urbanization at the local level was strongly affected, therefore, by the form of export production (Balán, 1976). At the same time no simple relationship between product type and urban development can be detected. Since the production methods of the same product often varied, the urban consequences were very different in different regions. Thus wheat production created very distinct urban systems in Argentina and the United States. Similarly sugar, which helped to create the Mexican Revolution in Morelos by the way the plantations expanded and took over peasant land, had less marked and possibly more beneficial effects in Northern Peru (Roberts, 1978: 58; Womack, 1969). In some cases different technologies and forms of social organization have varied for the same product even in the same country. In Brazil, for example, Balán (1976: 158) notes that 'coffee has been produced by slave workers, plantation tenants and share croppers, and independent farmers. Although technology has changed, it has not done so in any drastic way.' Thus it is a combination of the linkage effects, together with the methods of production, that determine the local impact of an export product. As a consequence, the local manifestations of dependent export development varied dramatically from product to product and from region to region. Indeed Roberts (1978: 60) has warned that students should 'pay particular attention to the way in which capitalism expands within underdeveloped countries and not simply focus on the mechanisms through which the dominant world economies have extracted a surplus from under-developed countries.'

This warning clearly includes those regions in which export production was not located, but which were affected by such expansion. The national conse-quences of success for export expansion also had important repercussions on regions that remained outside the main export zones.

First, the expansion of export production often although not invariably led to the annexation of land from indigenous groups. Such annexation might be carried out by force, as in Latin America in the seventeenth century, or through the extension of a commercial market for land, as in Mexico in the nineteenth century. Sometimes the alienation of land would occur so as to permit export production, sometimes to supply export areas with food supplies. Export expansion, especially in the nineteenth and twentieth centuries, often went hand in hand with the commercialization of domestic agriculture. In British South and East Africa concessions granted by, or forced upon, local populations constrained indigenous agricultural expansion. Clearly the consequences of land alienation differed according to the total cultivable area available, whether or not indigenous groups were turned into wage-earning labour forces and according to the social and economic systems established in the rural areas. But since a common element in such land alienation was the concentration of wealth in the hands of the expanding élites and the reduction of land available to the displaced groups, the consequences were always likely to truncate urban development.

Second, the expansion of the export sector was likely to weaken the political autonomy and the economy of provincial regions and thereby undermine the growth of major provincial centres. Not infrequently export expansion attracted imported manufactures which undercut the markets of indigenous enterprises based in provincial cities.

The growth of export revenues gave national governments a new source of income which was often many times greater than their previous revenues. While the provinces might be relieved of their former tax bill, they were now forced to request funds from the national government and they lost their previous power to control or withdraw contributions to the exchequer. In Peru guano and nitrate exports, which financed Lima and the national exchequer, left the provinces without any real autonomy (Romero, 1949). Elsewhere control over the national export surplus gave political control to the dominant élites of the capital cities and led to stagnation of the provincial economies. In many cases regional economies have never recovered from this reversal.

Industrialization, Modernization, and Bureaucracy

The world depression of the 1930s and the effects of the Second World War led to a spontaneous process of industrial expansion in the larger Third World nations, especially those in Latin America. Protected from imports of manufactured goods from the developed countries, first by the fall in the prices of primary exports and therefore a shortage of foreign exchange with which to purchase consumer imports, and later by the shift of industrial production in the developed countries away from export activities towards the war effort, Latin America's industry prospered (Frank, 1967). This experience suggested that a new and more successful strategy of development might be embraced. Rather than continuing to rely on imports of manufactured products, Latin American nations could themselves industrialize. Intellectual justification for such a strategy was provided by Raúl Prebisch (1950). His study of trade between Latin America and Britain between 1870 and 1930 demonstrated that the terms of trade had turned in favour of Britain and against Latin America. The prices of primary exports from Latin America had fallen relative to the prices of manufactured products from Britain. Every ton of coffee or tin exported from Latin America bought less in the way of manufactured products in 1930 than in 1870. It was this shift in the terms of trade that lay at the heart of Latin America's under-development. The solution to the dilemma was for Latin America to industrialize. Questionable though much of the argument and statistical evidence was, the report had an enormous influence in Latin America. Through the United Nations Economic Commission for Latin America, which he directed, the industrialization strategy was propagated throughout the region. By the 1960s no Latin American country had failed to adopt the recommendation. Import tariffs had been raised, quota restrictions introduced, infrastructure was being erected, and encouragement offered to manufacturing enterprise.

As countries in other parts of the Third World approached and obtained independence the industrialization/import substitution strategy became conventional wisdom among most new administration. Only in the Republic of Korea, Taiwan, and more recently, Brazil have export-oriented industrialization policies been implemented, often of course with spectacular success (Balassa, 1980;

Mason et al., 1980). India had adopted an import-substitution policy even before independence, as the British encouraged the industrialization of the country. After 1949 this strategy was continued during the first and second national plans and led to the establishment of major steel and engineering complexes. India, of course, was something of an exception, if only because of the size of her population. In the smaller countries of the Third World import-substituting industrialization could never achieve the same credibility. Nevertheless even in the smallest newly independent African or Caribbean state elements of the policy were embraced. If a steel industry was too ambitious, plastics, food-processing, or light engineering was clearly not; most governments went ahead with infrastructure, industrial parks, and incentives to foreign and local investors.

This is not the place to examine in detail the benefits and costs of import-substituting industrialization in different parts of the Third World. Suffice to say that in few places was it an outstanding developmental success. In most places it brought economic growth, but the majority of the population failed to participate in the benefits of that growth. In the largest and more affluent Third World nations the process led to the development of a sophisticated and diversified manufacturing sector. Even in Brazil, Argentina, or Mexico, however, it failed to resolve the recurrent problems of too few jobs and too much foreign technological and financial dependence (Bergsman, 1970; Furtado, 1971; King, 1970). In the medium-sized and poorer countries it led to the creation of inefficient companies producing, at costs well above competitive world prices, a small, rather privileged industrial work-force, and the promise of an industrial miracle which would never be satisfied. In the majority of Third World countries the results were derisory. Perhaps novelist Naipaul's (1969: 215–16) ex-minister of a newly independent Caribbean state best sums up the worst consequences of import-substituting industrialization:

We encouraged a local adventurer to tin local fruit. This was a failure. It hadn't occurred to anyone concerned to find out whether local people wanted local fruit tinned; no one else did either. The same man went in later for tinning margarine and was a success. The margarine was imported, the tins were imported. Our effort was to operate a machine that turned the flattened tins into cylinders. We capped one end, filled the cylinder with the imported margarine, and capped the other end. I remember the process well. I opened the factory. Our margarine was slightly more expensive than imported tinned margarine, and had to be protected. I believe the factory employed five black ladies, whom we photo-graphed looking grave and technical in white coats. Industrialization, in territories like ours, seems to be a process of filling imported tubes and tins with various imported substances.

The locational consequences of industrialization were clear-cut. Throughout the Third World industrial development occurred most rapidly in the largest cities and encouraged the accentuation of metropolitan and primate city development. The tendency to concentration was both cause and effect of other centralization processes and of the efforts to promote rapid economic growth.

In Mexico it led to the national capital increasing its share of manufacturing employment from 35 per cent in 1950 to 47 per cent in 1975; in Brazil to the state of São Paulo increasing its employment share between 1950 and 1970 from 39 per cent to 49 per cent. Admittedly, the process of metropolitan development has been accompanied by a spontaneous process of industrial deconcentration (Gilbert, 1974a; Rofman, 1974). Rising land prices, traffic congestion, urban taxes, and pollution controls have encouraged existing companies to move and new companies to be located away from the central city areas. But few have moved more than a few kilometres from the metropolitan centre. Indeed, the process of deconcentration seems almost to have strengthened industrial growth in the centre region by reducing avoidable costs arising from urban diseconomies while retaining many of the benefits from primate city and metropolitan locations. The advantages of a central location are legion in most capitalist countries, but in less developed countries the benefits are possibly greater still (Alonso, 1971; Gilbert, 1974b). Underlying these advantages is the fact that the export-orientation phase of development tended to create a highly concentrated urban complex which contained the bulk of the higher-income groups, the greater part of the social and economic infrastructure, the termini of the transport system, and the national government bureaucracy. In choosing their locations, few foreign and national enterprises were reluctant to eshew the advantages of these concentrations; advantages which were magnified further by the forms of industry being established.

The initial stage of industrialization saw the establishment of companies producing directly for the consumer market. Textiles, foodstuffs, and clothing were followed by electrical, plastics, and light-engineering companies making vacuum cleaners, refrigerators, and other consumer-durable products. Many of these products were limited to the higher-income groups in society, most of whom lived in the major cities. Consequently, most market-oriented companies tended to concentrate in the largest cities. In turn the establishment of modern plants had a detrimental effect on existing manufacturing and artisan industry. Small companies amalgamated with the new, local artisan activity failed to compete with the new plants. The consequence was that the dynamism of labour-intensive industry in the smaller urban centres was undermined.

Primate city location was favoured further by the dependence of so many new industries on imported parts, machines, and fuel. Indeed, one of the greatest ironies of import-substituting industrialization was its failure to cut imports. Rather than importing the finished refrigerator, the various parts that would make up the finished product were imported and assembled locally. On occasion the various parts would cost more than the final item would have cost ready assembled. In locational terms the dependence on imports emphasized the advantages of coastal cities. Thus, those primate cities that were ports or were closely linked to ports gained a further stimulus to their industrial expansion.

Many of the new industrial enterprises were associated with, or financed by, foreign corporations. Quijano (1971) and Castells (1973) have argued that such links encouraged the 'very unbalanced' pattern of urban development which characterizes Latin America. Certainly there is evidence to support the contention that foreign-owned industry is more concentrated in metropolitan centres than in other cities, whether the country be Argentina (Rofman, 1974) or, for that matter, the United Kingdom (Holland, 1976). But numerous exceptions suggest that the link between foreign ownership and spatial concentration is not so straightforward. In Colombia, for example, foreign investment during the fifties led to the expansion of neither of the main industrial cities, but to the industrialization of Cali and Barranquilla (Gilbert, 1970). It was only foreign investment that was sufficiently mobile to take advantage of the locational advantages offered in those cities. Much the most plausible argument, therefore, is that foreign investment locates in the most advantageous location; this is usually the primate or capital city. In this sense foreign investment responds to existing centralization more than it creates it.

In fact all industrial companies, irrespective of the source of their capital, seek access to the national government bureaucracy. For throughout the Third World national governments wield increasing economic influence. In most Third World countries the state manipulates exchange rates, import tariffs and licences, public utility charges, infrastructural provision, wages, and industrial prices. As a consequence, managers are engaged in constant dialogue with the government. Such contact would be maintained by telephone, cable or by regular visits to the capital city; however, the nature of business relationships in Third World countries dictates that such contacts are made personally with the minister or director of a government institute. In such circumstances it is not surprising that access to the government machinery is a much quoted rationale of industrial location in Third World countries (Gilbert, 1970; Lavell, 1971).

In many countries, indeed, it can be argued that it is the location of government and the paraphernalia of modernization rather than industrial growth *per se* that is the principal source or urban and regional concentration. In most African and Caribbean countries, where industrial growth is limited, expansion of the government bureaucracy has been a major stimulus to urban concentration. Well-paid government bureaucrats constitute an important market for imported manufactured products, and for the shops which sell them, for the construction industry and for domestic services. One of the incidental outcomes of 'modern' administration and efforts of planning economic development has been the accentuated growth of urban complexes. Whatever the level of industrial development, national governments have sought to mobilize savings and to centralize decisions over the allocation of investment. Thus the surplus created in rural areas and in the hinterlands of provincial cities tends to be channelled towards the primate city. The growth of banking taps savings from every region and allows investment in projects anywhere in the nation; but most of the viable projects are located in the major cities. Sometimes the mobilization of funds is manipulated through state institutions. The Cocoa Marketing Board of Nigeria long financed industrialization and other national growth policies through surpluses extracted from peasant producers. In so far as these funds were invested in Lagos and Ibadan, rather than in the production areas, the large cities grew at the expense of lower-order centres (Bauer, 1954). Variations of this transfer of funds have been described in numerous countries (Baer, 1964; Fitzgerald, 1976), invariably with the result that the metropolitan centres have grown at the expense of provincial cities.

Hand in hand with industrial concentration, and in Africa and the Caribbean often independently, economic activity increasingly develops in the major city. Commercial and service activities proliferate to service the manufacturing companies, the government bureaucracy, and other growth sections. As cities become larger, governments attempt to maintain political stability by controlling the prices of basic foods and transportation and by permitting land invasions or illegal urban subdivisions. Middle-income groups receive subsidized public housing and health services. Industrialists are wooed by governments turning a blind eye to environmental pollution; private-sector real-estate interests are allowed to dictate the terms of urban development and land use. Once under way, urban growth is rarely channelled into directions that will maximize the public good. Rather, such growth is allowed to continue under its own implacable logic, whatever the eventual outcome. Few governments can afford to face the political consequences either of a genuine policy of decentralization or of effective urban planning. Most groups who command political support are linked to the metropolitan cities and to the economic activities generated by their growth. Many of the problems we discuss in the following chapters are the consequence of this uncontrolled and unmanaged expansion.

3

THE RURAL-URBAN INTERFACE AND MIGRATION

The history of the last half-millennium has been shaped by the expansion of the capitalist system (Wallerstein, 1974; 1980). Ever more outlying regions were incorporated into the emerging world economy. Existing cities were integrated into the new system, their functions transformed. New cities sprang up to establish political control and to channel resources to the metropolitan centres. Rural populations were drawn into the new activities in the mines or on agricultural estates, or to become peasants, all producing for urban markets, and subject to political control and cultural penetration from the cities.[1]

In the past many rural populations lived in what were by and large subsistence economies, but their isolation has broken down. The self-centred society with only limited contact with the outside has virtually disappeared. For many peoples the integration into the world capitalist system was traumatic: they were enslaved, were forced into the *encomienda*, or suffered as indentured labour. They were thus tied to the land even while the product of their labour entered world markets. In Brazil before 1930, for instance, the mobility of labour was restricted by economic and psychosocial ties that bound tenant farmers, *parceiros*, and colonists to the landowners. These ties were backed by bands of armed thugs who in some areas came to constitute real 'armies of the sertão' (Singer, 1975: 455). But such bonds have largely been broken. Today rural populations raise the cash they need to settle taxes, to purchase manufactured goods, and to pay school fees, by selling some of the products they grow as independent producers, as tenant farmers, or as share croppers. Or they find employment with local landowners, in other rural areas, or in the cities. Whether they sell produce on the market or their labour to an employer, they are part of a far-reaching economic system beyond their control. They experience the vagaries of the world economic system when they lose their jobs during recessions or when a sudden drop in world market prices depresses their earnings from export crops.

Incorporation in the world system brought considerable differentiation to what had frequently been quite egalitarian societies. Certainly, many had known severe inequalities in the past. Captured enemies were held as slaves, entire people were subjected and made to provide goods and services for their masters. Still, a measure of equality based on general access to land was the more common pattern. In any case, as these societies became part of larger societies, new elements of differentiation came to the fore. The first to be converted by missionaries and to attend their schools had a headstart in employment as teachers, government officials, or commercial clerks; the first to accumulate a little capital in employment or from the sale of their crops established themselves as traders or transporters; the first to become agents for the colonial government or the independent state expanded their control over land or derived the benefits that flow from wielding patronage. Rural populations now came to experience relative deprivation. As incorporation proceeded, they recognized their own poverty: they saw a few in their midst rise to levels of affluence undreamt of in the past, and they came face to face with the lifestyle of outsiders — missionaries, traders, government officials, foreign experts, and tourists.

Some rural areas were exploited to the point that the living conditions of their populations declined. Elsewhere specific groups experienced pauperization. But for most rural dwellers living conditions improved; in terms of better health and longer life the change was usually dramatic. However, these very improvements accelerated population growth, and population pressure on the available land became severe in many areas.

With the perception of a better life enjoyed by some locals, and by visitors from the outside, came an awareness of the means towards such an end.[2] Throughout the world today very few are those rural dwellers who have not sold and bought in markets or shops, who have not seen what a school certificate can do for the future of a child, who have not listened to first-hand accounts of what it is like to work in the city. Some improve their condition while staying in rural areas or by moving to other rural areas, as farmers, traders, or artisans. But for many, rural prospects appear dim and the urban scene more promising.

The Rural–Urban Gap

Cities are centres of power and privilege — such a summary statement holds throughout the Third World today.[3] Certainly, many urban dwellers live in desperate conditions. In a survey of various street occupations in Djakarta in 1972, average daily earnings ranging from 120 to 365 *Rupiah* (equivalent to US$ 0.30 to US$ 0.90) were reported in different trades. Most of those interviewed could barely feed their families; the very poor could manage only because they were single. However, even those in the poorest trades reported that they were better off than they had been in the rural areas. There was an increase of nearly two-thirds in reported income in terms of the unweighted average for the different trades (Papanek 1975: 9). In a survey of squatter settlements in Delhi in 1973-4, 54 per cent of household heads were reported to be employed as casual labourers. They found work for only 240 to 260 days a year on average, but this was more than twice the working days they had in the village. And while their wages were low, their average earnings over the year were two and a half times what they could earn in the rural areas (Majumdar 1978: 41). Rural–urban migration in Third World countries can be fully understood only if we grasp the condition of the rural masses.

Comparisons of rural and urban incomes are notoriously problematic.[4] The usual basis is some index of urban wage rates and a crude index of agriculture incomes, such as the prices fetched by cash crops. These measures provide an indication of sudden shifts in urban or rural incomes, e.g. the rapid rise in urban wages in most African countries just before and shortly after the attainment of independence. But they have serious shortcomings. Over time they fail to take into account changes in the productivity of labour in agriculture, which may be decreased by growing population pressure, but increased by improvements in farming techniques. Also, adjustments for differences in the cost of living between rural and urban areas are difficult to make.

The central difficulty for any comparison of urban and rural incomes intended to explain and predict migratory behaviour is the need for disaggregation. Average urban wage rates have little relevance for the unskilled migrant. And rural opportunities will vary according to the endowment of the region of origin and the migrant's local position, i.e. access to land and capital inputs. The point is well illustrated by Shaw's (1976: 74–105) analysis of rural out-migration within and among Latin American countries. Variations in the system of land tenure are significantly related to the rate of rural out-migration from different provinces in both Chile and Peru. Comparing sixteen countries, Shaw shows further that it is not absolute population pressure, but access of labour to land, as mediated by land ownership, that affects rural out-migration (table 3.1). The average rate of out-migration was highest for that group of countries in which more than half the land was held by *latifundios* and where more than half the farms were *minifundios*: Mexico, Peru, and Venezuela.

Table 3.1

Average yearly rates of rural out-migration for sixteen Latin American countries classified by patterns of farm size, 1950–1960[a]

Distribution of farms	Distribution of land	
	Less than half held by *latifundios*[b]	More than half held by *latifundios*[b]
Less than half are *minifundios*[c]	0.56	1.60
More than half are *minifundios*[c]	1.48	2.33

[a]These rates present the arithmetic yearly averages of net rural–urban migration during census periods around the 1950s as a percentage of rural population at beginning of census period. The estimates are based on vital statistics using average rates of natural increase from *United Nations Demographic Yearbooks* and population data from national censuses (Shaw 1976: 5).

[b]*A latifundio* is defined as a farm in excess of 500 hectares.
[c]*A minifundio* is defined as a farm less than 5 hectares.
Source: Shaw (1976: 103).

An evaluation of the rural–urban balance of opportunities has to take into account not only individual incomes but also public amenities. The urban areas, and especially the major cities, invariably offer more and better facilities than their rural hinterlands, and afford superior education and training, for the migrant's children in particular. Piped water assures clean water and releases women from the drudgery of fetching water over long distances. Expert medical care and drugs are available. Electricity replaces the kerosene lamp and the open fire. A few successful migrants even move into subsidized housing. Clearly, here again there is a serious problem of disaggregation. Migrants frequently experience severe discrimination in access to these urban amenities, indeed, for some, housing and sanitary conditions may well be worse than where they came from. Still, on balance most enjoy more amenities than those who stayed behind.

Rural–urban differences are best assessed with an indicator that measures well-being directly. Health and life are universal values and thus provide measures with cross-cultural validity. Mortality data are an obvious indicator. Estimates of infant and early childhood mortality broken down by rural versus urban residence have been assembled recently for a number of Third World countries (table 3.2). The reliability of many of these data is problematic, but there is reason to assume that they tend to understate rather than exaggerate urban–rural differentials. Information on infant and child mortality is usually derived from retrospective surveys. Characterization as urban or rural depends on residence at the time of the survey. Thus some of the births and deaths reported as urban occurred in rural areas, before the migration of the mother, and to that extent high rural mortality rates increase the urban average. And the major source of error, underreporting of children who have died, is more common in rural than in urban areas. Still, the problem of disaggregation remains. At the urban end in particular, mortality rates among migrants can be expected to be higher than the average. The difference should not be exaggerated though: migrants usually constitute a large proportion of the urban population and hence strongly affect urban averages. In most countries the rural–urban differential is so large as to suggest a very real improvement in living conditions for migrants.

Why People Move

A substantial body of research on rural–urban migration has accumulated over the last two decades, and the evidence is overwhelming: the great majority of people move for economic reasons.[6] When people are asked their reasons for moving, the better prospects in the urban economy usually stand out. Also, migration streams between regions can be shown to correspond to income differentials between those regions.[7] And over time, as economic conditions at alternative destinations change, migration streams switch accordingly.[8]

That material considerations are of prime importance in decision making appears to be a universal fact. Certainly, for poor people to behave otherwise

Table 3.2

Infant/early child mortality rates in urban and rural areas[a]

Country (date of survey/census)	Infant deaths[b] Urban	Rural	Deaths to age 2[b] Urban	Rural
Algeria[c] (1970)	122	150		
Bangladesh (1970–4)	115	137		
Benin (1961)	45	117		
Bolivia (1971–2)			166	224
Brazil (1970)	98	101		
Central African Republic[c] (1959–60)	173	194		
Chile (1965–6)			84	112
China (1979)	12	20–67[d]		
Colombia (1970–4; 1968–9)	52	84	75	109
Costa Rica (1968–9)			60	92
Cuba (1973–5)	26	31		
Dominican Republic (1970–1)			115	130
Ecuador (1969–70)			98	145
El Salvador (1966–7)			139	148
Gabon (1960–1)	78	133		
Ghana (1971)	94	132		
Guatemala (1968–9)			120	161
Guyana (1969–73)	60	48		
Honduras (1969–70)			113	150
India[c] (1979)	69	139		
Indonesia (1970–4)	60	96		
Iran (1974)	75	110		
Iraq (1975)	75	98		
Jamaica (1969–73)	37	46		
Jordan (1970–4)	62	78		
Kenya (1977)	91	110		
Liberia (1971)	126	171		
Malaysia[c] (1964–8)	35/34[e]	53		
Mali (1960–1)	99	123		
Mexico (1976–7)	79	97		
Morocco (1961–2)	100	170		
Nicaragua (1966–7)			143	152
Panama (1970–4)	32	36		
Paraguay (1967–8)			69	77
Peru (1971–5; 1967–8)	84	128	132	213
Philippines (1973)	49	61		
Senegal (1973–7)	71	137		
South Korea (1970)			31	48
Sri Lanka (1969–73)	52	120/49[f]		
Sudan (1973)			146	178
Syria (1970)	81	112	112	154
Tanzania[c] (1973)			82/75/115[g]	110
Thailand (1970)	31	74		
Togo (1961)	113[h]	142[i]		

[a] The reader is cautioned against making comparisons of mortality rates across countries. The reliability of the data varies a great deal, and the urban/rural differentials in particular will be affected by varying definitions of urban versus rural populations.
[b] Deaths are per 1,000 live births.
[c] The survey/census did not cover the entire country.
[d] Official data put the rate at 20 to 30. However, an official reported the countrywide rate at 56 which, using the urban rate and assuming that one-fifth of the population is urban, leads to the upper estimate.
[e] The first rate is for metropolitan areas, the second for other urban areas.
[f] The first rate is for estates, the second for other rural areas.
[g] Rates for Dar es Salaam/larger towns/small towns.
[h] Rate for Lomé, the capital city.
[i] Rate for all of Togo except Lomé.
Sources: see n. 5, p. 199.

rapidly leads to a threat to their very survival. Migration entails costs, economic
and frequently psychological, as well as substantial risk much of the time. Those
who engage in it without the prospect of significant material rewards are a
minority and do not substantially affect the aggregate outcome. The 'bright
lights theory' of rural–urban migration has enjoyed a certain vogue, but the
simple fact is that most new arrivals do not have the means to spend much time
in bars, dance halls, or movie theatres. Indeed, many people, rather than move
to the city, prefer to stay in the rural environment in which they have grown up,
provided it offers a similar standard of living to them and equivalent prospects
to their children.

Migration is rarely a solitary affair. Potential migrants do not weigh their
decision in isolation, rather, they are members of groups, such as family, local
community, classmates, which evolve patterns of behaviour which are modified
over time as experience dictates. Even where individuals migrate alone, others
are involved in implementing the move, in adapting to the urban environment,
and in securing a foothold in the urban economy. Frequently migrants have to
make arrangements so that parents are taken care of, that wife and children who
stay behind are assisted.

Many villagers have opportunities to listen to the accounts of migrants who
return briefly or to stay. Some visit kin or friends in the city before making the
move. They thus have a measure of information about urban conditions before
making a decision. When they come to town they more often than not are
given a hand by kin or home people already established there. In a sample
of blue- and white-collar workers who had moved to Bombay, over three-quarters
had one or more relatives living in the city. More than half gave this as an important consideration for coming to Bombay rather than another city. Nine out of
ten reported that they had been assisted by relatives or friends on their arrival:
about two-thirds received free accommodation and food, and two-thirds of the
blue-collar workers and over one-third of the white-collar workers acknowledged
help in finding a job (Gore, 1971: 48–52, 62–7). Similar accounts abound.
Indeed, in some cases potential migrants can afford to wait in the village until
their urban contacts signal a job opportunity.[9]

Extended families usually constitute the central element in such networks.
Relatives are most likely to assist in paying school fees and expenses for uniforms
and books, to provide a home for children who have been sent to town to
pursue their education, to offer the newly arrived migrant shelter and food for
a while. The extended family can be seen as an agent or urbanization in many
parts of Subsaharan Africa and India (Flanagan, 1977, 1978; Eames, 1967).
Gone are the days when elders disapproved of the young men 'running away'
and they literally absconded at night (Banton, 1957: 48 ff.; Rouch, 1956: 78;
Skinner, 1965: 67). Today migration is an accepted behaviour virtually everywhere, and frequently the remittances of migrants furnish villagers with what
for them are the luxuries of life. In some cases, and notably in Southern Africa,

rural areas have become dependent for survival on the earnings passed on to them.

Once a pattern of migration is established, going to town may become the thing to do and the urban experience take on positive connotations. Thus in many parts of the Sudanic belt young men were expected to have spent one or several spells of seasonal migration in Ghana (Rouch, 1956: 194). Such norms usually emphasize the experience to be gained and the challenge to the young to prove themselves. Sometimes they become so generally accepted that individuals are swept along, even when they do not share the economic rationale for going to the city. Migration may in this way become the rule for a community, but once economic circumstances change, collective migration behaviour adapts quickly to the new reality.

The sight of severe and widespread poverty in Third World cities easily leads to the assumption that migrants did not know what to expect, that illusions about the prospects lying ahead brought them to an urban enivronment in which they are trapped. This happens occasionally. Grindal (1973), in an acount of a group of northern Ghanaian immigrants in Accra, suggests that they had indeed been misled by stories told by returned migrants who described the South as a land of great wealth, where the buildings are many stories high, where the people ride in cars or on bicycles, were the 'social life' abounds, and where one can earn money for things such as bicycles, clothing, and finery. Such myths were perpetuated by return migrants who wished to convey a positive image of themselves and their experiences. They talked much less about the problems they had encountered in the cities of the South. In contrast with the expectations thus raised, the successor migrants' first contact with southern urban life was an unexpected and often shattering experience. Many were then forced by pride to remain in the South in order to spare themselves the humiliation of coming home in poverty.

Studies not limited to a small ethnic group tell a different story. Caldwell's (1969: 120 ff.) survey of predominantly migrant areas in the four principal cities of Ghana gives little support to the contention that rural–urban migrants have false expectations. Nearly two-thirds of the migrants interviewed stated that life in the town was just what they thought it would be. Among those who found their impressions markedly astray, almost half had been too apprehensive about urban conditions. Only about one in six immigrants had been disappointed. The unexpected deficiencies of the town divided almost evenly into lesser economic opportunity than anticipated and greater social problems or insufficient facilities to cope with problems of urban living. Studies throughout the Third World similarly report time and again that the great majority of migrants consider that they have improved their condition and that they are satisfied with their move.[10]

The push from rural areas and the pull of urban areas are often distinguished in discussions of migration. Reference to push or pull serves to emphasize the importance of a particular motive in the decision to migrate. Refugees may be said to be pushed out of their rural homes. During the civil strife that accompanied the Partition of India in 1947, about 16 million people fled across the newly established boundaries; most of those uprooted from rural areas sought a new beginning in cities. War, the man-made calamity, has frequently made rural areas so insecure that peasants packed up and left for the relative security of cities. During the many years of the blood bath in Indochina some peasants sought shelter in the cities, though many others were relocated by force. In Indonesia the independence struggle, as well as regional rebellions after the attainment of independence, led to a mass exodus from the affected rural areas. Civil wars in Korea, Malaysia, the Southern Sudan, and Zaïre made peasants abandon their ancestral lands. In Colombia *La Violencia*, the violent conflict in the countryside which lasted for over a decade, was a major factor in rural-urban migration according to some observers.

Elsewhere droughts, earthquakes, cyclones, volcanoes, or floods have posed immediate physical danger as well as usually bringing threats of hunger and disease in their wake. Droughts in Africa and India made rural dwellers abandon their homes and seek relief in urban areas. Although such disasters are commonly referred to as 'natural', they are man-made to the extent that political action, or more typically inaction, increases their severity and impact on the affected population. Anticipatory measures could have limited the impact of the long drought of the 1970s in the Sahel, and mass starvation need not have occurred if more vigorous relief efforts had been initiated in time. In India local crop failures have led to famine time and again while grain stocks elsewhere in the country were hoarded by traders and public authorities impeded the movement of supplies across state boundaries. Indeed, in this age of highly productive agriculture in major parts of the world and of efficient global transport, there can be no justification for hunger anywhere.[11] When men instigate wars, when they are unable to control the elements or are unwilling to help fellow men in their struggle with nature, entire populations become refugees. But there are also less noticed individual refugees, persons who have fallen foul of the rural community or the locally powerful and who seek refuge in the city.

The push from rural areas is dramatized in the case of refugees. But even in these extreme cases it can easily be seen that a comparison is involved: refugees move to more secure settings. Invariably the decision to migrate involves an assessment of alternative locations; people move to a more promising environment. Such is also true where the pull looms large. To take the archetypal case, joining the gold rush implied a perception of more limited opportunities at home.

Migrating to Urban Centres of Unemployment and Underemployment

Great masses of rural people are potentially mobile. And they appreciate the gap between rural and urban standards of living. A great many are prepared to move to town if they can be sure of a livelihood there. Although the days when migrants found work in town for the asking are long gone, substantial numbers nevertheless continue to come to face widespread unemployment and under-employment.

Some migrants come with exceptional qualifications or the right connections and can count on securing a satisfactory income in the urban setting. Many others are not so fortunate. Two interpretations have been advanced to explain migration to cities characterized by unemployment and underemployment. Both argue that the decision to migrate is a rational response to economic conditions. The difference between the two interpretations is accounted for by variations in the structure of urban labour markets.

In Tropical Africa analysis focused on migrants coming in search of jobs that offered wages and working conditions regulated by legislation and/or collective bargaining. They would spend several months trying to secure such a job, but, if unsuccessful, eventually return to the village. Thus in Kampala Hutton (1973: 61–2) found a clearly established pattern in the middle 1960s. Of the unemployed men she interviewed, three-quarters planned to leave if they could not find work, typically within less than six months. More than three-quarters of these intended to return to their rural home. Going home, however, was only a temporary measure; only 11 per cent of the unemployed surveyed felt that they would stay there.

In the 1950s and 1960s much urban unemployment in Tropical Africa appears to have been a function of this pattern. With independence urban wages rose substantially in many countries. Frequently independence was also accompanied by a significant expansion in urban employment. Rural–urban migration surged, the labour shortages that had plagued colonial governments vanished, and urban unemployment appeared. Since much labour migration had been short-term up to this time, recent immigrants faced little competition from entrenched workers and their descendants. The recruitment of unskilled labour approached a random process. Since minimum wages were high, compared with rural incomes, even a lengthy job search constituted a rewarding strategy. Joining the urban unemployed, the rural–urban migrant tried his luck at the urban job lottery (Gugler, 1969).

The proposition that potential migrants take into account not only the rural–urban real-income differentials, but also the probability of securing urban employment, was incorporated into a model by Harris and Todaro (1968; 1970).[12] The probability of obtaining urban employment was defined as the proportion of the urban labour force actually employed. The assumptions underlying this definition were problematic even at the early stages of urban unemployment in Tropical Africa (Gugler, 1976). The most comprehensive test of the proposition was based on a survey of 5,500 households in seven Tanzanian towns in 1971. An analysis of the propensity to migrate according to level of education provided evidence for the significant role of both rural–urban income differentials and urban employment probabilities. In contrast to Harris and Todaro, the employment probability was defined as the ratio of the net number of jobs created over four-month periods (the estimated average time spent in the job search) to the number of unemployed (Sabot, 1979: 120-7).

In retrospect it is clear that the urban job lottery pattern occurred in circumstances that were exceptional. The situation in Tropical Africa increasingly resembles the pattern that prevails in other parts of the Third World, where most rural–urban migrants have little prospect of gaining access to the better earning opportunities. In particular, even an extended search is unlikely to enable the new arrival to join the 'protected' labour force whose wages, working conditions, and perhaps tenure are regulated by legislation and/or collective bargaining, and who are increasingly covered by social-security legislation. Protected workers usually enjoy considerably better conditions than much of the remainder of the work force and therefore cling to their jobs. Competition for any openings is severe and access restricted. Employers have established criteria for recruitment into different job categories, e.g. formal educational qualifications, experience, age, sex. And workers in these firms take advantage of opportunities to assist family members, kin, and friends in joining them.[13]

In a period of transition the hiring process within a major skill category may be quite haphazard, approaching the nature of a lottery, as was the case for unskilled labour in Tropical Africa around the time of independence. But when the urban population becomes stabilized, committed to at least a working life in town, and urban opportunities expand slowly, those migrants who come without the right connections or exceptional qualifications have to settle for the less attractive opportunities. They become part of what Quijano (1974) characterizes as a marginalized labour force. Some find employment in sweat shops at wages well below the minimum wage, subject to dismissal at a moment's notice; they are not covered by labour legislation or it is not enforced; and they do not qualify for social security benefits. Others pick up such casual work as becomes available from time to time. Others again work on their own, perhaps as street vendors, in lines that are open to newcomers, but where competition is fierce and earnings are low.

Who Migrates?

Given the rural–urban gap, wholesale emigration from the disadvantaged rural areas might be expected. But the cities are less than hospitable to new immigrants and only the highly trained, well connected, and hardy venture there. The stream that appears formidable at the urban end constitutes only a small proportion of the rural population. In only a few highly urbanized countries – Argentina, Chile, Venezuela – does out-migration exceed natural population increase in rural areas. In nearly every Third World country the rural population continues to grow.

There are major differences among migrants in terms of socio-economic background, and their urban prospects vary accordingly. At one end of the spectrum are the many who are poor and ill equipped for any but the most menial tasks: some come for regions where poverty is the common fate of the peasantry, e.g. much of Upper Volta; others originate from the lower strata of quite differentiated communities, e.g. village India; with few exceptions they have little schooling and are barred from most of the more rewarding opportunities. At the other end of the spectrum is the migrant from an unusually developed region, or more typically a member of a privileged rural minority, who attends the better schools and climbs the educational ladder high enough to gain access to a promising career in public administration, with a major company, or as a professional.

Young adults always predominate where migration in search of employment is concerned.[14] They are usually unmarried, but even when married have less at stake in the rural areas than their elders. They frequently lack control over resources, land in particular, and wield little power in local affairs. To put it into universal terms: they are at a transitional stage between adolescence and adulthood and not yet firmly committed to an adult role in the local setting. For that very reason they enjoy an advantage in the urban economy: they are not just physically strong, they are more adaptable to the different demands of the urban environment. And if migration entails accepting marginal earnings in the hope of eventually securing a protected job or satisfactory self-employment, then the potential rewards are highest for the young starting on a lifetime urban career.

Clear patterns of sex selectivity can be discerned within major regions. In most of them men outnumber women in the cities, frequently by a substantial margin. This pattern, however, does not hold across the Third World: notably in Latin America and in the Philippines where women predominate in the cities. A review of census data recorded between 1965 and 1975 documents the major regional differences. In Oceania, the unweighted average for six countries showed 128 men for every 100 women in urban areas; in Asia, the average for 13 countries was 109; in Africa, the average for 22 countries came also to 109.[15] In Latin America, in contrast, the average for 23 countries indicated 92 men for every 100 women in urban areas (United Nations, 1980: 117).[16]

The common colonial heritage of Latin America and the Philippines suggests that the predominance of women in rural–urban migration is related to the pattern of land tenure inherited from the colonial period. Indeed, many rural dwellers in these areas own little or no land. Their situation is thus quite unlike that in other regions where women continue to exploit the farm while men migrate, a pattern I shall discuss shortly. However, severe shortages and landlessness are common also in many parts of Asia where men outnumber women in rural–urban migration. In any case, arguments as to why women accompany husbands in migration are insufficient to explain the Latin case where women outnumber men among the rural–urban migrants. We need to understand why substantial numbers of women move on their own, a pattern rarely encountered elsewhere in the Third World. If young adults are the most likely to move because they are at a transitional stage between adolescence and adulthood, then the length of this stage varies a good deal, especially for women. The common heritage of Latin countries includes a religious ethos that exalts the status of the single woman, but most other Third World cultures encourage early marriage and childbearing.[17] Young Latin women thus are potentially mobile independent of a spouse. Faced with limited rural opportunities, they turn to the cities where many households can afford to offer them the low pay and limited benefits that go with domestic service.[18] There may be a second flow of independent women: those who have brought their children up and join the young family household of a son or a daughter in the city — to resume a role of housekeeping and child-rearing.[19]

Patterns of Migration

The movement of individuals is the focus of much migration analysis, and this tendency is encouraged by the fact that migration frequently involves young single persons. However, in many cases migration is not just a once for all move, rather there are a number of moves over a lifetime, a migratory career. Just as the initial decision to migrate is rarely taken in isolation, so the migratory career is best understood with reference to family and community. Three principal patterns of rural–urban migration in the Third World then stand out:

(*a*) temporary migration of men separated from their families;

(*b*) family migration to urban areas followed by return migration to the community of origin; and

(*c*) permanent establishment of urban family households.

These are not fixed statuses. The man who left his family behind may decide that it should join him; the family that expected to return to its community of origin may settle down in the city forever. While changes in migratory status, as perceived by the migrant, typically go in the direction of an increasing commitment to the place of destination, they are clearly affected by changing circumstances in both the urban environment and the area of origin, e.g. deteriorating urban conditions may force men to send their families back to the village.

The preponderance of men over women in rural–urban migration in most of Asia, in Africa, and in Oceania reflects a widespread tendency for male migrants to leave wife and children in their rural area of origin. If the Industrial Revolution engendered the distinction of home and workplace, the separation of worker and dependents has been drastically magnified for many Third World families.[20] Extended family support typically facilitates such simultaneous involvement in the urban and the rural economy. Indeed, the assistance of male kin in certain tasks and the protection they afford frequently appears as a prerequisite for a wife to manage the farm and to hold her own in a male-dominated environment. In contrast, lack of extended family support in the rural setting, characteristic of much of Latin America, probably fosters the migration of entire families.

The migration of individuals, whether single or separated from their family, has distinct economic advantages: it optimizes labour allocation, it minimizes the cost of transport, and, more important in many cases, especially in rural-urban migration, it may minimize the cost of subsistence. Employers save on wages and fringe benefits, and public authorities face less demand for housing and infrastructure, but there are also gains to migrants that motivate them to accept family separation. Living costs in the city are high, while urban earning opportunities for women are usually very limited. Typically wife and children remain on a family farm growing their own food, and perhaps even raising cash crops. Where land is communally controlled and cannot be alienated, as is the case in much of Tropical Africa, there is no compensation for those who give up farming it. A wife who comes to town has to abandon an assured source of income to join a husband on low wages.[21]

Family separation has commonly taken the form of circular migration. After a period of employment lasting six months perhaps, or a couple of years, the migrant returns for an extended stay with his family. In the ideal case the return coincides with peak labour requirements on the farm. In some areas such migrants go as contract labour, i.e. they are recruited for a fixed period of time at, or close by, their home place, and provided with return transportation. Repetition of the circular movement is common so that many migrants build up extended urban experience. It is tempting to speculate that circular migration is the initial response of a 'traditional' society to new opportunities to earn wages and acquire manufactured goods, to visualize 'tribesmen' making short forays into an alien environment. The facts indicate otherwise. Bedford (1973: 126) concludes his review of research in the Pacific islands by emphasizing the persistence of circular migration during 150 years of European contact. In Indonesia, where circular migration was well established during the colonial period, Hugo (1977) reports that it has greatly increased in importance since then, particularly in the last decade.[22] Circular migration in these areas today, as in Tropical Africa in the past, is a function of the recruitment of men at low wages. Where employees have access only to bachelor accommodation, both aspects – the cheap labour policy and the limitation of recruitment to men – are brought into sharp relief. Most strikingly, in environments thus characterized by circular migration, major employers are able to establish a more stable labour force by providing conditions that encourage workers to bring their wives and children.

Circular migration was common in Tropical Africa in colonial days, and high rates of labour turnover and absenteeism were of major concern to employers. However, in the copper mines in what is now Shaba Province, Zaïre, the Union Minière du Haut Katanga changed its labour policy as early as 1927; a measure of compulsion was involved in that workers had to bring their wives, but the region soon boasted a stable labour force. By 1957 the average length of service of African employees in the Katanga mines was eleven years. On the Copperbelt, in what is now Zambia, a policy to establish a permanent labour force was initiated in 1940: permanent accommodations for married employees were made available and the standard of housing improved, adequate schooling in the urban areas was provided, and a pension scheme instituted. The average length of employment of African workers increased from four and a half years in 1956 to seven in 1964.[23] In contrast, the South African gold mines continued to recruit labour on short-term contracts from adjacent areas throughout these years (Wilson, 1972a: 123–7).

In parts of British colonial Africa, as well as on some Pacific islands, circular migration was not just the outcome of policies adopted by employers; the non-settlement of indigenous workers in urban areas was politically intended and administratively enforced. In South Africa the gold mines are prohibited by law from providing family accommodation for more than 3 per cent of their African work force. Many men are recruited on short-term contracts not only for the mines but for various other sectors of the economy. The number of African migrants in the country has been estimated at about half of those in registered employment (Turok and Maxey, 1976: 241). Furthermore, over the last two decades, major efforts have been directed toward uprooting the many Africans who have been long settled in urban areas. Racial oppression has thus created a paradox: the most industrialized country on the continent, where much of the African population has worked in mines, factories, and services for several generations, has the highest proportion of short-term recruits in its labour force.

Circular migration constitutes an adaptation to family separation: the migrant returns regularly to his wife and children for extended periods of time, and he remains actively involved in the extended family, and indeed in village affairs.[24] This strategy fails with the appearance of urban unemployment. If the search for a job takes months, then circular migration is no longer a viable proposition. The migrant who wants to be assured of urban employment has to cling to his job.[25] Instead of extended stays with the family there are such short visits as employment conditions and distance will permit.[26] What had been an economic cost to employers — a labour force characterized by high turnover and absenteeism — becomes an increase in social costs for workers: more severe strains in their relationship with wife, children, extended family, and village community. The frequency of visits varies a great deal. As improved means of transport are introduced, and their cost decreases, monthly or even weekly commuting are becoming more widespread. But in a country such as India many migrants cover considerable distances and can visit their families only during their annual leave. As a folk song in rural Uttar Pradesh laments:

> The field is turning a jaded wasteland.
> In their home the flowers are withering.
> She is fading in her father's place,
> Her husband is wasting away in Calcutta.[27]

A decline in the excess of men over women in rural–urban migration may be taken to indicate that family separation is becoming a less common pattern.

This appears to be the case in many countries in Tropical Africa over the last three decades. There is little evidence to suggest that urban earning opportunities for women have markedly improved. Certainly, as the period of urban employment has lengthened, family separation has become a less satisfactory pattern. At the same time, the increase in wages has diminished the significance of the rural income forgone and of the urban/rural differential in the cost of living. Also, in some areas, land shortages entailing a decline in output or the, often related, breakdown of communal control over land transforming it into an asset that can be realized, have reduced the opportunity cost of abandoning farming.

Settling down in town with a family is usually for the long term, perhaps for a working life, but it does not necessarily signify a permanent move. Strong ties to members of the extended family who have stayed behind, and to the village community, can make an eventual return an attractive proposition. At the same time most migrants, even when managing to support a family in the urban setting, enjoy little economic security. Unemployment and underemployment are rampant, but few qualify for unemployment compensation. And social security systems covering disablement and old age are still in their infancy. For many urban dwellers the solidarity of the village provides an alternative social security, meagre but reliable. Plentiful land under communal control is still a common pattern in Tropical Africa and the Pacific.[28] In such a situation the migrant can maintain his position in the rural community and even during an extended urban career remain assured of access to land on his return.[29] A review of survey data for five West African countries showed in every case a substantial proportion of the migrants indicating the intent to retire in their home area (Gugler and Flanagan, 1978b). A large-scale survey conducted in 1963 in Ghana reported that four-fifths of the long-term migrants over the age of sixty-four had gone back (Caldwell, 1969: 196). In communities in which return migration is a common pattern there is a tendency for it to be established as a cultural norm, just as in the case of rural–urban migration. Rather than acknowledging the economic imperative, the norm of return migration is typically articulated as an ideology of loyalty to the home community.

In parts of Africa, in much of Asia, and especially in Latin America, most migrants have little prospect of maintaining access to agricultural land because of population pressure and/or institutional constraints.[30] They have no plans to return. Instead they press for the provision of social security to urban workers. And they search for sources of earnings outside employment. Escaping the vagaries of employment is a major attraction in establishing one's own business. Also, ownership of a home, however rudimentary, gives the assurance of accommodation and offers the possibility of deriving income from rentals. Hence the strength of squatter movements (see chapter 7 below).

The demands made by migrants on the urban system will thus vary according to their plans for the future. Single migrants expect little. Indeed, the limited prospects they face are the key reason the married left their family behind. They will tend to opt for a minimum of expense for housing so as to shorten their stay or to increase their remittances and savings. Return migrants will remain concerned with conditions in their home area. For permanent migrants the provision of security in the urban setting, especially in old age, becomes crucial.

In delineating these three patterns of migration I have given considerable emphasis to intended as against actual migratory behaviour. There may be reason, however, to discount what migrants have to say about their plans to return to their area of origin, and thus it is frequently assumed that the majority will end their lives in the cities (Lloyd, 1979: 136). I am not so sure. What little data there are suggest that many migrants do realize their aspirations to retire to the rural community. In any case, whatever the broader picture may be, many of the implications of return, as distinct from permanent, migration hold, whether the intention to return is ultimately realized or not; they hold as long as migrants act upon their assumption that one day they will settle down 'at home'.

4

EMPLOYMENT IN THE CITY

Industrialization and urbanization are frequently assumed to be intimately connected. In developed countries cities appear as the necessary outcome of the concentration of people required for the operation of industry. World-wide there is a close correlation between the level of urbanization and the level of development, i.e. the richer countries tend to have a greater proportion of their population living in urban areas. But the relationship between industrialization and urbanization is not as clearcut as it may appear at first sight. Before the Industrial Revolution various regions around the globe boasted cities which were the focus of religious activities, the seats of governments, the centres of trade.[1] An urban population is dependent on the acquisition of an agricultural surplus, but such a surplus may be obtained through offerings to priests, as tribute to rulers, or in exchange for goods.

Colonial cities similarly had little industry, but primarily performed functions of control and commerce. In India and in the larger Latin American countries some industries were established early and a substantial range of industries had developed by the 1940s, but most Third World industrialization came only following the Second World War or even later – e.g. around 1960, the time of independence in Tropical Africa – and was based on imported technology. There are advantages in having access to advanced technology, but in one crucial respect the technology is inappropriate for poor countries: it is geared to the factor availability in highly industrialized countries. As capital stock expanded in those countries, the productivity of labour has risen dramatically. Labour is relatively scarce and expensive, hence modern technology seeks to minimize its role, as witness automation and data processing. Transposing this capital-intensive technology wholesale to poor countries means a heavy drain on scarce capital and foreign exchange resources, and employment for only a few from a burgeoning, low-productivity labour force. But most Third World countries foster such industrialization, if not explicitly, then implicitly through overvalued exchange rates which subsidize the importation of capital goods.

Third World governments and private investors alike might be thought to have a strong interest in technologies that take full advantage of the cheap, abundant labour, but the obstacles are several. For one thing, in many cases labour-intensive technology is simply not available. Research and development, as well as machine-tool industry, are concentrated in rich countries and demand from poor countries is too limited to have much effect. This may change as international funding for 'intermediate technology' becomes available.

Also, in recent years countries such as India and Brazil have become important producers and exporters of machinery. Second, national élites are typically concerned that their country should have the very best equipment, that it should be up to date; this particularly affects the choice of techniques in the public sector.[2] Third, most industrial production takes place in large production units operated by major companies. They tend to provide higher wages, more generous benefits, and considerable job security for reasons I shall discuss in chapter 7, thus increasing the cost of their labour. Fourth, in most Third World countries much of the investment is carried out by foreigners who tend to opt for the more capital-intensive techniques. In a study of the large-scale manufacturing sector in India, Agarwal (1976) found foreign firms to be somewhat more capital-intensive than domestic firms. He adduced a number of considerations: foreign firms paid substantially higher wages, had better access to capital and financial markets, were less constrained by foreign exchange and important regulations, and had greater experience in capital-intensive technologies and operations; domestic firms were less hesitant to hire large numbers of workers because they were more 'at home' in the indigenous labour market.

The modern factory provides little employment in comparison to its fore-runners during the Industrial Revolution. At the same time, industrial expansion is severely limited by the structure of the market in most Third World countries. Much of the population is so poor that it can afford few industrial products: textiles and footwear, food and drink, tobacco, enamelware, paint, plastic utensils, and bicycles are the more common industries for the mass market.[3] Producers of most consumer durables, most strikingly the automobile industry, face the fact that only the small middle- and upper-income groups have the means to acquire their output. In very large countries, of course, even a relatively small middle class constitutes a sizeable market, e.g. in India, Indonesia, Brazil, Mexico, and perhaps Nigeria. A few small countries have established export markets for a large part of their industrial production, e.g. Hong Kong, Taiwan, Singapore, South Korea. These are the exceptions. Few Third World cities are hubs of industry, some are mining centres, but most are primarily nodes in networks of trade and transport and/or seats of government.[4]

Unemployment, Underemployment, and Misemployment

There have been times when employers clamoured for workers, when they complained about high rates of turnover and widespread absenteeism. In the early stages of the incorporation of the rural economy, subsistence farmers saw little reason to sell their labour elsewhere. After the abolition of slavery, colonial governments resorted to forced labour. Then a more subtle means of coercion was found in the imposition of taxes: unless people grew cash crops or parted with some of their cattle, they had to earn wages to pay their taxes. However, nearly everywhere incorporation soon created new demands in the rural areas that only money could satisfy. The high degree of self-sufficiency of the traditional farmer was shattered as he became dependent on goods and services to be purchased in the market. Some raised the cash within the rural economy, but many went to work on plantations, in mines, and in the cities.

Even where rural areas were effectively incorporated, labour shortages were not unheard of, and the urban work force was frequently described as uncommitted. At issue were the level of urban wages and urban living conditions. Thus much of colonial Africa was characterized by a cheap-labour policy which encouraged the circular pattern of labour migration discussed in chapter 3. The policy was buttressed by the proposition that migrants would work less at higher wage rates because they would stay in town only as long as necessary to meet a fixed objective, that they were target workers. In most settings the proposition that the labour-supply function was thus backward sloping bore little relationship to reality; rather, it was a myth that provided the ideological underpinning for a cheap-labour policy (Berg, 1961). Today turnover and absenteeism are no longer of concern; in the major firms they are frequently at levels below those prevailing in industrialized countries.

Third World cities are characterized by an excess of labour with limited skills. Open unemployment constitutes only one facet of urban surplus labour. A second element is underemployment, i.e. the tasks at hand could be satisfactorily carried out by fewer persons. Finally substantial numbers, while perhaps fully employed, produce goods or provide services that can be judged to contribute little to social welfare; such persons may be labelled 'misemployed'.

Information on open urban unemployment in developing countries is notoriously problematic. First of all, there are few data. The most comprehensive effort at compilation, Turnham's (1970: 193-5), provides figures for twelve Asian countries, seven African countries, and twenty countries and dependencies in the Western Hemisphere. The data are limited to one or a few major cities for several African and nearly all American countries, and the rates vary from 26.6 per cent in Algeria to 1.6 per cent in India. Berry and Sabot (1978: 1212) provide more recent data for open urban unemployment for seven Asian, one African, and five Latin American countries. The rates range from 16.9 per cent for Sri Lanka to 1.3 per cent for Thailand. Regional estimates by the International Labour Office for 1975 put open urban unemployment at 6.9 per cent for Asia, excluding China and other centrally planned economies; 10.8 per cent for Africa; and 6.5 per cent for Latin America. In China the urban unemployed were reported to number 10 million in 1979 or about 5 per cent of the urban population (Murphey, 1980: 104); given that about half the urban population is in the labour force (Rawski, 1979: 29-30), this implies an unemployment rate, i.e. the unemployed as a proportion of the labour force, of the order of 10 per cent.

Second, there is good reason to doubt how completely urban populations are covered by censuses, how accurately they are represented in surveys. There is probably a systematic bias in that low-income groups tend to go underreported; in so far as their unemployment rates diverge from the average, the overall unemployment rates reported are affected.

Third, the extent of unemployment reported is very much a matter of definition.[5] Is it restricted to those actively seeking work or does it cover all who are available for work, including those who have become discouraged about finding work? The distinction is likely to affect in particular the unemployment rate reported for women. This is even more the case for a further definitional issue: are those searching/available for part-time work to be included? Finally does part-time work disqualify a person from being considered unemployed?

The unemployed are obviously unproductive, but they are usually not representative of the most desperate urban living conditions. Being unemployed in most cases signifies enjoying the support of parents, spouse, kin, or friends. Thus unemployment is frequently reported to be lower among migrants than among the urban born, who are presumably supported by families already well established in the urban economy. An extended search for a satisfactory job can be a rewarding strategy, especially for those with better qualifications.[6] Comparatively high levels of unemployment among the better educated, a common pattern, may be seen in this light.[7] Also the more educated tend to come from families who can support them through an extended period of unemployment. This is an optimizing approach in so far as accepting a low-level job impedes effective search for the more attractive opportunities. In contrast the poorest, whose relatives and friends cannot help them, and those recent migrants who have nobody to turn to, are forced to find some livelihood: unemployment is a luxury they cannot afford.[8] But productivity is low for the many who are underemployed.

We define 'underemployment' as the underutilization of labour.[9] Such underutilization is most conspicuous where labour is idle part of the time. This is a widespread pattern in agriculture. In the urban sector seasonal fluctuations are prominent in industries related to the agricultural production cycle, in construction, and in the tourist trade. Underemployment is not limited to these sectors, however, but is much more pervasive.

Underemployment takes three distinct forms. In one guise it is related to fluctuations in economic activity during the day, e.g. at markets; over the week or month, e.g. in recreational services; or seasonally. As activity ebbs, casual labour is laid off and many self-employed are without work. Underemployment takes a second form where workers are so numerous that at all times a substantial proportion are less than fully employed, i.e. a reduction in the number of workers would not affect aggregate output. In terms of numbers affected, street vendors constitute the most important category in many countries.[10] A third type of underemployment is what may be appropriately called 'hidden unemployment'; solidarity groups that continue to employ all their members rather than discharging them when there is insufficient work to keep

them fully occupied. Such guaranteed employment is typical of family enterprise, but social ties other than kinship proper, e.g. common origin or shared
religion, can also provide a commitment to maintain every member of the
community.[11]

In his study of the urban labour force in Tanzania, Sabot (1979: 149-77)
defined as underemployed those urban wage earners and own-account workers
whose earnings were below average rural income. By this criterion 10 per cent
of the urban labour force was underemployed in 1970; another 10 per cent
was unemployed — a fifth of the urban labour force could thus be considered
surplus labour. Still, in the context of Tanzania, the loss in potential output
was limited. Since the urban labour force was rather small, perhaps 6 per cent
of the total labour force, the output to be gained by the transfer of the urban
surplus labour to the rural sector was unlikely to add more than 1 or 2 per cent
to national income. In countries in which larger proportions of the labour force
are urban, similar levels of urban unemployment and underemployment suggest
a much more substantial loss of potential output.

Finally there is what we have called misemployment. Labour may be employed
full time, but the tasks performed contribute little to social welfare. Begging is
a clear-cut example. More respectable, but also rather unproductive, are the
activities of the hangers-on in the entourages of the more powerful and affluent.
The role of hanger-on is institutionalized in inflated bureaucracies.[12] There is
also a wide range of illegal activities. It might be argued that the thief who
redistributes resources from the wealthy to his poor family is performing a
service not dissimilar to that of many bureaucrats in a welfare state.[13] And indeed
the productivity of an activity is ultimately socially defined.

Much misemployment focuses on getting crumbs from the table of the rich.
The member of the local élite or middle class, the foreign technical adviser, or
the tourist is begged for a morsel, or made to maintain a company of syco-
phants, or has his wallet snatched. The relationship is vividly portrayed by three
activities: the army of domestics that cleans and beautifies the environment
of a small section of society;[14] the prostitutes who submit to the demands of
those who can pay, and who in the bargain become outcasts; and the scavengers
who subsist on what the more affluent have discarded, who literally live on
crumbs from the rich man's table.[15] Admittedly, most forms of misemployment
make some contribution to social welfare. To take domestic service, the effect
can be substantial where women with qualifications that are in short supply are
released from household work. What is at issue here is that large numbers of
people are employed in a wasteful manner because their labour is so cheap —
compared with the incomes of the élite and the middle class. The point is well
demonstrated by the fact that the requirements of middle-class households
for domestic help rapidly decrease as domestic wages rise.

Throughout much of the Third World today, rural families send their sons
and daughters to the city so that they will be able to partake, however little, in

whatever demeaning way, of its riches. As Lomnitz (1977: 208) put it in her study of a shanty town in Mexico City:

The settlers of Cerrada del Cóndor may be compared to the primitive hunters and gatherers of preagricultural societies. They go out every day to hunt for jobs and gather the uncertain elements for survival. The city is their jungle; it is just as alien and challenging. But their livelihood is based on leftovers: leftover jobs, leftover trades, leftover living space, homes built of leftovers.

Bienefeld's (1979) account of the persistent employment problems in the feudal cities of medieval Europe suggests close similarities. Trade and tribute, labelled 'taxes' these days, played a predominant role in the city's economic life, and there was a proliferation of personal services, including an omnipresent army of peddlers, beggars, jugglers, and thieves. Once labour had been transformed into a commodity, the inducement to invest in productive activities was impaired in a number of ways that have striking parallels in present-day Third World cities: alternative activities, such as trade, continued to offer higher profit rates; greater security was found in the acquisition of real estate − in modern times foreign investments provide a haven from political turmoil; there was little expansion in internal demand because of low wages, undeveloped transport networks, and the modest rate of growth of agriculture; and it was difficult to secure large external markets for manufactured goods.

Unemployment, underemployment, and misemployment add up to a massive problem in Third World cities related to three dimensions of inequality. The sharply differentiated incomes of the affluent and the masses which allow the few to pay so little for the services of the many foster misemployment. The privileged position of the protected labour force compared with that of the bulk of urban workers causes unemployment where it encourages workers to hold out in the hope of joining the protected labour force, and it leads to underemployment as the mass of urban workers, with little capital equipment, compete for limited markets. Finally rural–urban inequality encourages substantial rural–urban migration which contributes to the rapid expansion of the urban labour force.[16] Reductions in inequality on any of these dimensions can be expected to lead to a more productive allocation of labour.

Women and Children in the Labour Force

Unemployment is usually reported considerably higher for women than for men, even though many women do not actively look for work because they are aware that the opportunities open to them are severely limited. Among the underemployed, women are found in disporportionate numbers in many countries. The ubiquitous traders of West Africa are legendary; less is known about the women who work in family enterprises. And many women are misemployed. Substantial numbers make a living from prostitution.[17] But it is domestic service that provides the largest category of employment for women in many countries.[18] The waste of women's labour in their own households, on chores which are to some extent superfluous, may be seen as part of the same issue.

The incomes and working conditions of women and children are a matter for concern, but they have received little serious attention to date. Nici Nelson's (1979) detailed study of the economic activities of women in a squatter settlement in Nairobi is an outstanding exception. She found women to be much more restricted than men in their choice of economic activity. Only a small proportion of the local business establishments were run by women, and most working women were involved in illegal beer brewing or prostitution. Women were handicapped because they were less well educated than men, had fewer skills of commercial value, and supported and cared for children. Indeed, a disproportionate number of successful women entrepreneurs were barren. Other women began to expand and consolidate their business only in their late forties when most or all of their children had grown up and perhaps contributed to a joint household income.[19]

Certainly, marginal forms of employment are attractive to women who need to supervise their children. Hence women accept work put out at low rates, for example sewing, and trade from their homes. In China many women are reported to be working in neighbourhood workshops. They usually enjoy neither the wages nor the fringe benefits that come with comparable work in state enterprises, but can stay close to home (Whyte, n.d.b: 17; Howe, 1978: 178-9). However, there is clearly also a strong element of discrimination against women in the urban labour markets of the Third World, as indeed in industrialized countries. Domestic service is the prime example. In many countries it is largely women who accept the long hours and low pay. They are usually not allowed to keep their children with them, but have to entrust them to the care of others or leave them to their own devices.

Here again, if there is inequity, sex discrimination also entails high costs for the collectivity. If women were fully integrated into the urban economy, a smaller population would have to be accommodated in urban centres to perform the same economic tasks. Accordingly a lower investment would be required in key elements of infrastructure, such as housing and sewerage, which are considerably more expensive than their rural equivalents. There could also be savings in the requirements for services such as the provision of fuel and the distribution of staple foods, which are similarly more costly in the urban setting. The wives and daughters of the predominantly male work force require infrastructure and services, but they remain largely unemployed, underemployed, or misemployed (Boserup, 1970: 206-8). That substantial numbers of men are unemployed or underemployed as well does not invalidate the argument. To the extent that urban employment goes preferentially to men, migration by men is encouraged. Opening up employment opportunities for women would probably attract only a few women from rural areas, given the numbers of women already in urban residence who would have considerable advantages over new arrivals.

Child labour is all too common in Third World countries. Many children are found in services, others in construction and in factories. Children working in underground mines have been reported in India and Colombia. In Seoul shoe-shine boys are integrated into crime syndicates. They work twelve hours a day, seven days a week, every week of the year, stopping only if they are sick or if it is raining. They are part of a team that works together, eats together, and lives together. They associate only with each other. The boys' lives are totally con-trolled by the syndicate that houses and feeds them, provides them with the implements of their trade – and takes about 85 per cent of their earnings (Kang and Kang, 1978).[20]

Many families have no choice but to put even quite young children to work (Leiserson, 1979). The alternative, families abandoning their children, is not uncommon. In Bogotá an estimated 5,000 *gamines* survive by their wits: eight- to fourteen-year-old boys beg, steal, and rob, band together, and sleep in the streets, covered with cardboard and plastic sheets.[21] Children working and children abandoned – in both cases the consequences in terms of education and health are serious.

The Informal Sector

A common approach to the unemployment problem contrasts two sectors that, it is argued, differ sharply in their labour requirements. Dualistic conceptions of Third World economies have long been current. An early distinction was between 'modern' industry and 'traditional' artisanship, but the unsatisfactory nature of these labels soon became obvious. 'Modern' activities, such as servicing and repairing imported automobiles or television sets, are frequently carried out in a quite 'traditional' manner, i.e. in small, poorly equipped shops.

In the 1960s renewed attention was drawn to the 'murky' sector because in country after country substantial additions to the urban labour force failed to show up in employment statistics. While there was concern about unemploy-ment, there was also an increasing recognition that a large and growing number of people were engaged in non-enumerated activities. They were thought to be working in the service sector. However, statistical enumeration is primarily a function of the size of a firm's work force, and small enterprises in the primary sector, e.g. peri-urban gardening, and in the secondary sector, shoe-making for example, are just as likely to go unenumerated as are street vendors.

Hart's (1973) classic paper, first presented in 1971, introduced a new termin-ology, distinguishing an 'informal' from a 'formal' sector. On the basis of research in a low-income neighbourhood in Accra, Ghana, he emphasized the great variety of both legitimate and illegitimate income opportunities available to the urban poor. Subsequently McGee (1976) explored various approaches towards what he called the 'protoproletariat'. The response to Hart's plea that a historical, cross-cultural comparison of urban economies in the development process must grant a place to the analysis of 'informal' as well as 'formal' structures was nothing less than overwhelming.[22]

Hart's terminology was adopted by a mission to Kenya organized by the International Labour Office. It argued that the informal sector provided a wide range of low-cost, labour-intensive, competitive goods and services, and recommended that the Kenya government should promote the informal sector (ILO, 1972: 223–32 and *passim*). The report characterized the two sectors in the following terms (ILO, 1972: 6):

Informal activities are not confined to employment on the periphery of the main towns, to particular occupations or even to economic activities. Rather, informal activities are the way of doing things, characterised by —

(*a*) ease of entry;
(*b*) reliance on indigenous resources;
(*c*) family ownership of enterprises;
(*d*) small scale of operation;
(*e*) labour-intensive and adapted technology;
(*f*) skills acquired outside the formal school system; and
(*g*) unregulated and competitive markets.

Informal-sector activities are largely ignored, rarely supported, often regulated and sometimes actively discouraged by the Government.

The characteristics of formal-sector activities are the obverse of these, namely —

(*a*) difficult entry;
(*b*) frequent reliance on overseas resources;
(*c*) corporate ownership;
(*d*) large scale of operation;
(*e*) capital-intensive and often imported technology;
(*f*) formally acquired skills, often expatriate; and
(*g*) protected markets (through tariffs, quotas and trade licenses).

This characterization of the formal sector is quite persuasive. In every Third World country large-scale enterprises play a major role in various sectors of the economy. Their status ranges from public-sector companies to multinational corporations to locally owned firms, but they are invariably closely related to the state. Their power *vis-à-vis* the state and other participants in the economy raises questions about their impact on the autonomy of the national polity and the threat of monopolistic control over sectors of the economy. A major part of the formal-sector labour force typically enjoys a measure of protection in terms of working conditions, job security, and social security. The establishment of such a 'labour aristocracy' has political implications that will be addressed in chapter 7. For present purposes, concern focuses on the employment implications of the tendency of large-scale enterprises to rely on imported, and hence capital-intensive, technology. Their recruitment of expatriate personnel for the highly skilled positions adds a further irritant.

In contrast, the informal sector appears to offer a panacea for the urban employment problem, while at the same time providing scope for the eclosion of local entrepreneurial talent. The size of the informal sector is impressive enough. Admittedly, attempts to assess its share of the urban labour force encounter serious difficulties. Not only, as we shall see, is the informal sector nearly impossible to delineate, but many of its workers have reason to evade attempts to record them. Nevertheless, there can be no doubt that in most Third World countries a large proportion of the urban work force is found in this sector. Estimates for cities in six Latin American and two Asian countries suggest that between 39 and 69 per cent of the urban labour force work in the informal sector (Souza and Tokman, 1976: 358; Mazumdar, 1976: 659).

The view that the informal sector provides the answer to the urban employment problem is strengthened by the notion that government policy towards it contains few elements of positive support and promotion, and many elements of inaction, restriction, and harassment, as the International Labour Office (1972: 226) mission argued in the case of Kenya. It should be noted, though, that Kenya gained independence only in 1963, and that its European settlers had established regulations expressly keeping African enterprise out of the cities.[23] And while formal–sector firms typically enjoy privileged access to credits, foreign exchange, and tax concessions, entrepreneurs in the informal sector can be seen to enjoy competitive advantages *vis-à-vis* large-scale industry in so far as they escape taxation, social-security levies, and government regulation of wages, working conditions, and job security. Eckstein (1977a: 141-7) describes such a pattern in Mexico and suggests that the implied support for the informal sector is intended by the government.

The central difficulty of the two-sector model is that any multidimensional definition can be applied to only one of the sectors, leaving the other sector as a residual category. A multidimensional definition of the formal sector, such as that advanced by the Kenya report, fits large-scale industry reasonably well. It characterizes also, by and large, major commercial, financial, and service organizations, and government administration. If we accept it, we are left with an informal sector which does not conform to a similarly distinctive ideal type, but rather covers a varied range of activities. While none of these activities has all the characteristics taken to define formal-sector activities, the postulate that the informal sector has the obverse characteristics of the formal sector is clearly untenable. To take the characteristics used in the Kenya report, entry into much of the informal sector is far from easy;[24] a self-employed repairer of television sets is dependent on imported supplies; it is quite common for small-scale enterprises to employ non-family labour; illegal activities may be organized on a large scale; the owner-operator of a taxi uses capital-intensive technology which has not been adapted to the resource constraints of a poor country; skills are acquired in the formal school system and in formal-sector employment; and there is sometimes monopolistic control of markets.[25]

The shortcomings of the informal-sector concepts are not just of analytical concern; rather, they invalidate any attempt at policy prescription. As Bromley

(1978: 1034) put it,

It is often mistakenly believed that a single policy prescription can be applied to the whole informal sector, so that governments should adopt similar programmes towards artisans making furniture, towards artisans illegally manufacturing fireworks, towards sellers of basic foodstuffs, and towards prostitutes or drug-peddlers. The informal sector is large enough to permit and diverse enough to necessitate a wide range of different policy measures, allowing governments to mix incentives, assistance, neglect, rehabilitation and persecution within the total range of policies.

In particular, the assumption that the informal sector is the province of the poor is subject to important modifications. On the one hand, low incomes are common in the formal sector; many firms employ substantial numbers of casual workers at low wages, without fringe benefits, and unprotected by social security. On the other hand, large variations in earnings occur not only across the informal sector but even among more narrowly defined categories of workers, e.g. the self-employed and those in tertiary activities (Mazumdar, 1976). Any comparison of incomes in the formal and the informal sector has further to allow for the fact that the informal sector disproportionately recruits the very young and the very old, women, and the less educated. Still, earnings differentials between the sectors remain substantial even when sex, age, and education are controlled for (Mazumdar, 1979; Merrick, 1976).

The Kenya report dichotomized the urban economy into the formal and the informal sectors and recommended strengthening the linkages between the two sectors as a strategy of promoting the informal sector (ILO, 1972: 228–31 and *passim*). Since then studies in other countries have shown significant existing linkages.[26] Such linkages provide the basis for a good deal of informal-sector activity. However, the informal-sector participants in such relationships tend to be in a subordinate position. In particular, the informal sector can be argued to subsidize the formal sector: its low-wage labour produces low-cost inputs for the formal sector and provides cheap goods and services for formal-sector workers (Portes and Walton, 1981: 67–106).

The interrelation of the informal and the formal sectors is strikingly illustrated in Birkbeck's (1979) account of garbage pickers in Cali, Colombia. The largest proportion of potentially saleable garbage is collected and started on its way by garbage pickers working on their own, and most of their production is destined for large factories. In the paper industry waste paper provides a third of raw material requirements, and some 60 per cent of that waste paper comes from individual pickers. The earnings of the majority of pickers are about a third of the lowest wage paid by the major paper company, and they are neither assured of a fixed and regular income nor enjoy employee and social security benefits. Throughout the informal sector many of those conventionally described as self-employed are thus in fact disguised wage workers, such as outworkers or commission sellers, or dependent workers who depend on one or more larger enterprises for credit, the rental of premises or equipment, a monopolistic or oligopolistic supply of raw materials or merchandise, or a monopsonistic or oligopsonistic outlet for their production (Bromley and Gerry, 1979: 58).

Quijano (1974) moves beyond the two-sector distinction and explores the articulations in a three-sector model for Latin America. Monopolistic formations dominate the manufacturing sector; they are oriented towards complex technology imported from the industrialized countries and tend to exclude labour. An intermediate level of competitive manufacturing, semi-manufacturing, and artisan production has neither the stability nor the capacity for expansion necessary to admit in a stable way the labour force that assembles around it or to retain that which it already has.[27] Finally, a 'marginal pole' lacks stable access to basic resources of production that serve the dominant levels of each economic sector; under such conditions the occupations and mechanisms for their organization can operate only around residual resources and, for the most part, residual activities:

A growing sector of the labour force is produced which with regard to the employment needs of the monopolistically organised hegemonic levels of activity is *superfluous*; and with respect to the intermediate levels organised under the competitive form and consequently marked by permanent instability of its weakest enterprises and its peripheral occupations, this labour force is *floating*, since it tends to be intermittently employed, unemployed or underemployed according to the contingencies affecting this economic level. As a result, it inevitably tends to be forced to take refuge in the roles characteristic of the 'marginal pole', where it fluctuates among a numerous range of occupations and labour relations. In this sense, the principal tendency of this labour force is to turn 'marginal' and to differentiate itself and establish itself as such within the economy. (Quijano, 1974: 414–15)

Clearly any assessment of the prospects for the informal sector, and of policy options, has to be both specific and comprehensive, i.e. it has to focus on particular activities and those engaged in them and to take full account of linkages, with the formal sector in particular. Beyond that, any attempt to alleviate the problem of urban surplus labour is confronted with the prospect that its very success will attract additional migrants from the rural areas.[28] The urban employment problem cannot be solved within the urban arena, unless it is sealed off by a break in the rural–urban connection. This is the policy in South Africa, in Indonesia for the capital city Jakarta, and generally in socialist countries. It is implemented through controls on migration designed to curtail rural–urban movements. Indeed, the universal pattern of a net rural–urban flow was reversed in China when middle-school leavers were sent to rural areas during the Cultural Revolution, in Cambodia when the Khmer Rouge regime imposed a wholesale urban exodus. If the costs have been staggering in the latter case, the effectiveness of migration control is limited, even where drastic measures are taken to enforce them. Half of the residents in the African township of Soweto, on the outskirts of Johannesburg, are said to live there illegally. Large numbers of Soviet citizens are thought to have moved to Moscow without the required permit. In China hundreds of thousands of rusticated middle-school leavers have returned to the cities on their own.[29]

Where the rural–urban flow continues unimpeded, no solutions to the employment problem can be effected within the urban labour market, let alone by promoting the informal sector. Rather, the issue of rural–urban inequality has to be addressed. This is of necessity a long-range proposition, and it faces formidable obstacles everywhere. Yet if there is an urban employment problem, it can be solved only in the rural areas.

The Fragmented Labour Market

So far we have looked at migration and the urban labour market in very broad terms. In reality labour markets, like most markets, are invariably fragmented in a variety of ways, i.e. different categories of people enjoy differential access to earning opportunities. This is obvious in geographical terms: the better opportunities tend to be concentrated in urban areas, inaccessible to those who are beyond commuting distance. But even within any one local labour market considerable fragmentation is to be found. Migration streams in turn can be seen to be differentiated as migrants respond to opportunities. Two major sources of differentiation stand out: labour markets are stratified and segmented.

Wages, job security, social security, and working conditions stratify the urban labour force in a manner that is the more highly visible as it translates into differences in dress, mode of transport, and housing. The labour market appears composed of several distinct layers of earning opportunities. Formal education qualifications are frequently a prerequisite for entrance at various levels. They may be thought to be related to the functional requirements of a given job; however, beyond certain minimum requirements, it is probably more accurate to see such entrance prerequisites as a function of the educational characteristics of the labour pool. Across countries the educational prerequisites for a given job tend to be higher in those countries where the labour force is more educated, and within countries the demands put on applicants invariably increase along with the expansion of the educational system. 'Credentials' thus appear as a screening device, and their relationship to functional job requirements becomes increasingly tenuous as first primary, then secondary, and finally tertiary education reach an ever larger proportion of the population.

The labour market may be compared to a geological formation composed of a sequence of quite distinct horizontal layers. This image corresponds closely to the patterns established by formal organizations. And public discourse tends to focus on the access various population groups have to formal education as the prerequisite for entry at various levels. However, labour markets are not only thus stratified, the horizontal layers are also segmented vertically. Rather than one, there are several geological formations, separated to the extent that entrance to each is controlled by networks of patronage that give privileged access to certain categories of people and deny access to others.

We have seen in chapter 3 that most migrants expect and obtain assistance from urban contacts. The urban host, to help the new arrival, to relieve the burden of housing and perhaps even of feeding him, has good reason to find him work. Thus migrants who have secured employment introduce their relatives and other people from 'home' to their firm. Employers on their part may find such 'family brokerage' convenient and even advantageous. They know that skills and knowledge are not as important for many positions as other qualities, e.g. dependability, potential for training, persistence, or initiative. Further, in many cases any advertisement will generate all too many applications from people with similar qualifications. In such circumstances the employer prefers to use a broker. He selects among his employees one or two persons he trusts and asks them for suitable candidates, whom they will probably have to train. The broker will look to his extended family for suitable candidates and draw up a short list. He may coach a candidate on how to fill in the application forms and on how to react at the interview. A close and complex relationship thus grows up between the employer, the broker, and the employee. The broker has increased the socio-economic position of his kin group and his own standing within it, his recruit has obtained a job, and the employer can exert leverage over his employee through the broker (ILO, 1972: 509–10). In small-scale enterprises the owners themselves may initiate their relatives and other people from 'home' into their trade.

Because of such particularistic recruitment patterns, migrants of common origin tend to cluster in certain jobs and trades. In a survey of fourteen villages in West Java, Indonesia, Hugo (1977) found that the two narrowly defined occupational categories most common among migrants from any one village accounted for over two-fifths to four-fifths of migrants and commuters (table 4.1). In Accra the timber market was controlled by immigrants from one village in faraway Niger in the 1950s (Rouch, 1956). And migrants from the community of Mexticacan are involved in the manufacture and sale of ice cream throughout Mexico (Rollwagen, 1971).

The fragmented character of the urban labour market in turn affects the composition of migrant streams. The role of formal educational prerequisites in screening entrance to the more privileged strata motivates parents in rural areas and small towns to make every effort to secure the maximum education for their children. For those who have advanced sufficiently far on the educational ladder there can be little doubt but that attractive opportunities are awaiting them in the city. Others, while not so fortunate, feel assured of a future there because their contacts give them privileged access to a particular niche in the urban economy.[30]

The vertical and horizontal differentiation of the urban-labour market is thus mirrored in the stream of migrants. If their prospects vary widely, these prospects

Table 4.1

Occupational clustering of migrants and commuters from fourteen West Java villages working in urban areas, 1973

Village	Number of migrants and commuters	in most common occupation	(%)	Proportion of migrants and commuters in second most common occupation	(%)	in two most common occupations (%)
I	74	Groundnut hawker	65	Government/Army	15	80
II	55	Cooked food/cigarette hawker	35	Day labourer	22	57
III	91	Cooked food hawker	43	Jewellery hawker	21	64
IV	70	Becak driver	57	Day labourer	16	73
V	82	Becak driver	41	Factory worker	34	75
VI	100	Labourer	35	Hospital worker	13	48
VII	87	Kerosene hawker	32	Household domestic	15	47
VIII	77	Airline/hotel worker	32	Household domestic	10	42
IX	87	Miscellaneous goods hawker	60	Government/Army	12	72
X	88	Driver	27	Government/Army	26	53
XI	87	Becak driver	38	Construction worker	20	58
XII	92	Carpenter	49	Government/Army	28	77
XIII	99	Barber	31	Bamboo worker	20	51
XIV	104	Bread hawker	42	Driver	32	74

Source: Hugo (1977: 64). Reproduced by permission of the Editor, *Bulletin of Indonesian Economic Studies*, and the author.

are at least reasonably well defined for many. The integration of new arrivals into the urban-labour market is thereby eased. Discontent over discrimination does not crystallize as long as the criteria for privileged access vary from one little niche to the next. In many countries, however, rather large fragments of the labour market appear as the exclusive preserve of a racial, ethnic, religious, or political group. Such a situation shapes the contours of political conflict, an issue which will be addressed in chapter 7.

5

THE HOUSING OF THE URBAN POOR

Housing is a highly visible dimension of poverty. Perhaps that is why it represents such an emotive issue in so many Third World cities. The sight of thousands, and often millions, of people huddled in shabby accommodation with a minimum of servicing is certain to evoke some reaction from politicians and governments. In this chapter I examine the nature of low-income housing and the changing policies of governments towards it. How successful are the poor in building their own homes, what are their main priorities, and how do they order these priorities? To what extent is the success of so-called self-help housing limited by the structural conditions of Third World cities? To what extent are there signs of improvement or deterioration in urban housing conditions? How have governments reacted to the housing issue and why have these policies been adopted? To what extent have governments acted in the interests of the poor and how far have their actions worsened urban conditions? By asking such questions, I hope to provide not merely a description of Third World urban housing conditions but also an explanation of why such conditions persist.

The Dimensions of Poverty

It is only too easy to demonstrate the effects of poverty on housing in most Third World cities. On any index of service provision, household density, or physical quality, a majority of the urban population is living at standards that are clearly unacceptable when compared to the way most Europeans or North Americans live. In India more than half the urban households occupy a single room, with an average occupancy per room of 4.4 persons (Rosser, 1972). In Greater Bombay 77 per cent of households with an average of 5.3 persons live in one room (Misra, 1978: 375-6) and many others are forced to sleep on the pavements at night (Ramachandran, 1974). In Ghana room densities range from 2.5 to 3.2 in the cities of Takoradi, Kumasi, and Accra (Hinderink and Sterkenburg, 1975).

In terms of service provision, the situation is equally alarming. In Djakarta only 8 per cent of houses were supplied with both electricity and water in 1969, and 76 per cent had neither facility (Oliver, 1971: 66). In Cape Coast, Ghana, 73 per cent of houses lacked water and 25 per cent electricity (Hinderink and Sterkenburg, 1975: 293).[1] In Brazil, in 1970, 47 per cent of Recife's houses lacked running water and in Greater São Paulo, 41 per cent (IBGE, 1970). In Calcutta 77 per cent of all families share lavatories with other families and more than 10 per cent have no facility at all (Lahiri, 1978). In the middle-sized Colombian town of Buenaventura, 86 per cent of all households lacked water in 1964 and 84 per cent lacked electricity (DANE, 1967).

I could continue to list figures of this kind but the level of neglect is already more than clear. Instead, I shall use the space to offer the warning that three points need to be borne in mind in evaluating data of this kind. The first is that services in Third World cities compare very favourably with those of the surrounding rural areas. In Malaysia, for example, 61 per cent of urban dwellings lack an inside flush toilet but the proportion in rural areas is 91 per cent; while 17 per cent of urban dwellings lack an electricity supply, in the rural areas it is 69 per cent (Wegelin, 1977: 61). In Colombia only 11 per cent of urban households lacked piped water in 1973 and a similar proportion electricity, but in the rural areas the figures were 71 and 86 per cent respectively (DANE, 1977). While this comparison in no sense condones urban conditions it does warn against over-reacting to so-called urban squalor and romanticizing the rural life. If services in urban areas are thoroughly inadequate, those in most rural areas are usually much worse.

The second reservation is that most of the criteria by which we judge housing conditions in poor countries are highly subjective and ethnocentric. While the poor of India would no doubt welcome flush toilets in their homes, it is unlikely that they view the lack of such a facility in the same cataclysmic way as would a European or North American. Families unaccustomed to such 'luxuries' often view their real needs differently. For many Third World poor, 'our' standards are often irrelevant because they have more urgent needs. To a hungry family food is of far greater importance than shelter, especially where the climate is dry and warm. The importance of this reservation will become clearer when we discuss architectural norms and public housing provision. But the needs of the poor, or at least the ordering of their priorities, are frequently misunderstood by professionals, let alone by those of us who have lived most of our lives in the comfort of a developed country.

Thirdly, judgements about housing conditions must also take into account different cultural, social, and environmental conditions within Third World cities. Those who compare conditions in large and small cities need to recognize that the manifestations of poverty differ. In large cities poor housing conditions are likely to be represented in the high proportions of people living in one room and paying high rents. Jobs and services may be available in the central areas of those cities, but space is at a premium. In small cities the problems may be just the reverse. Regional differences are also important in international comparisons. In many African and Asian cities renting a home is much more common than in most Latin American cities; in Lagos and Bangkok most families rent rooms (Achunine Obi, 1979; Romm, 1973). In Latin American terms high rental levels may be judged detrimentally, but the different situation may not be due entirely to poorer economic circumstances. Peil (1976, 1981) and Muench (1978) note that renters in West Africa and Kampala are not poorer than owners. In some cases renters do not purchase homes in the city because they have every intention of returning to the countryside, in other cases they prefer to invest surplus funds in a business, to avoid the responsibility of home ownership, or to maximize their residential mobility (Muench, 1978). Similarly renting may not constitute as exploitative a situation as that in many developed countries. Frequently, as in Lagos or in Bucaramanga (Colombia), owners live in the same dwelling and rent to poorer members of their family at relatively low rents (Piel, 1981; Edwards, forthcoming; Marris, 1979; 426). Similarly standards of physical construction should be viewed with caution. It is no coincidence that most pictures of bad housing conditions are taken in hot climates. To most European eyes a bamboo house is inferior to one built of brick; wood inferior to cement. Had the story of the three little pigs been written by an African, it might well have ended differently. In a hot climate bamboo and wood are entirely adequate construction materials and it may be the poor of more temperate brick-built cities, such as Quito, La Paz, or Buenos Aires, who suffer the 'worst' housing conditions. As Peil (1976) suggests, it is often far more pleasant to live out of doors in tropical countries.

Local factors must be considered carefully, therefore, when making comparisons of conditions across the Third World. At the same time the positive correlation that exists between the level of national wealth and the quality of housing means that there are higher proportions of poor urban dwellers in Asia or Africa than in Latin America. In addition it is probable that the African and Asian urban poor live in worse conditions than do their Latin American counterparts. Standards of servicing, for example, are superior in Latin America to those of Africa or Asia. In Latin American cities the poor must wait several years for electricity or running water to be installed, but services normally arrive. By contrast, the poor of most Asian or African cities may never receive services. Such variations are in large part an outcome of differences in the levels of national and urban prosperity. Cities such as São Paulo or Buenos Aires, which concentrate large proportions of the total wealth of countries which by African standards are immensely rich, will naturally possess better conditions than those of African capitals. While these superior services and resources may be disproportionately concentrated in middle- and upper-income housing areas, even the Latin American poor benefit to some degree from the higher level of national and urban resources. Clearly there are other sources of variation between cities. Societal organization is a vital consideration; in terms of service provision, if not in terms of living space, the poor of Havana live better than those of other Caribbean islands (Acosta and Hardoy, 1972). But, as many socialist leaders would be the first to admit, there are limits to what can be done with reduced financial resources.

Rationality among the Poor

The differences in housing conditions in different Third World cities are a function of differing levels of per capita income, the distribution of wealth, the rate of urban growth, and the form of societal organization. But they also reflect differences in the responses of the poor in each city. Such responses vary dramatically according to the poor's own expectations of their life chances, their own view, reasonable or untenable, of what kind of housing they want and the degree to which they are organized to improve their housing situation. It is difficult for the poor to escape their poverty given the economic and social situation in most Third World countries. But, within the limits we shall discuss, the poor's response to that poverty is rational, innovative, and nearly always more perceptive than often they are given credit for.

Perhaps no two people have played a greater role in drawing our attention to the rationality of the poor with respect to their housing situation than Mangin (1967) and Turner (1967, 1969). In their work in Peru they demonstrated that the shanty, which was so often, and of course sometimes rightly, denigrated as the ultimate in penurious living conditions, was frequently the basis of an adequate shelter. Rather than merely being a shack without services, it was the foundation upon which the more fortunate, better off, or more innovative sought a way out of their poverty. Over time, spontaneous housing tended to improve as inhabitants built outside walls, extra rooms, a solid roof, and sometimes a second floor. *In favourable circumstances* the poor could produce substantial, spacious, and reasonably serviced homes.

Turner and Mangin did more, however, than merely show that over time many poor families are able to consolidate their housing. They also demonstrated that the reaction of the poor to poverty was rational and that families recognized the most sensible ways of improving their living conditions. Such an argument was diametrically opposed to the conventional wisdom of the day which owed much to the ideas of Oscar Lewis. Lewis's (1966) concept of a 'culture of poverty' had achieved widespread popularity. At its crudest, this view encouraged the idea that the poor are poor because they are poor. Poor children eat badly, receive a poor education, and receive from their families and cultural peers a training that encourages them to accept their poverty as inevitable. As Portes (1972: 269) notes, the concept came to 'denote a situation in which people are trapped in a social environment characterized by apathy, fatalism, lack of aspirations, exclusive concern with immediate gratifications and frequent endorsement of delinquent behaviour.'

The 'culture of poverty' view of the poor persists to this day among many higher income groups. It persists, perhaps, because it is a highly convenient explanation to the wealthy; by implication poverty is the poor's own fault. In this sense it serves as 'a vehicle for interpreting the social reality in a form which serves the social interests of those in power' (Perlman, 1976: 247). But, convenient though it may be, it has little basis in reality. Mangin and Turner showed how the poor responded sensibly and rationally to the choices and opportunities open to them in their housing situation. And while the poor undoubtedly contribute at times to their own poverty, the basic causes of that poverty are beyond their control. The poor are not a separate sub-society but act much like everyone else. In Perlman's (1976: 234) words: 'In short, they have the aspirations of the bourgeoisie, the perseverance of pioneers, and the values of patriots. What they do not have is an opportunity to fulfil their aspirations.'

Rejection of myths such as the 'culture of poverty' is gradually leading to important changes in housing policy. If the poor are considered to be incapable of helping themselves, then they have to be helped. In a housing context this tends to mean that only governments are capable of building satisfactory housing for the poor. By contrast, the major policy recommendation in Turner's work is that governments are best advised to help the poor to help themselves. Such a recommendation has the additional virtue that self-help housing often produces superior shelter to that produced by governments, if only because the poor understand more clearly the role that housing plays in their lives. Architects, by contrast, are too often concerned with their own self-image and by their frequently erroneous views of what the poor really want. Turner has consistently argued that architects believe too strongly in the idea that good housing is an end in itself. Shelter should not be judged only in terms of whether it has a good roof and adequate drainage or would satisfy the board of examiners of an architectural faculty. While no one doubts that in an ideal world most houses would be well designed and serviced, in conditions of poverty another criterion is more important. That criterion is whether housing suits the needs of particular poor families. Turner (1976) demonstrates the choices facing two Mexican families, comparing the situation faced by a family living in an architecturally satisfactory house with that of a family living in seemingly more squalid physical conditions. In architectural terms the former mason's house is superior since it is both modern and supplied with services. Unfortunately, as a result of moving from his previous residence in the shanty town, the elderly mason's unreliable main income is no longer supplemented by the earnings of a small shop serving tourists. The family's income, in fact, is quite inadequate to cover the costs of the modern house which they have long coveted. Around 55 per cent of the family's total income is now devoted to maintaining the house and paying for the services compared to only 5 per cent previously. Given the present circumstances of the family, the 'quality' of the house is an irrelevance; it constitutes oppressive, not good, housing.

By contrast, the 'supportive shack' occupied by the ragpicker, while offering nothing in the way of good architecture or services, does match the family income. In fact it provides just the support needed by the family at a time when the man's employment as a car sprayer became unprofitable. Since the shack is in the back garden of a godparent whose house provides the services used by the family, they do not suffer the inconveniences of many shanty dwellers. And because the family is young and healthy, there is a good chance that they will obtain superior housing in the future.

The point of Turner's comparison is not to justify bad housing but to demonstrate the futility of poor people living in shelter of high architectural standards when it does not match their needs and incomes. Good housing should not be designed on the basis of assumptions about what the poor's needs ought to be, but should provide the flexibility by which the poor can trade off one need against another. In an earlier paper (1972) he suggested that all families have three basic needs; security, identity, and opportunity. Each income group within a city tends to make a different trade-off between these three needs. In the context of housing the poor value proximity to unskilled jobs (opportunity) much more highly than either ownership (security) or high-quality standards of shelter (identity). By contrast, a middle-income family gives much higher priority to modern standards of shelter and freehold ownership than to proximity. The policy implications of this argument are that the poor's needs are usually badly understood by governments and the kinds of housing provided by them are therefore inadequate. Much better, in Turner's view, is to give the poor greater flexibility to design and construct their own housing. It is not a recommendation for every family to build its own home, but for some kind of intermediate position between the somewhat autocratic dictates of large-scale enterprises, especially government, and the anarchy of letting every family build its own house (Turner, 1976). Give individual families greater choice over their housing design and location and the match with their needs will be closer.

The major criticism of this view is not that the poor, or for that matter the rich, are incapable of deciding their own best interests, but that in most circumstances the choices they make are tightly constrained. For example, we may argue that families made a choice between renting accommodation that is close to work (the classic 'bridgeheader' location) and building their own home in a more peripheral location (the classic 'consolidator' location). No doubt those families who earn an adequate household income can decide wisely which of those two alternatives they prefer. But of course most renting families do not have the choice. Their only possibility is to settle wherever they can obtain cheap rented housing. For the old, infirm, and very poor, the trade-off is nonexistent because it is determined by income level and the nature of the housing market in their city.

The same argument can be extended to cross-cultural comparisons. As we have seen, the balance between rental, spontaneous, and conventional housing varies greatly between cities, often within the same country, but notably between continents. To some extent the fact that more West African families rent homes in urban areas is a matter of choice. But, clearly, the availability or otherwise of adequate rental accommodation, the ease with which families can occupy land, the cost of building materials, the size of city, and therefore the transport problems involved in getting to work, are all factors determined by the organization of society rather than by the families themselves. The fact, therefore, that the poor in Lima invade land, those of Bogotá buy land, and those of Lagos rent accommodation, is only partly due to different preferences. Much more important are the structural conditions that limit the choice.

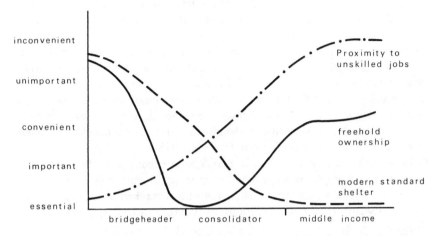

5.1. The housing priorities of middle-income groups, consolidators, and bridgeheaders, according to J. F. C. Turner (1972)

What I am essentially arguing is that poor individuals are rational and make trade-offs which improve their welfare level. At the same time, their poverty and the conditions facing them in most Third World cities effectively limit their choices. Of course all our choices are limited by something, but in conditions such as those found in Calcutta or Kinshasa, the choice is so limited as to be effectively compulsion. In such circumstances the poor do not choose location, but are pushed into any available accommodation. The only alternative in the long term is if the range of choice is enlarged by rising income levels or by changes in the housing or land markets; an argument to which I return.

The Nature of Spontaneous Housing

The archetypal shanty hut on a hill is not the only, and indeed is often not the worst, form of housing in many Third World cities. At the same time it is the principal form of poor housing in the sense that most owners, squatters, and renters live in housing that began as some kind of spontaneous accommodation. But such an argument begs an important question: what is spontaneous housing? Unfortunately, there seems to be no simple anwer. Drakakis Smith (1981; 1976b: 297) argues that 'the most acceptable definitions rest on the illegality of occupation of land, house or both.' Similarly Leeds (1969: 44) suggests that the 'only uniform identifying characteristics are their illegal and unordered origins by accretitive or organized invasion and, because of their origin, their continued juridically ambiguous status as settlements.' But such definitions include uneasily the frequent case of the poor purchasing the land on which they construct their dwellings. While the purchase itself normally follows legal procedures, such land often lacks planning permission from the urban authorities because of its inadequate services, physical layout, ownership characteristics, or its location beyond the urban perimeter. Such settlements are well represented in Delhi (Bose, 1973), constitute the majority of low-income areas in Bogotá, where they are known as pirate urbanizations, and cover substantial areas of Mexico City, where they are known as clandestine sub-divisions (Losada and Gómez, 1976; Ward, 1976a). If Doebele (1975) is correct in his belief that more families in poor cities buy land than invade it, any definition must include this kind of semi-legal transaction. Similarly, any definition should include the common practice in parts of Africa and Melanesia to obtain permission from local officials or tribal chiefs to obtain access to communal land (Peil, 1976; Doebele, 1978).

In addition, it is not only poor people who occupy land illegally. In San Salvador, for example, while few low-income settlements have been approved by the urban-planning agency, most settlements share their illegal situation with Colonia Escalón, the most luxurious of the upper-class residential suburbs (White, 1975).

Another common definition of low-income housing is that it has been constructed through self-help. And although most people would agree that self-help is a vital ingredient in the building of spontaneous settlements, it is inadequate without qualification, since few among the poor build their houses alone. They normally contract help from skilled neighbours who can lay the foundations, complete the more difficult brickwork, install the plumbing, or design the electrical system. Even Turner (1969: 525) notes that in Lima the poor may often have built only one-quarter of the dwelling themselves; the rest having been contracted out. While this estimate would seem high for Bogotá's low-income settlements, the point is sound.[2] Spontaneous settlements contain an important and sometimes a large component of skilled, even professional, labour (Moser, forthcoming).

Clearly neither illegality nor self-help is an adequate definition. Nor can we rely on income as an accurate definition of spontaneous settlement, since many of the poorest urban inhabitants live in the old, now decaying, conventionally built residences of the élite. During the twentieth century the pattern in many Latin American and North African cities has been for the rich to move out from the central areas into newly expanding suburbs (Amato, 1970; Sargent, 1972; Blake and Lawless, 1980). Their previous residences have sometimes been occupied by middle-class families and sometimes subdivided into accommodation for the poor. In other cities, such as Colombo and Mexico City, speculative builders have actually built cheap housing to rent to the poor (Drakakis-Smith, 1981; Ward, 1976a). Nor, of course, can we define spontaneous settlers by specific income group, because the poor, however defined, include many renters. In addition, while spontaneous settlers normally fall into the lower-middle-income

group in cities such as Bogotá (Valenzuela and Vernez, 1974), they may constitute a more middle-income group in the poorer cities of Africa or Asia.

I do not wish to make too much of this definitional problem. Nevertheless,
it is essential to remember that different definitions reflect different philosophical
approaches to the housing issue and that spontaneous housing takes a myriad of
forms. Generalization in such a situation is dangerous. This diversity also means
that any of the pet terms to describe such housing, whether it be shanties,
irregular settlements, self-help homes, squatter areas, or even spontaneous
dwellings, are often misleading. The squatter settlement, for example, is a misleading term to describe houses built on purchased land; the term 'shanty' is
inappropriate for brick-built consolidated housing which might once have been a
shanty. Spontaneous settlement is misleading in the sense that many such urban
developments have been highly organized by their leaders to avoid eviction.
Not only are many invasions planned carefully but they are often supported, and
even initiated, by political groups, including those of the government. Nevertheless I defend my use of the term 'spontaneous settlement'; it raises something of
the sense of innovation that the poor bring to their individual housing problems
and also acts as a reminder that such housing, even if now solidly built, often
began on the fringe of the law, sometimes after an invasion, and was usually
built in some measure by the inhabitants themselves when resources became
available. I would not, however, defend my use of the term very vehemently
and would be equally happy, and unhappy, to use the terms 'irregular' and
'self-help' housing.[3]

As a broad definition, spontaneous settlements fall normally into two or
more of the following categories: (1) most of the dwelling was built by the
family which originally occupied or now occupy it, (2) the spontaneous settlement as originally founded suffered from some degree of illegality or lacked
planning permission; (3) when the settlement was first formed most forms of
infrastructure and services were lacking and in many settlements services are still
lacking; (4) the settlements are occupied by the poor, however defined. Obviously
this definition is neither tight nor concise but it does eliminate most of the non-
spontaneous forms of settlement that exist in Third World cities. Within this
term may be included as subtypes: *invasions* (of either public or private land,
whether organized or incremental), where no purchase of the lot is involved;
pirate settlements, where the land is purchased, but lacks planning permission;
rental settlements, where houses are built on rented land; and *usufruct settlements*,
where permission to use communal land has been granted by tribe, local government, or private owner. I am aware that in certain cases such subtypes overlap.

The Consolidation of Spontaneous Housing: Prospects and Barriers

In cities in which the poor are not threatened by eviction there is plentiful
evidence to show that they are capable of improving their housing conditions.

Many settlements which begin as unserviced collections of huts gradually achieve the status of ordinary suburbs of the city. Little by little the huts are transformed into solid dwelling units, the community and friendly politicians put pressure on the authorities until electricity, water, buses, drainage, schools, and health centres are provided.

For the populations of these consolidating settlements progress is slow but consistent. When money is available, they invest in improvements to their housing. When times are hard, they are not evicted because they do not pay rent. In times of inflation the price of food and transport may rise, but at least their investments in the house and the land are safe. To the successful consolidator the dwelling also offers a source of income either through renting or through turning the front room into a shop. *At their best*, spontaneous settlements offer a great deal of necessary flexibility to the poor. A large family which needs space can extend the structure at will, the small family which prefers high physical standards to space can achieve this goal. And where the community is not riven by political conflicts (see chapter 7) the whole settlement benefits as a result of sustained pressure on the service agencies.

The question that needs to be raised, however, is whether the process of consolidation is possible for the majority or merely for a minority. What proportion of the Third World poor in fact make the transition from bridgeheader to consolidator to middle-income dweller? To what extent do the proportions vary from city to city? Is consolidation mainly a phenomenon of the more prosperous Latin American city? Who actually are the consolidators? In short, what are the conditions under which successful consolidation can occur?

Turner (1967; 1969) emphasizes the importance of security of tenure in the consolidation process. Without a high level of confidence that they will be permitted to retain the land, no family will willingly invest time and money in consolidating their dwelling. But who or what ensures security? Where the poor buy land, the security generally follows, even where planning permission is lacking. Where the poor rent land on which to build, as in parts of the West Indies (Clarke, 1974) or South Africa (Ellis et al., 1977: 7), security depends more on the length of lease and upon being able to maintain rental payments. Where, as in many shanty towns of Montego Bay, there is no security, houses are designed so that they can be moved easily to another location (Eyre, 1972: 406). Where land has been obtained through invasion, security is still more problematic. Effectively it is the attitude of government authorities, together with the amount of political pressure that can be maintained, that establishes security. If the government changes, or its political power weakens, the settlement may be threatened. Security under such conditions is especially problematic where the right of tenure has little relationship with the letter of the law. In Caracas, for example, Pérez and Nikken (1979: 12) note that the law relating to building on other people's land has more relevance to nineteenth-century France than to Venezuela. Squatters are generally permitted to stay because 'action by the police against the squatters does not commend itself to the political authority and there are generally more reasons to side-step it than to undertake it.' A change of government, of course, may change the policy and with it tenure rights. Security is often as much a state of mind as a reality. And where, as so often occurs, the government decides to introduce an urban-renewal programme there may be little that can be done by the squatters to prevent it (see below).

Another critical factor determining the ability of the poor to construct and to consolidate spontaneous settlements is the availability of land. Clearly the nature of the land market and government policy are the key factors here. If land invasions are tolerated, it would appear reasonable that more families might gain land than where invasions are prohibited. In the latter case the availability of land depends upon the price of suitable land relative to the incomes of the poor. In some African and Melanesian societies communal land is made available by tribal chiefs or local governments so that the poor only face the problem of construction. In other exceptional cases, such as the Republic of South Africa, access to land is controlled according to racial type. A black African wishing to work in Cape Town is compelled to live apart from his family in a workers' hostel or run a high risk of eviction from the few available squatter areas. He is effectively prohibited from obtaining land which will permit him to consolidate.

As cities become larger, and unbuilt land becomes scarcer, more and more families are compelled to buy land (Payne, forthcoming). Once dependent on the market, availability is determined by price. Unfortunately the rates at which land prices increase in Third World cities are generally high. Evers (1975: 782) notes that in Asian cities 'population increase and other social processes have intensified the pressure on urban land and have led, in the 1970s, to a wave of land speculation and spiralling land prices.' In an earlier period the effects of the petroleum economy in Venezuela led to the total land value of the central 5.4 million square metres of Caracas increasing four times from 1938 to 1951 (Lander and Funes, 1965: 322). Today land prices in the centres of large Asian and Latin American cities are close to those in Central London and New York. While Walters (1978) is almost certainly correct that there is an upward bias in most estimates of land-price rises, there is no doubt that the profitability and low level of risk connected with land transactions, compared with other investment opportunities in Third World countries, attract large amounts of capital and push up prices. Land speculation is completely uncontrolled in most Third World cities and spectacular profits are possible for the shrewd investor. As Cornelius (1975: 34) reports, the dry Texcoco lake bed in Mexico City 'was bought up in the 1940s for a few centavos per square hectare by a handful of entrepreneurs — including some army generals — who were later to become millionaires from their miniscule investment.' In a statistical analysis of the effects of land prices Grimes (1976) shows that costs are ensuring that public housing is built on the cheaper edges of cities and that many of the poor are being priced out of the land market. What makes matters worse is that government servicing and zoning policies frequently have the effect of valorizing land and increasing prices still further (Da Camargo et al., 1975; Gilbert and Ward, 1978). And despite the efforts of some governments to hold down these rises, their interventions have more often accentuated land shortages and fuelled further increases (Payne, 1977).

Price increases are also having a major impact on the ability to consolidate once land has been obtained. Costs of building materials are rising rapidly in many countries either because of monopoly practices or because of failures to increase production. The signs are that in Brazil, Mexico, and Colombia the costs of cement, glass, bricks, and steel have risen much more rapidly than the salaries of most low-income workers. Clearly such real price increases are bound to slow the consolidation process.

The prices of construction materials and land relative to wages and salaries are critical issues in determining the rate of spontaneous settlement growth and consolidation. As Ward (1978: 47–8) has shown for three settlements in Mexico City, 'once certain tenurial assurances are met, residential improvement at the household level is a product of the investment surplus that is created.' This suggests that consolidation can only take place among those groups who have reasonably well-paid jobs. This point has indeed been recognized by Turner (1969: 526), who argues that the 'vital differences between the semi-employed "bridgeheader" and the more or less regular wage earning "consolidator"' are frequently overlooked. This failure to distinguish between the poor and the very poor leads to misleading generalizations about the poor and about the potential for spontaneous settlements to grow. Turner here, and elsewhere, clearly believes that the opportunities for consolidation are limited for the *very* poor. Squatters are an 'auto-selected community' who differ from poor non-squatters and who are able socially and economically to cope with the problems of spontaneous settlement (Turner, 1969: 513). The worrying implication of the argument is that within every city there will be a sizeable group of people who are unable to participate in the consolidation process. And as Dwyer (1975: 203–4) has argued, if this is the case in Latin America, the consolidation prospects of the majority in desperately poor cities such as Calcutta, Manila, or Nairobi are remote.

It may also be that the very process of urban growth may reduce the poor's chances of consolidating their housing. I have already noted that rises in land prices are being fuelled by urban expansion. But city growth may also accentuate other difficulties for the poor. For example, as cities grow physically larger, the journey to work will get longer. Already workers in cities such as Lagos and São Paulo are travelling for three to four hours per day between centrally located work opportunities and peripheral homes. Such journeys not only cut family budgets but also limit the time available for home consolidation. Of course such an outcome is not inevitable. Conscientious and effective planning might create conditions favouring employment decentralization, which would provide jobs close to homes. But such adjectives rarely describe the planning system in most

Third World cities (see chapter 8). Pessimistically, therefore, I must predict that the time and cost involved in travelling to work will pose an increasing burden on the metropolitan poor with an obvious effect on the pace of consolidation.

The changing physical size and shape of the city will also affect the desirability of certain residential areas. Such changes affect the poor almost as much as the rich, and may lead to deterioration in previously improving settlements. As Brett (1974: 186) puts it,

many of the earlier consolidators may move out, renting or sub-letting their homes to poorer newcomers squeezed out of the city centre, or to provincial migrants fresh to the city. Where this happens, the selective out-migration of 'high achievers' will tend to lead to a downturn in the investment cycle, so that the peripheral settlements of today may become the slums of tomorrow.

The presence of higher-income consolidators would seem essential to the prosperity of a spontaneous settlement. Such families contribute to the welfare of the rest of the settlement by creating a market for local stores, by providing casual employment, and by adding a more powerful voice in the petitioning for services (Doebele and Peattie, 1976). But in turn social differentiation within a spontaneous settlement raises a critical issue. While the richer families obviously contribute to the economy of the *barrio*, the poor may be an important source of income for the rich. For it is an undeniable fact that as settlements become older and consolidate, the proportions of renters increase; owners deliberately extend their houses to accommodate renters, thereby increasing their incomes. In Bogotá, where the author carried out household surveys in four spontaneous settlements, the proportion of renters in each *barrio* tended to rise with the age and the levels of servicing of the settlement (table 5.1).

Table 5.1
Age, renting, and servicing of Bogotá's barrios

	Casablanca	Atenas	Britalia	San Antonio
Age of settlement (years)[1]	9.5	12.1	2.9	9.2
Percentage of households who are renters	42	43	28	43
Services and utilities score[2]	12	15	6	11

[1] On 1 Jan. 1979. Defined as the average date when the owners who were interviewed arrived in the settlement excluding those who bought from a third party.

[2] Points are awarded to a settlement according to its level of servicing: e.g. 2 points for settlements where virtually all households have a legal electricity supply, 2 points where both public and private telephones are installed, 1 point for a daily police patrol, 4 points for a settlement where three-quarters or more of the roads are paved. The maximum possible score for any settlement is 20 points.
Source: Household survey of the project on 'Public Intervention, Housing and Land Use in Latin American cities'.

The implications of high levels of renting in spontaneous settlements are unclear. In Latin American cities many current owners were once renters, so that the presence of renters may be interpreted positively: they too will one day become owners. This interpretation would seem especially plausible in those cities in which the proportion of renters to owners is falling. On the other hand, where the proportion of renters is increasing it is probable that renters are finding more difficulty in obtaining land and building houses. In this case, rather than renting being a temporary stage prior to home ownership, it may be a permanent state. Such a trend may also signify that consolidation has become more difficult for those with land; in such circumstances the only way for owners to consolidate is to sub-let rooms. Unfortunately, few studies have considered the phenomenon of renting.[4] Consequently we have insufficient information to judge whether renting levels are increasing or whether the poor's chances to obtain property is increasing or decreasing.

Finally, the rate of settlement consolidation depends also upon the extent to which public agencies are able to provide infrastructure and services to the spontaneous communities. In some cities, notably metropolitan Latin America, electricity, water, and telephone companies are often highly effective. On the other hand, in 1966 the homes of 1.7 million people in the Calcutta conurbation lacked water and the per capita supply of filtered water had declined by half between 1931 and 1965 (Dwyer, 1975: 215). To a considerable extent, service availability is linked to levels of per capita city income, but a number of other variables are important. Water supplies are critically affected by the environmental and topographical characteristics of the city; Mexico City and Caracas both face major shortages, whereas many cities such as Calcutta, Bangkok, or Djakarta, are almost awash with undrinkable water. Similarly, electricity services are dependent on available fuel supplies; cities located in countries lacking both coal and oil, and distant from rain-soaked mountains, face graver difficulties than others. But external features such as income levels, topography, and fuel supplies are not the only important determinants. The level of servicing for the poor depends also upon the efficiency and the allocation procedures of public utilities. In Mexico City and Valencia servicing for the poor depends upon political patronage; where these links are effective, services are provided (Ward, forthcoming; Gilbert, 1981b). Universally, service variations are linked to income levels. In São Paulo services are available in middle- and upper-income *barrios* which can afford to pay the installation charges. In the poorer *barrios* community action is often required to install the services given the level of utility companies' charges. Indeed in some cities the poor even subsidize the services of the rich. In Cape Town 'the overcrowded, extensively used (and thus profitable) black [bus] services directly subsidise the white services which are sparsely used and which run at a loss' (Dewar, 1976: 16). In Port Moresby water, sewerage, and garbage collection was provided only to the rich who were long heavily subsidized owing to the low prices charged (Oram, 1976).

Are Conditions Improving or Worsening?

Having considered the parameters that limit the process of consolidation, it is interesting to ask whether general housing conditions in Third World cities are improving or deteriorating. To most readers this may seem a senseless question, for the balance of academic and planning opinion is clearly on the side of deterioration. A glance at the literature supports the belief that in most cities the situation is worsening. Abrams (1964: 7) argues that 'more than a million people . . . are homeless or live in housing that is described by the United Nations as a menace to health and an affront to human dignity. Worse still, in almost all the developing areas, housing conditions are steadily deteriorating.' With reference to Calcutta, generally recognized to be one of the world's housing disaster areas, and to the Indian situation generally, Rosser (1972: 180) notes that 'the housing shortage in urban areas has now reached staggering proportions, and grows annually worse as the rate of provision of new and satisfactory housing lags far behind the rate of population increase.' In China urban population growth generally has exceeded the rate of new home construction and in the fastest growing cities the housing shortage has undoubtedly worsened. In Sian the population 'increased more than threefold from 490,000 to 1.5 million during the period 1950 to 1965, while the floor space of dwelling units only doubled' (Sen Dou Chang, 1968: 150). Even Turner (1967: 3) has argued that 'with squatter settlement growth rates of 12 per cent or more per annum in Mexico, Turkey and the Philippines as well as in Peru and many other countries — double that of city growth as a whole — it is hardly exaggerating to say that city development is out of control.'

   A common element in these arguments is that larger absolute numbers and relative proportions of Third World urban populations are living in spontaneous settlements. The conclusion drawn from this observation is invariably the same; general conditions have worsened. Put as simply as this, the argument is unsatisfactory. If services such as water, electricity, and drainage are gradually extended to spontaneous settlements, if rooms are added and even a second floor constructed, then many dwellings will have more in common with conventional houses than with the flimsy shacks normally associated with the term 'spontaneous housing'. In such circumstances, therefore, a proportion, and possibly a considerable proportion, of the housing ought not to be classified with the poorest dwellings. To confuse the term 'spontaneous settlement' with slums and to assume that the quantitative increase in the former proves that a deterioration in housing standards has taken place, negates the useful work done in Lima by Mangin and Turner. If spontaneous settlement does improve through time, then perhaps different conclusions should be drawn. In any case, before the proliferation of spontaneous housing may be interpreted either favourably or unfavourably it is necessary to consider in detail the changing conditions of those dwellings. Are more dwellings provided with services than previously? How have changing land-use patterns affected the locations of squatter housing? Are the real costs of building these dwellings higher or lower than previously? Without such supporting evidence the proliferation of spontaneous settlements proves little beyond the fact that Third World cities are expanding rapidly and fail to provide conventional housing for all their inhabitants.

Even if it can be demonstrated that housing conditions have deteriorated, or for that matter improved, then accurate interpretation is still difficult. If, for instance, higher proportions of urban dwellers are living in bad housing conditions than previously, this may only be a symptom of the rapid movement of people from rural to urban areas. Since, as we have seen, poor quality self-help housing is virtually the only form of dwelling to be found in rural areas, the fact that it should spread in the urban areas over a particular time period may well reflect the movement of poor people to cities and the continuance of poverty in the society as a whole. Similarly a clear improvement in housing conditions needs to be interpreted carefully. It is common for housing improvements to have taken place in one or several cities at the expense of conditions elsewhere in the country. If, for example, governments have channelled investment resources into the major cities and neglected the smaller towns and rural areas, then housing improvements in the major cities are placed in a less favourable light.

Far too often, however, superficial arguments are used to support the idea that there is an urban crisis. For example, Abrams (1964: 51) argues that

the less industrialized the country, the less apt it is to have a housing problem. The moment it begins to develop industrially, its housing problem burgeons . . . The moment the family moves from village to city, its members surrender the home that is usually their own, as well as the more ample space on which it stands, the freedom from noise, smoke, traffic and danger, proximity to nature, and their place in community life.

One wonders whether Abrams had forgotten how bad rural conditions can be. For, despite the appalling conditions found in most Third World cities, more people have access to water, drainage, electricity, and health services than they do in rural areas. It is clear that drainage and fresh water is more necessary in crowded urban circumstances than it is in rural conditions, but in most rural areas few services are available. Since the quality of the construction is not dissimilar between urban and rural areas, this suggests that most urban families live rather better.

I am not trying to argue that there is no housing problem or to deny that in many cities it may well be deteriorating. My aim is to demonstrate that most statements about the situation are based erroneously on at best one or two criteria. Because the priorities of the poor may be different from ours we need to take care. And even if we have objectively weighed the evidence and can state categorically that urban housing conditions have deteriorated, we still need to interpret the importance and the causes of this trend. In short, care in interpretation is the watchword. The tragedy is that despite such care, we can so often diagnose a decline in housing standards.

Government Responses

Distinct phases have been apparent in government reactions to the housing question, but it is difficult to place these phases into discrete time periods, since some governments were faced by particular phenomena much earlier than others and needed to modify their policies accordingly. For example, shanty-town expansion affected Latin American cities much earlier than most African centres; what was happening in Buenos Aires, Rio, or Mexico City in the 1940s was often of little concern to Lusaka, Lagos, or Dar es Salaam until the 1960s. In addition, generalization is complicated by the fact that within the same country different attitudes have been manifest at different levels of government. Not infrequently the national government has maintained one policy, often one of benign neglect, while the real issues and policy decisions have been apparent at the local level, often in the form of slum demolition and residential segregation.

Despite these reservations, it is possible to make some generalizations about housing policy. At the national level the typical governmental response for many years was to ignore the country's housing situation and to restrict the growth of low-income housing in the main cities by limiting cityward migration. In parts of the British Empire population movement was controlled carefully through Pass Laws, a device intended to keep as much indigenous housing in the rural areas as possible (Peil, 1976; Tipple, 1976). Where native urban labour was required it was allocated employer-built rental housing (as in Zambia), or segregated into distinct residential areas (as in India) or forced into workers' hostels (as in the Republic of South Africa). While this attitude eased over time as the labour demands of industry and mining increased, the neglect component remained paramount in colonial policy for many years. Of course it was never seen in those terms. Rather it was rationalized in terms of racial differences in customs and needs or, more humanely, if equally unrealistically, in the belief that if economic growth and good administration were encouraged, the housing problem would eventually disappear. The later view persisted beyond independence; until recently in fact it was the learned opinion of most economists working in developing countries (Abrams, 1964). Only in the 1970s did an institution like the World Bank become actively interested in social infrastructure such as housing. Previously investment in housing was seen to be unproductive and most funds had been channelled into the growth-generating industrial, power, transport, and agricultural sectors. Most national plans, produced as they were by economists, failed even to mention housing until the 1960s. Only since doubts have been expressed about the ability of economic growth to remove poverty has the need for something to be done about the slum conditions of so many people been recognized. Certainly the realization that investment in housing could actually create income or that it could play a vital part in the economy of the poor has been very recent. Indeed, apart from one or two heretics (such as Currie, 1971), investment in housing was regarded as the classic means of slowing economic growth and of adding to the problems of the urban areas by attracting larger numbers of people from the rural areas.

Residential Segregation

The local counterpart of national and international neglect was, and in modified form remains, a policy of deliberate segregation. In India the British planned their cities carefully; Delhi was 'built for two different worlds, the "European" and the "native"; for the ruler and for the ones who were ruled' (King, 1976; 263). Perhaps the word 'built' should be qualified, for only the European sections were planned and constructed by the colonial powers. Planning consisted of showing how towns should be organized, in building comfortable residential accommodation, wide roads, and open spaces for those who 'knew' how to use these facilities. The indigenous areas were left to look after themselves, probably on the assumption that nothing could be done to help them. The result in most cases was that pre-existing or new indigenous housing areas were allowed to develop in certain areas and new European centres constructed adjacent to them (figure 5.2). Often the areas allocated to the native population were too restricted and led, under conditions of rapid in-migration, to very high housing densities. In Zaria the European residential area was clearly separated, grouped around a clubhouse with a racing track, a polo field, and a golf course. In Tunis there was an almost self-sufficient city outside the original indigenous centre, though in Cairo, while all Europeans lived together in a colonial quarter, they never constituted more than half of the population in that area (Abu Lughod, 1976: 35-6). In some cities the demarcation according to housing standard and race was carried to extraordinary lengths. In Singapore Sir Thomas Raffles delineated separate quarters for Europeans, Chinese, Indians, Malays, and Buginese; in Batavia, the capital of the Netherlands East Indies, there were at least fifteen distinct racial-tribal districts (Wee, 1972: 217; Evers, 1975: 780). Since independence this pattern of complete racial segregation has begun to break down as the new indigenous administrators have begun to occupy the European residential areas. Only in the Republic of South Africa is the degree of segregation rigidly maintained as a matter of 'principle'. But while on the whole racial segregation, at least as a deliberate policy, has diminished, segregation of another kind has persisted and grown. As Evers (1977) argues for Asian cities, racial segregation is giving place to class segregation. Urban authorities no longer zone their cities according to race, but implicitly according to income and housing density. African and Asian cities are moving closer to the pattern, long apparent in Latin America, whereby income determines where people can live.[5] In case this form of segregation should fail to operate effectively, élite groups are additionally protected by zoning laws. As a consequence, beautifully planned élite *barrios*, the equal and better of the colonial townships, have emerged in all Latin American cities and are clearly separated from the spontaneous settlements. A case can be made, in fact, that planning has become popular in Latin

America mainly as a method of protecting élite *barrios* from the incursions of squatter settlers and the like (Amato, 1970; Violich, 1944). Today zoning, income, and government housing projects maintain residential segregation on the basis of class, not only in Latin America but throughout the non-socialist world.

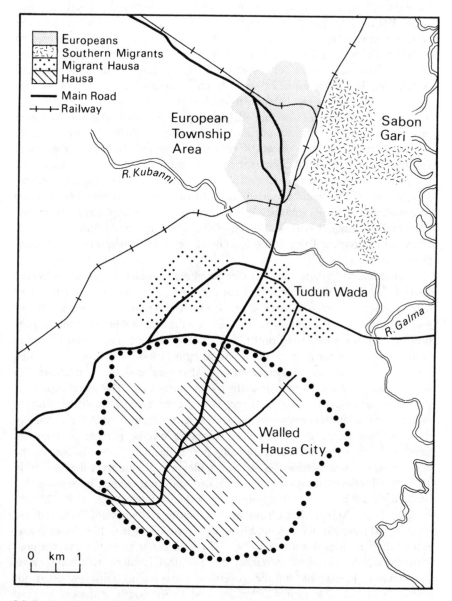

Europeans
Southern Migrants
Migrant Hausa
Hausa
Main Road
Railway

European Township Area

R. Kubanni

Sabon Gari

Tudun Wada

R. Galma

Walled Hausa City

0 km 1

5.2 Residential segregation in Zaria

Urban Renewal and 'Slum' Removal Policies

Normally linked to the policy of segregation has been one of demolishing undesirable housing. Indeed, the destruction of low-income housing is as old as the policy of separating populations according to their ethnic origins. In Singapore, for example, there are recorded cases of demolition occurring as early as 1840 (Wee, 1972; 220). Sometimes demolition was to discourage migration into the city, but more often it has been part of an urban renewal project or used to maintain the zoning laws. Unfortunately, urban renewal and demolition programmes have never been very effective in the sense of helping the displaced population. Too often the new housing has been unsuitable owing to its distance from work places, the regularity with which rents or mortgage payments have to be paid, and because of the limited house space provided. The most frequent reaction among the removed populations has been gradually to move back to areas similar to those from which they were removed. In the massive *favela* removal programme in Rio de Janeiro, large numbers of *favelados* sold their homes to higher income families or 'fiddled' the system in other ways (Valladares, 1978b; 18-23). In Nairobi most of the former squatters required to move to new sites in Kariobangi sold their lots to more prosperous applicants who moved in instead (Weisner, 1976). In Manila, of the 5,975 squatter families moved 35 kilometres to Sapang Palay in 1960, only 41 per cent remained in 1969 (Hollnsteiner, 1974: 313).

Such removal programmes have come under considerable attack in recent years as it has become obvious that the removed population seldom relish their new accommodation and that the reasons for the removal are often motivated less by interest in the conditions of the poor than in clearing land for prestige buildings or for speculative profit.[6] Frequently, indeed, demolishing housing is the worst of all possible strategies. As Abrams (1964: 126) long ago pointed out, 'in a housing famine there is nothing that slum clearance can accomplish that cannot be done more efficiently by an earthquake. The worst aspects of slum life are overcrowding and excessive shelter cost. Demolition without replacement intensifies overcrowding and increases shelter cost.' Unfortunately it seems that vested interests and/or ignorance on the part of planners has prevented this common sense from being heeded in many cities. In Nairobi the main squatter areas outside the Mathare Valley and Kibera were demolished in 1970 and President Kenyatta later defended the local council by arguing that he did not want Kenya's capital to turn into a shanty town (Stren, 1975: 272-3). In Cape Town 20,000 blacks living in the squatter settlement of Crossroads are regularly threatened with removal to the Transkei, 1,000 kilometres away, 'where they are legally entitled to be'.[7] Even the coloured population, the non-white racial group permitted to remain in Cape Town, is subject to urban-removal programmes. In its wisdom the government is building two new cities for coloureds at Mitchells Plain (27 km by road to the south of the centre), and

Atlantis (45 km north). While by Third World standards the accommodation being built is both cheap and of reasonable quality the fact remains that the new cities have few commerical or industrial employment opportunities, the proposed rail links to Cape Town are nowhere near completion, and it is less than evident that the poor actually want to move (Ellis et al., 1977; Dewar and Ellis, 1979).

Government Housing

The higher costs of transportation, rents, and services, and the disruption of informal social networks which previously had helped to sustain the low-income economy, have often been the main results of these removal plans. But many of the difficulties are rooted in the very notion of governments building housing for the poor in Third World cities. The universal error has been that governments have built at too high an architectural standard for the poor and without a clear understanding of the needs of the recipient population. The result has been that government housing has generally been too expensive, has offered very little flexibility in use, and has often been in unsuitable locations. The general experience throughout Third World cities has been that the poor have begun to move out of the accommodation and middle-income groups have surreptitiously begun to move in. Such public housing as has been built in San Salvador (Grimes, 1976), Bogotá (Laun, 1976), Rio de Janeiro (Portes, 1979; Valladares, 1978b), Mexico City (Cornelius, 1975), Lagos (Aradeon, 1979), Kuala Lumpur (Wegelin, 1977), or Manila (Hollnsteiner, 1974) has mainly been occupied by middle-income people. This does not mean that the poor have not benefited at all, for often they have sold their rights to the new families. But building for middle-income families is not what many agencies believed, or at least pretended, that they were doing. On occasion the poor have been forced into government housing against their will and have suffered from conditions of 'oppressive housing', to use Turner's apt phrase. The *rancho* dwellers of Caracas forced by dictator Pérez Jiménez's national guard into the 'super blocks' are a classic example of the unpredictable consequences of such a policy. Not only did they treat the new accommodation badly and fail to pay their rents, but they also turned into a potent opposition force which helped to remove the dictator (Myers, 1978).

Indeed, a question mark must be placed against the desirability of governments building houses at all in most Third World cities. By necessity, governments are building housing that cannot be occupied by the poor because of their extraordinarily low incomes. Most commonly the accommodation is occupied by the upper- and lower-middle-income groups; in many countries it is government workers or those with appropriate political links who benefit from the accommodation. For these groups government housing is undoubtedly popular and waiting lists are long. Of course there may be advantages for the poor as a result of housing construction for higher-income groups. The total housing supply will increase and vacated middle-income accommodation may become available for the poor, thus easing housing pressure. But equally common is the situation whereby ownership of the vacated accommodation is retained by the original occupants and let at exorbitant rents. Perhaps the greatest danger in government housing projects is that they are provided with a substantial subsidy which benefits groups who are less in need. As Van Huyck (1968: 71) notes, in Calcutta most funds for subsidized housing come through indirect taxes from the poor. In short, the poorest families are called upon to pay the burden of rehousing the fortunate few who live in the public housing projects. This, perhaps, is the key issue for government housing agencies. If they build housing for the poor, it can be provided only with the aid of large subsidies. Since the countries are poor, few subsidies can be provided and in any case regressive taxation systems force the poor to pay for the housing. If the standard of housing is reduced, governments end up building one-room concrete shacks or apartments which all too often the poor could have improved on at much lower cost.

In certain circumstances this judgement may be too harsh. Clearly, reactions to living in multi-storey accommodation will depend upon previous housing experiences. It would seem that in Singapore, for example, the degree of over-crowding in the central areas was so great that the Chinese community adapted without major problems to apartment living. On the other hand, Malay house-wives in the same city, who were more accustomed to village-style housing adapted less successfully; one comment on concrete floors was that it was like 'trying to make a home on the main road' (Wee, 1972: 227–8). Similarly, many socialist governments are persisting with the idea of government-built accom-modation and often discourage the idea of self-help.[8] In general, however, the experience of governments building houses in Third World cities has been of dubious value. Most such housing has been either of high quality which has benefited few families or of such low quality that it has alienated the recipient families (Drakakis-Smith, 1981). With the possible exceptions of Singapore, Hong Kong, and China, nowhere has a government building programme succeeded in stemming the tide of spontaneous settlement, presumably its primary objective.

Some economists would argue that the principal reasons for failure are that too few government houses are built or that governments have failed to stimulate the private sector to build more (Currie, 1971). An increase in the national rate of housing construction would give a major boost to employment opportunities, since construction is on the whole a labour-intensive industry. Variations on such programmes have been tried in Singapore, Hong Kong, Brazil, and Colombia. In Colombia housing construction was the central plank of the National Plan in the early 1970s. Funds were generated through index-linked savings plans and the resultant construction boom undoubtedly helped the employment situation in Bogotá where most of the funds were invested. Whether in fact the plan helped the poor, since construction was concentrated on upper- and middle-income housing, or whether it stimulated the rapid inflation that ensued are more open questions. A definitive verdict on the Colombian experience is difficult, since political support for the plan was removed in 1975 before the full consequences had worked themselves out.

Where such a strategy has been employed, it has been associated with, but has not necessarily been the cause of, rapid economic growth. In all four countries in which some variation of this policy has been applied, the national economy expanded rapidly. On the other hand there is considerable danger of stimulating a speculative housing boom which further concentrates incomes, unless complementary urban taxation reforms accompany the introduction of the new strategy. In addition it is less than certain that where the accommodation is constructed for the poor it is suitable to their needs or, in places such as Brazil and Colombia, whether it benefits the poor at all. Clearly, more detailed evidence is required on this kind of economic strategy.

Rent Controls

Another approach to improving conditions for the poor has been the institution of rent controls. Unfortunately the general experience seems to have been less than successful in the long term. In Mexico City 'rent controls, initially applied in 1942 to *vecindad* housing with a rent below 300 pesos per month and maintained ever since, have hastened the deterioration of the central city tenements, whose owners have little incentive to invest in their upkeep' (Cornelius, 1975: 27). Generalizing on the basis of several urban experiences, Grimes (1976: 98) has argued that rent controls can only be effective in the short term and in combination with strict controls on prices and incomes. Employed in other circumstances they have either cut the rate of new construction and maintenance or have encouraged the development of illegal rationing systems such as the payment of 'key money'.

Site-and-Services and Upgrading Programmes

In one sense there has been progress in government responses to the housing situation. There is now a consensus that most capitalist Third World governments are incapable of building sufficient homes to remove spontaneous housing and that greater reliance must be placed on some kind of self-help policy. Major institutions such as the World Bank, government planning agencies, and many architects are beginning to accept the advice of John Turner and others that more should be done to provide and service land and to leave the actual building to the people themselves. Two general policies can be classified under this general description, the one to upgrade existing settlements, the second to ease the development of new settlements (sites and services). The two policies obviously go hand in hand, promising to channel more resources directly to the poor and to give them greater security on the tenure of their land. At its best, a sites-and-services programme would offer a family a plot of land, gradual servicing, access to credit, advice on construction and materials, all at a price not beyond the family budget. The security afforded to the family would allow consolidation to take place and community action programmes to be introduced. Government service agencies would directly benefit from lower costs if people no longer occupied land on hillsides and river-valley bottoms which is expensive to service. Lower unit costs in turn might encourage such agencies to service larger numbers of people.

Self-help programmes have been taken up vigorously by numerous governments and by the World Bank; Laquian (1977: 291) notes that in 1974 there were 'eighty proposed or completed schemes in 27 countries'. Similarly Grimes (1976: 20) reports that 'as of 1973 sites and services projects were a part of the national development plans for 13 countries. By the same year, Turkey, Chile, India, Pakistan and Iraq had each completed more than 50,000 sites and services plots.' Site-and-service and squatter-upgrading programmes have undoubtedly arrived on the international scene, and as Doebele and Peattie (1976: 9) have noted, represent 'one of the most important reforms in the housing policies of developing countries in the last decade.' At the same time, such a policy is not without many dangers: not least the risk that it may be turned into a universal 'answer' to the housing problem.

Certainly, as recent literature is at pains to point out, self-help is no panacea. That same literature records a catalogue of failures to put against the obvious common sense which underlies its adoption. Stren (1975: 270) describes how in Nairobi the government managed to spend less than one-fifth of its site-and-service project budget between 1969 and 1972, and how in Tanzania the government managed to build only 795 site-and-service units between 1969 and 1974, compared with the annual target of 5,000. Similarly slow progress was a characteristic of Papua New Guinea (Oram, 1976) and Bogotá (Gilbert, 1981b); and in Kuala Lumpur, where nine schemes were tried between 1965 and 1971, Wegelin (1977: 91) reports that 'the experience . . . has not been a very happy one.'

Most of these failures have been attributed to poor administration, due in part to lack of enthusiasm on the part of the local authorities. As the Chief Planner of Nairobi was reported to have said recently, 'The Kenya government is still committed to the ideal that every urban family must have two rooms and a toilet and a kitchen and not everyone who matters is converted to a lowering of standards' (*Guardian*, 15 Dec. 1977). This reluctance to lower standards has been fairly general and has kept costs above those necessary to cater for most of the poor. Oram blames several failures in Port Moresby on over-strict building standards demanded of site owners. Stren (1975: 281) reports of one Nairobi site-and-service project: 'concrete slabs were provided for foundations. The cost of the slabs plus high standards of infrastructure put the project beyond the reach of most lower income families. The government was therefore obliged to heavily subsidize the project in order that low-income families could be settled in the plots and repay loans for building materials.' Rather than being accused of building, or condoning the building, of slums, government administrators have often prepared over-elaborate and hence over-costly programmes. In a sense, of course, this criticism opens sites-and-services projects up to the very problem that self-help schemes are trying to avoid. If costs rise, the only alternative is to provide a few families with large loans or subsidies or to spread funds thinly over a large number and gamble that the programme will still be viable.

In any case there is some doubt whether the very poor wish for higher standards if it means that they are to be burdened by debt repayments. Commenting on Zambian experience, Tipple (1976: 168) argues that a squatter resettlement scheme was unsuccessful because 'it was based on a false assumption that squatters would want to move to a serviced area and pay for the services provided rather than living in an unserviced area for no apparent cost.' Clearly responses will vary according to income level and to aspirations among the poor; very poor people are much more likely to settle for no services. It is likely, however, that more affluent spontaneous settlers would accept a serviced plot and related debt payments. Unfortunately, even where this is the case, bad administration all too often makes them wait too long for their lots (Oram, 1976) and services (Hollnsteiner, 1974: 315) or reduces the number of lots available.

Some degree of poor administration can be put down to teething troubles and inexperience. But in the case of self-help programmes this is a dangerous excuse. For one of the supposed beauties of such a policy is that it should be relatively free of bureaucracy. If in fact it demands extensive administration, then costs will rise and one of the main virtues of the programme is lost. Clearly, if administration cannot be kept to a minimum, the programmes will not work and planners must search for a new answer to the needs of the poor. Equally, if Third World governments are too incompetent to administer such conceptually simple programmes, the wisdom of sites-and-services and squatter-upgrading programmes must again be questioned.

In addition, self-help solutions have to answer two more profound criticisms. The first is that self-help is a cover for non-action by governments on critical issues such as urban reform, progressive taxation, and land speculation. As Wilsher and Righte (1975: 138) have expressed it,

the doctrine of self-help is deeply attractive. It appeals to everyone's belief in human ability, neighbourliness, ambition and good sense . . . [however] it also, less nobly, encourages people to believe that there is nothing much to worry about, that the less interference that there is with natural forces the better, and that everything will work itself out in the long run.

A related, but still more sinister, accusation is that of Drakakis-Smith (1976a: 2): 'By satisfying some of the minimum housing desires of the urban poor, self-help projects can be said to maintain the status quo and as such have been eagerly adopted by urban power elites as multi-lateral funds have become available over the last few years.' Such a charge has been made specifically against the Chilean government of Eduardo Frei (1964–70). The introduction of the famous Operation Site project led to the development of paternalistic government policies aimed at winning votes and were a substitute for its intended attacks on the structural causes of the housing problem (Kusnetzoff, 1975: 292).

The second major criticism of self-help is that if it becomes widespread it will re-create the difficulties which it aims to conquer. Doebele and Peattie (1976: 6), for example, argue that sites-and-services schemes are likely to cream off the more affluent and innovative poor. Such creaming would leave the poor settlements without leaders who might have pressed government for more services and help. It would also lower internal demand for services and commercial activities in the poor settlements, 'breaking the ties with the neighbourhood store, the local food vendor, the seamstress, the firewood distributor, and all the dozens of other more marginal persons who depended on them for their own economic survival.' The same criticism is valid with respect to the effects of self-help on the land market, jobs, and city growth. Laquian (1977: 297) has criticized *early* site-and-service efforts because they were 'located in urban peripheries, requiring relocation of inner-city squatters and slum dwellers, resulting in economic, social and personal dislocations.' But this problem is inherent in any system that operates under an uncontrolled land market. Given the structure of land prices in Third World cities, only peripheral areas are available for low-cost programmes. And if self-help programmes should proliferate, the subsequent incorporation of a huge number of families into the conventional land market would further push up prices, relegating government site and service schemes to the cheapest most peripheral land. The major consequence of self-help schemes, without modifications in the land market, would merely shift the burden of finding cheap land from squatters or pirate urbanizers to the state. Without severe land taxes or direct government intervention in the land market, insurmountable problems would paralyse the self-help programme.

Similarly, site-and-service programmes would contribute only partially to helping the employment situation. Self-help would create more opportunities within low-income communities for skilled and semi-skilled labour. But without large-scale programmes aimed at creating well-paid jobs, too few people would be able to participate in even the cheapest self-help programme. Some observers would even argue (cf. Bromley (ed.), 1978) that the incorporation of spontaneous settlements into the official sector through self-help schemes would open up the door to greater exploitation by the capitalist sector. Such schemes might make it profitable for large-scale construction companies to provide prefabricated housing, thereby threatening still further job opportunities in activities such as bricklaying. It might also make the supply of building materials more profitable for large companies and undercut local small-scale manufacturers who now provide employment for many of the workers in the spontaneous settlements. Clearly, the validity of such an argument varies from city to city and opinion will differ according to ideological position. Nevertheless a fundamental issue is raised, which in my opinion is sound. To generalize self-help without reforming some of the basic inequalities of the Third World city will undermine the programme.

To be successful, therefore, sites-and-services and squatter-upgrading programmes need to be accompanied by structural reforms of the land market, taxation and zoning, and urban-planning policies. Without such reforms self-help programmes may help the less destitute but in no sense will the majority benefit, even in the more prosperous Latin American countries. Of course the more intelligent advocates of self-help recognize the limitations of these programmes in the absence of complementary reforms and they are clearly correct in their belief that self-help is more likely to help the poor in the absence of reforms than most other housing policies would. Site-and-service or squatter-upgrading is no more than a partial palliative to the problems of the poor, and such programmes increase rather than obviate the need for reform. Let us hope that this common sense prevails and that the new orthodoxy does not become too well established, for if it does, the argument that self-help will constitute a counter reform may well prove correct. In that case, G. K. Chesterton's aphorism may well be proved right: 'a new philosophy generally means the praise of some old vice.' In short, the poor would be left to their own devices in a hostile urban world, this time with official sanction.

The Logic of Governmental Response

I have described how different governments have responded to the issue of poor housing. What we now seek to answer is why those policies have been adopted and why different governments have reacted in different ways to similar kinds of problems. In order to answer this question we need to know more about the state in Third World societies. Clearly, the form of the state varies with the organization of society; dictatorships often represent only a small élite group which manipulates the state in the cause of its interests; in some socialist countries the state may genuinely represent the masses and introduce policies that aim to improve housing and social conditions. Most countries fall somewhere between these extremes; the state is under pressure to represent a wide range of social groups, but tends to represent certain groups much more than others. In many capitalist countries the state represents primarily the interests of upper- and middle-income groups. But even dictatorships find it necessary to offer some benefits to the poorer sectors of society in order to gain a measure of legitimacy for their regime.

The role of housing and urban planning agencies in this context normally is to legitimize the policies of the state before the middle- and low-income groups. The extent to which such agencies are allowed to bring about real improvements for the poor will depend on the nature and the ideology of the state. In those countries in which serious taxation of the rich is absent, where land speculation is rampant and practised by government ministers themselves, we can expect little success on the part of the housing and planning agencies. On the other hand, where resources are channelled into social infrastructure, where some effort is made to control the rise in land prices, and where serious attempts have been made to channel the growth of major cities in directions that will economize on the cost of services, something more than superficial improvements may take place. In any case the housing issue is always as much a political as a technical matter. For government agencies only receive large sums to engage in the housing battle when a favourable political decision has been taken. Similarly, politicians rather than technicians determine whether land speculation is being controlled, prices of building materials allowed to increase faster than average incomes, and infrastructure provided for the poor or for the rich.

Politicians, though, are always limited in their actions by social and economic realities. However Utopian the intentions of governments, a limit is posed by the resources of the nation. While Communist China managed to redistribute a meagre national income, it is difficult to redistribute to the masses what is not being produced. In addition, many Third World governments have been severely limited by their lack of technological and managerial competence. While I shall emphasize the political dimension in the subsequent discussion, these limits on action need to be remembered.

Having made these general points, I wish now to consider the major reasons for governments having adopted specific urban policies. Why were slum removal and urban renewal projects so common, why has government housing so often been beyond the reach of the poor, why have sites-and-services projects now been taken up so enthusiastically? Are universal explanations possible or do government policies vary too much to fit into convenient boxes? Let me begin by considering why spontaneous housing is often demolished.

A common argument in the literature is that planners are hostile to the idea of the poor constructing their own dwellings; such housing is badly designed, uses poor materials, and is difficult for governments to service. While this attitude is understandable, it is usually irrelevant to Third World urban conditions and is a product of the education received by architects and planners. Since most professionals are trained abroad or in schools whose curricula are based on those used in colleges in Europe or the United States, they imbibe the conventional wisdom of those societies. In ex-British colonies the influence of British architectural and planning schools continues to be strong (Dewar, 1976; Dwyer, 1975; Aradeon, 1978), and Rosser (1972) complains of the 'mental barrier' against the 'brute realities' of the Indian city which this influence creates. The typical reaction of architects is to recommend high-quality governmental construction. Many believe that standards will be lowered if the poor are encouraged or permitted to build their own housing. But, as Turner (1972: 148) correctly points out, 'the standards the objectors have in mind . . . are not something which can be achieved with available resources but, rather represent the objectors' own notion of what housing ought to be.' This notion is obviously an imported and Utopian idea of little relevance to reality. Planners see only the bad elements of spontaneous housing without seeing the good. Paper plans are seen to be the reality and the solutions of the people themselves and their problems become, in

Grennels's (1972: 97) term, 'invisible'.

This blindness is the result of a genuine desire to improve the living conditions of as many people as possible; a fixed idea of what constitutes 'good' housing; a recognition of severe limits on public and private commercial sector resources to attain these goals; an emphasis on standardization of design and production efficiency; and a consequent discounting of the role of the dweller in the provision of housing. The latter is based on assumptions that public participation is inefficient and time consuming, that people 'don't know what they want', or simply that trained technicians 'know better' about laymen's needs than they do.

There are many examples of the 'image' of the squatter settlement being so bad in the minds of professionals and politicians that it has led to instant demolition. Aradeon (1978: 1) recalls 'the military governor of Lagos state who, on arrival from an Australian visit, announced that his government was going to clear the slums of traditional Lagos and rebuild it with modern apartments and shopping centres.' Such views are both inconsistent and superficial and lead to inappropriate policy responses.

While such misguided attitudes have an important influence in the formulation of inappropriate responses, it would be unwise to overstress them. When, as happened in the Ford Foundation's International Urbanization Survey, most reliance is placed on greater and improved professional training, it diverts attention from solid political reasons for squatter areas or poor neighbourhoods being obliterated. In many countries demolition serves an important role in national political strategy and often serves to support particular social groups. In British Northern Rhodesia, for example, demolition maintained an important colonial policy: 'The urban areas were the milieu of the white population and legislation was enacted to keep it that way' (Tipple, 1976: 167). Such a policy is still that practised in South Africa (Wilson, 1972; Ellis et at., 1977). In the Republic the state requires that accommodation be built for the migrant labourer; spontaneous housing is prohibited in the cities, but permitted in the rural areas. The policy against spontaneous housing in the cities is clearly not intended to help the poor black as much as to control the influx and to maintain white living standards. The transparency of South African housing policy is useful not only to warn us of the evils of apartheid but also to point to the way that governments manipulate housing policies.

The traditional Anglo-Saxon explanation of poor governmental performance is to blame it on short-sightedness on the part of the authorities and their advisers. All too frequently, however, the explanation lies elsewhere; it is in some group's interest that things continue the way they do. Many urban-renewal and squatter-relocation schemes clearly fit such an explanation. Consider the case when land close to the commerical business centre is occupied by low-income settlement. The technical explanation that it constitutes a health hazard or that the population would be better served by government-built accommodation elsewhere is simply too convenient. More often groups commanding political support persuade the planning authorities to act in this way and the project is legitimized in terms of the public interest. In Rio de Janeiro the *favela*-removal programme between 1962 and 1966 was supported on the grounds that the land was needed for mass-transit systems; in Mexico a similar programme was justified in terms of the construction of a metro; in Lagos 60,000 people were removed as part of a road-widening project. Of course, where a project is genuinely in the public interest, any group physically blocking its completion should be moved. Unfortunately too many renewal schemes harm the poor and bring them few real benefits.

Not infrequently, therefore, technical criteria, often based on European or North American 'experience', are intoned to benefit higher-income groups. To some extent we can agree with those who argue that sensitive housing and planning policies depend less upon an awakening in professional attitudes than upon more political pressure from the poor. Collier (1976: 133) argues that the authorities in Lima have permitted land invasions because of pressure, albeit limited, from the poor. 'In other countries, the extensive eradication of settlements suggests that they are even more powerless in their relations with the government than in Peru . . .'. Support for this contention comes from Ibadan where the political dominance of the central area population over the city council prevents slum clearance (Laquian, 1971: 65). Similarly '[in] India it appears from observation that the majority of low-income areas in the cities vote for the ruling Congress Party and that this has resulted in improvements to the physical environment of such areas even when this is in blatant contradiction to the government's own master plan' (Payne, 1977: 63). Political influence is clearly a vital ingredient in the orientation of housing policy.

Perhaps the role that political interests play within the capitalist system in determining governmental policy towards the poor is best shown by reversing my original question. Instead of asking why urban renewal schemes have been introduced and spontaneous settlements destroyed we should examine under what circumstances spontaneous housing has been permitted to develop. As broad hypotheses I can perhaps suggest that spontaneous settlements are allowed to develop when: (1) major political parties or governments require the political support of the poor; (2) land occupied by the poor does not directly threaten the principle of private ownership; (3) the operation of spontaneous settlements directly supports, or at least reduces the need for changing, the economic and social system.

We have already seen how in India and Nigeria partisan politics have prevented slum removal, but political interest can also lead to greater service provision and credit facilities. Drakakis-Smith (1976a: 12) argues that in Turkey, as the struggle for power between the two major political parties has become more evenly balanced, so the squatters have received *de facto* recognition of their occupation and have been provided with many facilities such as surfaced roads, electricity, and water connections. Similarly in Santiago land seizures rose from thirteen in 1968 to thirty-five in 1969 and 103 in 1970 as an election approached (Cleaves, 1974). According to Kusnetzoff (1975: 294-5), 'These figures demonstrate that, however strong the Frei repression, growing workers' organizations, the support of opposition parties for land seizures, and the proximity of a presidential election were altogether instrumental in overcoming that repressive power and thereby the planning and control capacity of the government.' The poor may also benefit, at least temporarily, under populist governments. In Peron's Argentina and Rojas Pinilla's Colombia the poor received more services and their settlements were threatened less frequently. In Lima the military government of Odría (1948-56) began to give away land as a means of undermining the political support of APRA.[9] Collier (1976: 64) claims that the long-term effect of this ploy was to set in motion a 'sorcerer's apprentice dynamic' which obliged new governments, both elected and military, to give away land and to service already established settlements. Consequently Lima's invasions are a direct result of government encouragement rather than a threat to the Peruvian system, as is so often claimed.

While the poor as a group may benefit temporarily from populist programmes or from political power contests which demand their vote, it is more common for particular settlements to be singled out for special treatment. In many Latin American cities service provision is a function of political patronage; *barrios* that promise to support a powerful political group or personality may receive telephones, water, or roads as part of the deal. Ray (1969) reports that in Venezuela many *barrios* are linked to particular political parties and benefit according to the fortunes of their parties. In Rio de Janeiro, according to Leeds (1969; 79), 'the larger the *favela*, the greater the flow of gifts or the more significant the gifts which can be commandeered: there are more votes to be delivered, more to buy . . . Thus, very large squatments . . . continue to grow, to improve, to wield political influence, while other considerably smaller *favelas* stagnate.'

In general, therefore, political interests are the critical element determining policy towards spontaneous settlements. How the poor as a group come out of the situation will depend on the degree of partisan political conflict as well as structural factors such as the prosperity of the country and the degree to which the poor can be helped without affecting middle- or high-income groups. These structural conditions are critical and lead us on to the second point.

The spontaneous settlers of Lima, Ankara, and Caracas have all been the beneficiaries of political competition. But in all these cities a major factor has been the availability of public land around the city. Throughout the non-Communist Third World, governments generally have tended to defend private land but have permitted invasions of public land. Only in exceptional circumstances have invasions of private land taken place. Luis Echeverría, the President of Mexico from 1970 to 1976, encouraged the occupation of land belonging to the Magazine *Excelsior* in reprisal for its critical attitude to his administration.

In Venezuela private owners have failed to discourage potential invaders when they have anticipated that the government might recompense them for their 'loss' (Pérez and Nikken, 1979; Gilbert, 1981b).[10] In Chile, in 1970, 'the situation was so topsy-turvy that owners of private land were encouraging *pobladores* to invade their land' (Cleaves, 1974: 301-2). Since land on the urban fringe could neither be farmed profitably nor sold privately for urban development, a land-owner's best course was to sell invaded land to the government at an inflated price, freeing the owner from his legal responsibility to install urban services.

Much more common is the invasion of public land, especially where extensive areas of state land lie close to the urban area. Gradually, however, rapid urbaniz-ation is reducing the supply of accessible public land and leading to much less relaxed reactions to invasions. In Ankara it is now more common for the poor to buy land and in Lima the last two years of the Velasco presidency (1974-5) saw a much stricter government response. Both governments now face the choice of cutting rates of city growth or preventing land invasion and thereby encouraging the purchase of land. In many Latin American cities, in fact, the poor purchase land in the same way as any other social group. In Bogotá, São Paulo, and Mexico City, many of the poor have purchased land in speculative subdivisions of fringe areas: in Bogotá over half of the city's homes have been built on such land. After paying a deposit, buyers are given three to four years to complete payment and are then given the title-deeds. The only important difference compared with that of the ordinary commercial market is that the land lacks planning permission and services. By most European standards it is strange that governments permit such extensive unregulated developments. On the other hand, these governments recognize that the poor need land and that if they compelled urbanizers to provide services it would force the poor out of the land market. The only alternatives to the process of pirate urbanization are higher levels of renting and, in the longer run, land invasion. While pirate urbanizations are often extremely expensive to service and encourage low-density patterns or urban growth, they provide land for the poor. More important still, they support the principle of private land ownership by reducing the need to invade and by turning large numbers of poor people into landowners. In Bogotá the state intervenes in pirate urbanizations only where the urbanizer is denounced by the population of the settlement (Gilbert, 1981b). Except for the over-grasping and corrupt, pirate urbanizers survive because government intervention would cause the state more problems than it would resolve. In addition, the system provides political interests with a source of patronage. Politicians seek planning permission, negotiate for services with the bureaucracy, and intercede with the pirate urbanizers. Less scrupulous politicans represent the interests of the pirate urbanizer before the authorities. In other cities, such as Nairobi, top politicians are themselves involved in sales of land and property to the poor and thereby have a direct interest in the maintenance of pirate urbanizations. Most commonly, however, the system of pirate urbanization survives because it offers the poor land without threatening the principle of private land ownership.

To some extent my second point overlaps with my third; the process of spontaneous settlement is permitted whenever it supports the existing social, political, and economic system. Whatever the fears and moral objections of élites to spontaneous housing, self-help keeps the Third World economy functioning. First, it lets the less poor into the housing market by keeping costs low, in a way moreover that does not threaten higher-income groups. Second, Marxists argue that the very cheapness of spontaneous housing allows the labour force to reproduce itself despite the low wages paid by modern industry (Pradilla, 1976; Burgess, 1978; da Camargo et al., 1975). Economic development occurs apace in dependent capitalist societies on the basis of cheap labour costs and the perpetuation of low-income housing helps to reduce the pressure for wage rises. While spontaneous settlements may offend middle- and upper-income groups, zoning regulations effectively segregate the different income groups. If spontaneous housing does not have to be seen too frequently, its advantages become manifest; it offers cheap labour to industry, a plentiful supply of servants, and the myriad of other cheap services available to Third World urban élites. Thirdly, the existence of spontaneous settlement, especially where there is an active process of consolidation, opens up profit opportunities for commercial and industrial companies. Glass, bricks, cement, tiles, and pipes are purchased in large quantities by the spontaneous settlers and provide a large market for construction material suppliers. In addition, spontaneous housing areas can help to channel the poor out of high-value central areas. As Collier (1976: 37) notes, 'out of sixty cases on which appropriate information was available, nearly 50 per cent in some way benefitted public or private urban development or real estate interests. The ambiguities of land ownership in Lima have unquestionably served the wealthy as well as the poor.' Fourthly, partisan political interests are served by the process. As Pérez and Nikken (1979: 73) argue,

squatting and the formation of *barrios* do not burden the state (or the party in power in local or national government) with any kind of obligation to provide land or services nor the task of sharing them. On the contrary, the state is granting a favour by not evicting the squatters . . . The provision of public services implies a new round of favours and the active cooperation of the *barrio* inhabitants can be made use of in installing the services.

My argument, therefore, is that while spontaneous settlement clearly brings problems for the state, it is generally functional to the maintenance and reproduction of the social and economic order. In turn, this raises an important question. If it has been in the interest of the Third World capitalist system to encourage spontaneous settlement, why has the state sometimes demolished such settlements and engaged in urban renewal? If spontaneous settlements have been so useful to the rich, why have the World Bank and the United Nations had to work so hard to sell the idea of sites-and-services programmes? This, in turn, raises questions about the validity of some Marxist explanations of the

Third World urban situation (Peattie, 1979). According to many writers, spontaneous settlement is functional to the system because it cheapens the cost of labour for industry and services. It thereby accelerates the pace of capital accumulation and allows the reproduction of the labour supply. At the same time, however, the monopoly capitalist sector increasingly enters the spontaneous settlement process. By purchasing land for speculation, by providing materials for construction, and by increasingly entering the retail market within such communities, large-scale companies increase their profits. But, in turn, their very entry into this market raises the costs of reproduction of labour and thereby puts pressure on wage levels, which spontaneous settlement is supposed to avoid. A contradiction is involved here which needs to be carefully considered.

One possible resolution is to explain the contradiction in terms of the mutually conflicting interests of different élite groups (class fractions). The state is subject to pressure from representatives of various capitalist groups; its housing response will therefore constitute a balance between these demands. Thus national governments may respond to industrial interests, vaguely sympathetic to spontaneous settlement because of the cheap labour it offers, by failing to formulate a consistent housing policy or by supporting self-help programmes. Meanwhile local government policy may respond to pressure from élite residential groups and the construction industry whose best interests are served by demolition. Such local action would be favoured when the poor have occupied high-value land awaiting development, when they have blocked prestige public works programmes, and when the poor have established themselves close to middle- and upper-income housing areas, thus threatening to lower land and property values. In other circumstances local governments may accept spontaneous settlement because they are incapable of handling the problem; they cannot build proper houses to accommodate the poor, they cannot service the settlers, nor indeed can they muster the political power to remove them. Since in any case the process serves the interests of the rich and since the poor seem generally content with the actions they themselves have taken, the most sensible policy has been to leave bad alone.

At the national level, governments are increasingly admitting the 'blight' of spontaneous housing into their national development plans; development, after all, is now understood to include much more than economic growth. International pressure from the World Bank and other loan agencies in favour of spontaneous housing may not be entirely welcome, but it is sweetened by hard currency loans. Further, urban problems can no longer be ignored by national governments because of the scale of the issue. Buenos Aires accommodates one-third of all Argentinians, Caraqueños make up one-fifth of the Venezuelan population, and Manilans represent one-eighth of all Philippinos. Since up to one half of the populations of these cities are spontaneous settlers, national governments are forced to intervene. The introduction of partial remedies such as sites-and-services projects can be expected to grow because Third World governments have no other solutions to offer. But the sorts of programmes that will be introduced are not those that have been recommended by the World Bank. For if national governments have been forced to intervene in the urban areas by political and economic realities, business interests have intervened because of the attraction of profits. A programme that would truly help the poor would involve attacks on land speculation, some subsidization of public services for the poor, and effective land-use planning which would reduce traffic congestion and unit costs of public service provision. But this is not the real world in a mixed economy and we are deluding both ourselves and the poor if we believe it. Sites-and-services schemes are both necessary and inevitable, but there can be no avoiding more radical changes which will redistribute the resources of the city and increase the rates of public service provision and job creation.

URBAN WAYS OF LIFE

Through the ages cities have elicited sharply contrasting responses. With the establishment of urban settlements humankind has wrought the most conspicuous changes on the planet's surface and profoundly altered the social relationships that distinguish the human species. But after 6,000 years of urban experience we still appear ambivalent about our creation. We can only speculate whether the early cities were primarily seen as the seats of despotic rulers, as the repositories of holy shrines, or as the kingpins in trade which spiced food and embellished life. To the philosophers of the Enlightenment the city represented virtue, but to later generations experiencing the Industrial Revolution the city appeared as a nest of vice and corruption. The *conquistadores* established their cities on the sites of the Aztec and Inca capitals they had destroyed, and they built their cathedrals with stones from the old temples, but their pride in their new creations ultimately came to be shared by foreign immigrant and *mestizo* alike. Calcutta stood for over two centuries as the symbol of foreign intrusion, but it was in Calcutta that the Bengal Renaissance challenged the West. The urban settlements of freed slaves on the West African coast, Freetown in 1792, Monrovia in 1822, Libreville in 1848, came to symbolize the struggle for abolition. But on the same continent Johannesburg stands as the foremost symbol of racial oppression today.

Our discussion also carries traces of ambivalence. The Third World city appears to us to be characterized by its dependent position in the world capitalist system, but it is also the locus where strategies for more balanced development can be adopted and set into motion. We have argued that the city holds out real promise to the masses it attracts from rural areas, but we have also emphasized problems of urban unemployment, underemployment, and misemployment.

Here we shall focus on the characteristics of social interaction in the city. Assumptions as to what constitutes the urban way of life abound, and they underlie many of the judgements about the merits and evils of the city. But a good deal of research has focused on urban social relations over the last four decades and, as we shall see, some assumptions commonly held are no longer tenable.

The stage for the contemporary enquiry into urban life was set by Wirth in 1938 in his classic essay 'Urbanism as a Way of Life'. He noted virtues of the city, but put greater stress on what he saw as its dehumanizing aspects. As Wirth (1938: 1) summarized his argument:

For sociological purposes a city is a relatively large, dense, and permanent settlement of heterogeneous individuals. Large numbers account for individual variability, the relative absence of intimate personal acquaintanceship, the segmentalization of human relations which are largely anonymous, superficial, and transitory, and associated characteristics. Density involves diversification and specialization, the coincidence of close physical contact and distant social relations, glaring contrasts, a complex pattern of segregation, the predominance of formal social control, and accentuated friction, among other phenomena. Heterogeneity tends to break down rigid social structures and to produce increased mobility, instability, and insecurity, and the affiliation of the individuals with a variety of intersecting and tangential social groups with a high rate of membership turnover. The pecuniary nexus tends to displace personal relations, and institutions tend to cater to mass rather than to individual requirements. The individual thus becomes effective only as he acts through organized groups.

A substantial body of research, however, has demonstrated that generalizations like Wirth's are not warranted. At the very time when Wirth wrote, Whyte ([1943] 1981) carried out research in a low-income Boston neighbourhood inhabited almost exclusively by Italian immigrants and their children. Middle-class persons looked upon the area as a slum, a formidable mass of confusion, a social chaos. Instead, Whyte found a highly organized and integrated social system; even young single men were integrated through the street-corner gang they had established. Twenty years later Gans (1962a) studied native-born Americans of Italian parentage in another Boston low-income neighbourhood. Again the area was perceived as a slum by the average Bostonian, but Gans found that the immigrants had created a stable, tight-knit community; he characterized it as an 'urban village'. What then of the millions of villagers arriving in Third World cities every year?

Peasant and Urbanite

Many urban dwellers remain firmly rooted in the rural community in which they grew up. This is a widespread pattern in Subsaharan Africa, much of Asia, and the Pacific. For the recent migrant to find himself isolated in the urban setting is not common. When it happens, the migrant may be lonely, but he is quite likely to feel secure in the knowledge that he continues to be a member of the community he came from. Wife and children who had to be left behind, members of the extended family, or the village continue to define for many a rural place as home.

The migration patterns distinguished in chapter 3 above are obviously related to the strength of the ties migrants maintain with their community of origin. Many migrants anticipate returning there. They continue to see themselves as members of a rural community, whether they want to be back in time for the next harvest, or plan to retire in the village after a lifetime of work in the city. The latter pattern prevailed in the 1960s in what was then Eastern Nigeria. Urban residents invariably stressed that they were strangers in town. Irrespective of his birthplace every Eastern Nigerian could point without hesitation to a community in which his forefathers lived and which he considered his 'home place'. It would be a rural community except for the few who descended from families long-established in pre-colonial towns. The home community conversely referred to them as 'our sons abroad'. They were expected to maintain contact and to return eventually (Gugler, 1971: 405).

Significant ties with their rural areas of origin are not uncommon even among permanent migrants. Such a commitment to the extended family and the village is reported from Meerut, a city in North India, where Vatuk (1972) studied first- and second-generation migrants holding white-collar jobs. Most consider their real home to be in the village and say that they are living 'outside' in the city, or 'in service', i.e. at their place of employment. Frequent contact with the village and a sense of belonging to the village home carry on over several generations. Couples return for a visit to the husband's place of origin during holidays, women visit their natal homes with their children. The exchange of money, goods, and services between rural and urban segments of the agnatic extended family is not only normatively prescribed but common in practice, particularly if the rural residents are the parents of the head of the urban household. However, with few exceptions, these urbanites have no intention of ever returning to live in the village, nor will their children settle there. True, many retain joint owner- ship of rural land and homes, but such property apparently has little material value for these white-collar urbanites; it is not a significant source of present or potential income. Indeed, urban residents who have a claim to family property are reluctant to see the property divided because they continue to place high value upon the ideal of family 'jointness' (Vatuk, 1972: 131-4, 139, 141, 194).

Bruner (1972: 226; 1973: 376) reports a similar pattern among the Toba Batak, a Christian minority in Indonesia. They originate from Sumatra, and many of those residing in Medan, one of the two principal cities on the island, go to their home village for short visits to discuss lineage affairs, to look after property, or to participate in village ceremonials, but very few ever return there to live, even after retirement. Batak in distant Djakarta – a ten-day boat trip away – send money home, help the children of rural relatives to attend school in the city, and keep an active interest in home affairs. The urban Batak do not lose their place in rural society. Indeed, many continue to own a house and rice fields in their village, even after two or three generations in the city. However, ownership of village property eventually comes to have symbolic rather than economic value.

The commitment many migrants have to their community of origin may be taken to suggest that they remain peasants at heart, that they do not become urbanites. Short-term migration in particular encourages such an interpretation. But even when migrants come for only a brief stay – no longer the typical pattern, as was seen in chapter 3 – it does not follow that they continue to behave in rural ways while in town. Though they are used to rural behaviour and may well hold rural values, they are frequently aware of, and experienced in, urban ways. They have learned about urban conditions in school and from visiting or returned migrants. Some have been in towns before, be it to sell rural products, to make purchases or obtain services, or just as guests of kin or friends.

Certainly, as soon as the migrant arrives in town he has to adopt behaviour that will allow him to pursue his economic goals effectively. The point was made forcefully by Gluckman (1960: 57) when he dismissed an earlier perspective that saw African workers as 'tribesmen' in his classic dictum: 'An African townsman is a townsman, an African miner is a miner.' Yet such a model of situational change captures only one aspect of the migrant's adaptation. There is also a drawn-out process: the migrant continues to modify his behaviour as he gains urban experience, as he undergoes biographic change.[1]

Language use constitutes a conspicuous and important area of adaptation. Some migrants need only to make a few additions to their vocabulary or to modify their pronunciation, but others have no mastery, or only limited mastery, of the city's lingua franca. Many migrants in Asian and African cities have to switch to the national or regional language in common use. The transformation is particularly striking in those Latin American cities in which American Indian migrants come to be seen as *mestizos* as they learn Spanish, abandon their rural dress and hair styles, and modify their food habits. The switch in language use illustrates the propositions of both the situational and the biographic change model: as soon as the immigrant arrives in town he will need to employ what little he knows of the lingua franca; as he stays on, his language skills will improve.

Adopting urban patterns of behaviour does not require forgetting how things were done at home. Working-life migrants will continue to behave in urban or rural ways as the situation demands. Indeed, they have to be both peasants and townsmen in order to operate successfully in the dual system they have established (Gugler, 1971). Learning and acquiring new norms of behaviour through urban socialization, some individuals grow away from their rural ways, but most do not abandon the will or lose the ability to enter into social relations governed by rural norms, whether in the town or in their home areas. In other words, becoming urban involves an extension of cultural equipment, but it does not necessarily imply a commensurate rejection or loss.

Home People

Most rural–urban migrants make their first move to a city where they expect to be received by relatives or friends. They will be offered shelter and food for a while, they will be introduced to the urban environment, and efforts will be made to find them an opportunity to earn their living. This pattern of initial urban association encourages persons of the same origin to form residential clusters. A tight housing market or allocation of housing by public authorities or employers constitute countervailing tendencies. But even when residentially dispersed, people of common origin frequently maintain close ties.

Butterworth (1972) describes a group of men in Mexico City who migrated from Tilantongo, an isolated Mixtec community 300 miles away. Almost every weekend they meet at the house of a member who is the undisputed leader of the group. A member in need of aid turns to him first, but responsibility is corporate. For a member who had become an invalid, the group mustered considerable financial resources and spent a great deal of time and effort on gaining access to public agencies. Repayment of such assistance is not expected, even loans go mostly unpaid, but continued affiliation with the group and willingness to help other members is implied.

The migrants share information about strategies for coping with problems in the city and introduce new arrivals to the complexities, but the most popular topic of conversation is their *tierra*, Tilantongo. They discuss the current state of affairs in the community and deplore the decline that has taken place. They critically analyse the needs of the community and possible ways to meet them, hatch schemes to get rid of the reactionary incumbents in the community offices, and weigh suggestions to be made at the monthly meeting of the formal organization of Tilantongo migrants in Mexico City. Their leader makes regular calls on the president of the organization of Mixtec migrants in Mexico City, a former state deputy in the Mexican legislature with influence in government circles. Considerable efforts are directed towards getting him and officials from various government commissions to accept invitations to *fiestas* at the leader's home. Once present, the officials will be plied with liquor and a sumptuous barbecue *a la Mixteca* in an attempt to extract promises of aid to Tilantongo.

The solidarity of common origin, strengthened by feelings of mutual obligation, and shared long-term interest in the future of their home community, is complemented by sentiment. These men rarely associate socially with anyone other than migrants from Tilantongo. As they drink together, they recall their childhood in the village, the way things have — and have not — changed:

After the men have been drinking for a while, someone invariably brings forth a guitar to accompany sentimental songs about their beloved *tierra*. A favorite is the 'Cancion Mixteca.' ('How far away am I from the land where I was born / Immense nostalgia fills my thoughts . . .') Hardly a dry eye remains as the melody concludes: 'I would like to cry / I would like to die / of sentiment.' With tears streaming down his cheeks, one of the men is likely to stand and shout, 'I'm from Tilantongo!' (Butterworth, 1972: 39)

Formal organizations of 'home people' are prominent in parts of West Africa. Such ethnic unions go to considerable lengths to have all from home join in. They meet regularly, elicit intensive participation, and serve a wide range of explicit and implicit purposes. Members relax in each other's company, they evolve like responses to the urban milieu, provide assistance in personal crises, settle their disputes within the union, and are frequently involved in furthering the development of their home community (Gugler and Flanagan, 1978a: 81-8).

Three variables affect the pattern of association among migrants. Links with home people in the city and ties to the common home area tend to be mutually reinforcing as each enhances communication and social control in the other context. Mayer ([1961] 1971: 283–93) emphasizes a second variable, the interaction between cultural traits and the structure of social relationships. Immigrants who have a traditionalist outlook will tend towards encapsulation in a group of like-minded home people who uphold shared rules of behaviour. If Mayer's analysis represents cultural background as the prime determinant of patterns of association in the urban setting, Banton (1973) has focused attention on a third variable: opposition among social groupings in town. He suggests that the social density that characterizes the village is encouraged among urban groups both by the degree of discontinuity between the rural and the urban systems and by the extent and strength of structural opposition in the urban system. I shall address ethnic alignments in political conflict in the next chapter.

Lifestyle Alternatives in the City

Contrary to the assumption that urban life is characterized by the absence of meaningful personal relationships, we have seen how many rural–urban migrants, far from being uprooted, maintain strong ties with their community of origin, establish in the city new communities based on common origin or, indeed, do both. Other urban dwellers, first-generation migrants or the urban born, feel securely anchored in networks of kinship and friendship. In a survey in Kanpur, India, an industrial centre of over one million inhabitants, nearly everyone reported seeing friends in the city more than once a week, and most characterized these friendships as intimate. Furthermore, a large majority had relatives in the city, and many described their relationships as intimate or extending to mutual aid.[2] The survey covered three neighbourhoods which differed in type of location, length of settlement, and socio-economic status, but the patterns reported were quite similar across these neighbourhoods. In each of them the great majority of residents appeared to have intimate ties in the city. And within each there was a good deal of visiting and exchanging favours (Chandra, 1977: 89–122, 189).

Religious groupings play an important integrative role for some urbanites. Roberts (1978: 145) attributes the development of Pentecostal and other Protestant sects in predominantly Catholic Guatemala to the attempts of those lacking extensive social relationships to develop the basis for such relationships. In the two low-income neighbourhoods he studied, members of the sects were often those without kin in the city and included women separated from husbands or whose husbands were alcoholics. Catholic voluntary groups performed similar functions for other low-income residents, providing the opportunity for single women with children, for example, to have a stable basis of interaction with others who could help them to find work or to obtain benefits from social welfare agencies.

Many an urbanite establishes a quite close-knit network with kin or home people, or through involvement in a religious or political group.[3] The ideal type of such a network is the isolated village community, where everybody knows everybody else. In urban settings it is approached in those exceptional cases in which a group of people are in each other's exclusive company not only during leisure-time activities but also at work. Unlike the village, the city offers an alternative form of integration. An individual may have a wide range of meaningful relationships with people who do not know each other. Such loose-knit networks are specific to the city, a pattern impossible to implement in a rural context. Close-knit networks tend to be composed of like-minded associates who enforce conformity with the rules of behaviour prescribed by the group. The members of a loose-knit network, in contrast, tend to have a more open outlook; each one can take advantage of the choices the urban setting offers and has greater leeway in deciding with whom to associate and which cultural pattern to adopt. The moral pressures exerted by associates in the heterogeneous urban setting are frequently inconsistent, and changing one's behaviour, beliefs, norms, and values need not lead to general ostracism, but only to strained relations with some associates.[4]

Gans's (1962b) classic rejoinder to Wirth exposed the basic fallacy of a perspective that sees social relationships as determined by the urban environment, i.e. of ecological determinism. Reviewing urban neighbourhood studies in the United States, Gans showed conclusively that only a minority of the urban population lives in isolation, and that a considerable variety of lifestyles is to be found across neighbourhoods. From this observation the central argument followed: to the extent that urban dwellers can choose their location within this heterogeneous enivronment, they also, more or less deliberately, opt for a lifestyle; for many urban dwellers their lifestyle is thus not determined by a supposedly invariant urban environment.

The shortcomings of ecological determinism are well illustrated by a study of crime in Kampala which focuses on two low-income neighbourhoods (Clinard and Abbott, 1973: 142–65). Kisenyi was well known as a high-crime area, while Namuwongo had a better reputation. Indeed rates of crimes reported to the police and of arrests were considerably higher in Kisenyi for violent crimes and even more so for property crimes. The study proposed an interpretation in terms of differences in community integration and in the residents' perceptions of their communities. It failed to address the fact that for most immigrants in Kampala there was an element of choice in which neighbourhood to settle. Kisenyi was located near to the bus station, major markets, and the business centre, and had the greatest concentration of prostitutes in the city, a wide selection of bars, places in which illegally brewed beer was sold, gambling and dancing establishments, and drugs. Namuwongo, in contrast, was situated outside the city limits and bordered upon the industrial sector. We would expect there to be a measure of self-selection among the people who respectively settled in two so diverse neighbourhoods.

Even within the same neighbourhood different categories of people may pursue distinct lifestyles, a point strikingly demonstrated in a different context by Gans (1962b: 629–32) for the inner city in the United States. Anthony and Elizabeth Leeds (1970: 243–8) similarly emphasize the heterogeneous composition of the *favelas* on the hills of Rio de Janeiro. Some of their inhabitants are unable to earn a living and barely survive on handouts; they frequently die young. We may call them the trapped, for they have nowhere else to go. Others have experienced a crisis which left them no alternative but to seek refuge in the *favela*; they are going through a period of stress, but there is the prospect that they will surmount their problems and move out. A third category of *favela* residents live there by choice in order to economize; they could afford regular housing but are attracted by the opportunity to pay little or no rent and perhaps the possibility of raising fruit, vegetables, pigs, or chickens. Finally a few are well off – the Leedses encountered an accountant, a watchmaker, and a retired teacher; they have a taste for the freedom the *favela* offers from conventional constraints, and for the social recognition and prestige they enjoy among their co-residents. Lomnitz (1978) describes a category of relatively affluent residents who are bound to shanty towns in Mexico City for their very livelihood. Small entrepreneurs need close contact with relatives and neighbours who provide them with cheap labour or custom. Brokers similarly have to live in the shanty town, e.g. the leader of a construction gang who recruits labour, the jobber who puts out sewing to women in the neighbourhood, the local political boss.

Apart from these various motivations, residential heterogeneity is fostered through processes of change. Where a neighbourhood is invaded – for instance, when the original squatters sell out to more affluent people once their settlement has become legalized – there will be high heterogeneity during the transition period. Conversely, a measure of heterogeneity arises when people remain in a neighbourhood in spite of changes in their economic fortunes or household composition – for instance, because they feel attached to the locality or they continue to have significant social ties in the neighbourhood, or because housing shortages make it difficult to find a satisfactory alternative or moving out means giving up rent-controlled housing.

Neighbourhood relationships are important for most urban dwellers, but they are only part of the urbanite's social network. If the urban villager appears bounded by his neighbourhood, others have additional social relationships which reach farther afield. Many migrants, as we have seen, remain integrated 'back home'. Where a migrant finds himself among strangers, he may well lead the life of an exile, affirming his continued membership in a home community. Whether migrant or urban born, most urban dwellers have significant ties in other parts of the city and frequently beyond. The maintenance of such geographically extended social networks is facilitated as fast forms of transport become more easily and more cheaply available, and as other means of communication are improved. Modern technology has dramatically expanded the human environment.

The attempt to explain the behaviour of people in terms of their immediate environment thus runs up against three phenomena in the urban context; lifestyles vary to a considerable extent across the urban agglomeration, and most urbanites have a measure of choice where to locate; a considerable variety of lifestyles is found within some neighbourhoods; and urban dwellers, to the extent that they can take advantage of modern transport and communication, are not bounded by neighbourhood. Conversely, certain categories of urban dwellers can be seen to be constrained by their immediate environment. Many are forced into an environment not of their choosing, e.g. those who out of economic necessity work in the gold mines of South Africa and have no alternative but the minimal accommodation for single men provided by their employers. Others have no satisfactory alternatives within their immediate environment; they are outsiders in a homogeneous neighbourhood — for example, a lone minority household in an otherwise homogeneous neighbourhood. Finally, the environment is narrowly circumscribed for some, either because they cannot afford efficient transportation and communication or because they are homebound — for example, mothers caring for children, the young, invalids. Still, for most urban dwellers there are alternatives.

Indeed, what distinguishes the city from rural areas are the options it provides. There is not one urban lifestyle distinct from a rural way of life but a variety of lifestyles unknown in the village community. Some urbanites lead encapsulated lives, nearly as if they were in a village community, but others strike out, associate with like-minded persons, separate when they no longer agree, become individualists. The bigger the city, the better the chance for even the most unusual mind to find others so inclined. The city allows the unconventional, those labelled 'deviants' in the society at large, to establish social relationships with those of same ilk, and to develop viable social roles. In the city adherents of a new religion, protagonists of a new political idea, carriers of a new fashion can aggregate in sufficient numbers to support each other. Cities are centres of innovation because it is in cities that innovators can constitute a critical mass (Fischer, 1976: 37).

The opportunities the city offers dissidents, to associate among themselves and to leave others in the dark about their thoughts, and indeed about their activities, present a serious problem for regimes that aim at directing broad-based mobilization and narrowly circumscribing dissent. They invariably attempt to deal with it through grassroots organizations at the neighbourhood level (and also at the place of work). In China residents' committees are closely connected with the formal police structure (J. A. Cohen, 1968: 104–70, 355–60; Whyte, n.d.a). They are said to leave almost 'no place to hide', or, in the Chinese phrase, no 'dead corners', and are credited with a great reduction in urban crime, prostitution, and drug abuse. However, in the wake of the Cultural Revolution hundreds of thousands of rusticated middle-school leavers returned to the cities without authorization. In Cuba the functions of the Committees for the Defence of the Revolution have fluctuated over the years, but vigilance was considered a prime concern much of the time. If its focus was local collaborators with foreign intervention in the early 1960s, especially around the time of the Bay of Pigs Invasion, vigilance has continued to be directed against political deviance as well as common crime (Domínguez, 1978: 261-7; Butterworth, 1980: 105-18).

Mental Stress and Crime in the City

Part of the negative image of the city is the assumption that mental stress is more characteristic of the city than of rural areas. The evidence from Third World countries is scanty and less than clear cut. The Harvard Project on the Social and Cultural Aspects of Development provides data on men aged eighteen to thirty-two in Argentina, Chile, India, Nigeria, and Pakistan (Inkeles and Smith, 1970). The survey asked about such psychosomatic symptoms as difficulty in sleeping, nervousness, headaches, or frightening dreams; more were reported among those with longer urban residence in four of the five countries, but the relationship was statistically significant only for Argentina and Pakistan. Similarly, when urban non-industrial workers were matched with cultivators on variables such as education and ethnic membership, the workers reported more psychosomatic symptoms of stress in four countries (no data are available for Argentina), and the differences were statistically significant in Nigeria and Pakistan. However, when long-time factory workers were matched with cultivators, while the workers appeared less well adapted in four countries, the only statistically significant difference obtained in India, where they reported less stress. A similar study in Kenya compared Abaluyia women who shared their lives between Nairobi and their rural home communities in Western Kenya, Kikuyu market women in Nairobi, and rural Kikuyu women (Weisner and Abbott, 1977). The rural Kikuyu reported substantially higher stress scores than either of the other groups, and the relationship held when education and age were controlled for; however, the differences were not statistically significant. Certainly, to date, research has failed to provide the consistent results that would sustain the popular stereotype that urban life is more stressful than rural life.[5]

Measurements of psychological adjustment have to be qualified as brave attempts at best. The data base is similarly precarious when it comes to addressing another salient facet of the negative image of the city; the belief that crime and vice are rampant there, in contrast to supposedly more idyllic rural areas. Usually all we have to go by are crime statistics. Clearly not all crime is reported, nor are all criminals arrested. Of particular concern for our purposes is the fact that the proportion of crimes reported and of criminals arrested varies not only by type of crime but also by kind of community.

Violent crime in Third World countries does not appear to be more prevalent in urban than in rural areas. The most comprehensive data available compare the national homicide rate and the rate for a major city in eleven countries (table 6.1). The countries divide about evenly between those in which the national rate is higher and those in which it is lower than the city rate. While every caution as to the reliability of crime statistics is in order, the major bias to be expected in poor countries — that rural crimes are more likely to go unreported and that rural criminals are less likely to be brought into the national system of justice — suggests that rural crime rates are understated compared with urban rates. We must conclude that the rural–urban dichotomy does not constitute a promising explanatory variable for the rate of homicide.[6]

Table 6.1
Homicide rates for eleven countries and major cities within them, 1960s[a]

country (period)	national rate[b]	major city	city rate[b]
Guyana (1966–70)	6.18	Georgetown	5.21
India (1966–70)	2.72	Bombay	2.85
Kenya (1964–8)	5.67	Nairobi	5.27
Mexico (1962, 1966, 1967, 1972)	13.24	Mexico City	13.34
Panama (1966–70)	11.07	Panama City	4.96
Philippines (1966–70)	7.98	Manila	23.86
Sri Lanka (1966–70)	6.09	Colombo	5.59
Sudan (1961–4, 1968)	5.67	Khartoum	30.25
Trinidad and Tobago (1966–70)	14.00	Port of Spain	15.31
Turkey (1966–70)	9.65	Istanbul	4.84
Zimbabwe (1966–70)	5.33	Harare	7.20

[a] The national rate includes the rate of the major city, hence the comparison given here underestimates the difference between the major city and the rest of the country. The reader is cautioned against making comparisons of homicide rate levels across nations or across cities. The definition and reporting of homicide varies considerably among countries, and the indicator used here, while identical for each country and city in it, is not consistent across countries.
[b] Average annual number of homicides per 100,000 inhabitants.
Source: Archer *et al.* (1978: 84–5, 94 n.8).

In contrast to violent crime, property crime as well as victimless crime appear to be more common in urban than in rural areas. Three types of explanation compete: the disorganization argument that may be identified with some of Wirth's writing, structural interpretations, and the compositional proposition related to Gans's approach.

The disorganization argument assumes that the urban dweller is no longer effectively integrated into a community and that he is therefore released from informal social controls over his behaviour while at the same time he lacks any firm commitment to community values; he is easily attracted by the promise of quick gains, seduced by the lure of vice. In fact, as we have seen, many urban dwellers are well integrated. Still some, especially young adults, may be quite footloose, accountable to none, ready to try their hand at theft or burglary, prepared to cash in on what has been outlawed as vice.[7] The psychological element in the disorganization argument carries less conviction since it fails to be confirmed by research on psychological adjustment. A different psychological argument might well be made. Some rural areas in the Third World are characterized by conspicuous inequality, but usually the contrast between rich and poor is more glaring in the cities. Rural–urban migrants tend to rest content that they have improved their position, they are preoccupied with establishing themselves securely in urban employment and housing, and their ambitions for social mobility in the urban context are cast in terms of hope for their children's future. However, some of the urban born look beyond their own status group and experience severe relative deprivation. Given limited opportunities for social mobility, a career in crime may well appear as the only avenue to fulfil their aspirations.

Structural interpretations emphasize the difference in objective conditions between rural and urban areas, and indeed among urban neighbourhoods. First, theft and burglary are facilitated in anonymous urban settings where the stranger goes unnoticed.[8] Second, rural dwellers are usually assured of subsistence, but urban indigents, unlike their counterparts in rich countries, may have no alternative other than to steal or rob for survival; sometimes they organize for the purpose as in the bands of *gamines* in Bogotá. Third, the city's underworld is sufficiently large for a division of labour among professionals to be established, indeed for organized crime. Fourth, the greater number of customers brings forth a wide variety of illegal services to cater to their wishes, whether they want sex, drugs, or gambling.

The compositional proposition shifts the focus to the characteristics of the people who come to live in different types of agglomerations, and in different parts of the same agglomeration. Where young men predominate among migrants, more or less outright prostitution is likely to be encouraged. Customers for illegal services visit to avail themselves of the greater variety of such services in the city. Criminal elements are attracted by better opportunities in the bigger cities. Some may find it advisable to depart from the village or small town where they are too well known for comfort; the city offers the opportunity to shed one's past – and to hide present activities.

The Subculture of the Poor

If the city is a less safe place for property, if it is denounced for pandering to the tastes of deviants, it is the urban slum that appears to signal the failure of humankind's urban endeavour. Indeed the contrast between rich and poor within one city – found everywhere but particularly striking in much of the Third World – dramatically exposes man's insensitivity to the plight of fellow man. However, a closer look at rural realities, at the condition of Untouchables in India, at the degradation of Indians on the Amazon, suggests that this is not a specifically urban phenomenon. Still, disregard for others is facilitated by cultural distance, or rather the perception of such distance, and the juxtaposition of locals and various migrant groups in the city readily provides bases for cultural distinctions to be made.

The middle-class visitor usually perceives urban poverty in distorted terms which are encapsulated in the notion of the slum. This is how Perlman (1976: 13), in an account reminiscent of Whyte's ([1943] 1981: xv-xvi) famous introduction to his study of a Boston 'slum', contrasts the outsider's perception of a squatter settlement in Rio de Janeiro with an insider's view:

From outside, the typical favela seems a filthy, congested human antheap. Women walk back and forth with huge metal cans of water on their heads or cluster at the communal water supply washing clothes. Men hang around the local bars chatting or playing cards, seemingly with nothing better to do. Naked children play in the dirt and mud. The houses look precarious at best, thrown together out of discarded scraps. Open sewers create a terrible stench, especially on hot, still days. Dust and dirt fly everywhere on windy days, and mud cascades down past the huts on rainy ones.

Things look very different from inside, however. Houses are built with a keen eye to comfort and efficiency, given the climate and available materials. Much care is evident in the arrangement of furniture and the neat cleanliness of each room. Houses often boast colorfully painted doors and shutters, and flowers or plants on the window sill. Cherished objects are displayed with love and pride. Most men and women rise early and work hard all day. Often these women seen doing laundry are earning their living that way, and many of the men in bars are waiting for the work-shift to begin. Children, although often not in school, appear on the whole to be bright, alert, and generally healthy. Their parents . . . place high value on giving them as much education as possible. Also unapparent to the casual observer, there is a remarkable degree of social cohesion and mutual trust and a complex internal social organization, involving numerous clubs and voluntary associations.

We have emphasized, against ecological determinism, the choices the city offers. But the range of choices available to urbanites varies widely, depending on the power they can wield in the political arena and in the market-place. Lack of leverage to affect the political process and lack of the economic means to compete effectively in the market severely circumscribe the choices open to many urban dwellers. Are their lives determined by their political position and their material condition? The notion of a culture of poverty, while recognizing similarities among the urban poor in different societies, emphasizes that the behaviour and values of the poor are not determined by their circumstances, but constitute a culturally evolved response.

The concept of a culture of poverty was introduced by Oscar Lewis, an American anthropologist with considerable research experience among American Indians, in India, in Cuba, and with Puerto Ricans, both in Puerto Rico and in New York City, but who is best known for his work in Mexico. Lewis (1959: 16) first proposed the concept in his account of the life of five families in Mexico City. He expanded and modified his arguments over the years, and I shall base my discussion on his last statement, published in 1970, the year he died.

The rather catchy phrase, 'culture of poverty', designates common cultural elements found among poor people in different societies. Within any one society attention is focused on cultural traits, i.e. patterns of behaviour and values, specific to the poor; these do not constitute a separate culture, but rather a variation on the national culture, a subculture. Lewis observes that these sub-cultures have a common core: the absence of childhood as a specially prolonged and protected stage in the life cycle, free unions or consensual marriages, a trend toward female- or mother-centred families, and a strong predisposition to authoritarianism. Critics first of all point out that many other elements listed by Lewis are not cultural traits, but rather part of the objective conditions of poverty, e.g. the lack of effective participation and integration of the poor in the major institutions of the society at large, the poor housing conditions and crowding they have to contend with.[9] Furthermore, while Lewis interprets the the subculture of the poor as both an adaptation and a reaction to their position in a class-stratified, highly individuated, capitalistic society, many of his critics tend to see the cultural traits of the poor as by and large determined by the economic and political reality they face, by structural constraints. The very similarities across countries are taken as an indication that the poor have little scope for innovation, that the constraints they face are so severe as to narrow the range of possible responses. The most profound disagreement in theory, and serious concern in praxis, arises over Lewis's ([1966] 1970: 69) contention:

The culture of poverty, however, is not only an adaptation to a set of objective conditions of the larger society. Once it comes into existence, it tends to perpetuate itself from generation to generation because of its effect on the children. By the time slum children are six or seven years old, they usually have absorbed the basic values and attitudes of their subculture and are not psychologically geared to take full advantage of changing conditions or increased opportunities which may occur in their lifetime.

If Lewis subscribes to early childhood determinism, he simultaneously affirms that any movement, be it religious, pacifist, or revolutionary, that organizes and gives hope to the poor and effectively promotes solidarity and a sense of identi-fication with larger groups destroys the psychological and social core of the culture of poverty. He ventures the proposition that the culture of poverty does not exist in socialist countries, and specifically comments on a slum in Havana which he first visited in 1946:[10]

After the Castro Revolution I made my second trip to Cuba [for five days in 1961] as a correspondent for a major magazine, and I revisited the same slum and some of the same families. The physical aspect of the slum had changed very little, except for a beautiful new nursery school. It was clear that the people were still desperately poor, but I found much less of the feelings of despair, apathy, and hopelessness which are so diagnostic of urban slums in the culture of poverty. They expressed great confidence in their leaders and hope for a better life in the future. The slum itself was now highly organized, with block committees, educational committees, party committees. The people had a new sense of power and importance. They were armed and were given a doctrine which glorified the lower class as the hope of humanity. (Lewis, [1966] 1970: 75)

Lewis returned to Cuba in February 1969 with several collaborators to carry out a three-year research project. A good deal of information had been collected by the time research came to an abrupt halt in June 1970. The project included a study of a housing development of 100 units in which residents from the very slum Lewis had visited previously, Las Yaguas, had been resettled in 1963. While the research was still under way, he wrote to a colleague: 'It is . . . clear that many of the traits of the culture of poverty persist in the housing project. I believe I was overly optimistic in some of my earlier evaluations about the disappearance of the culture of poverty under socialism. However, there seems to me no doubt that the Cuban Revolution has abolished the conditions which gave rise to the culture of poverty' (Lewis, Lewis, and Rigdon, 1978: 526 n.1).

Butterworth (1980), who co-ordinated research on the housing development for four months in 1970, provides an account which is limited in so far as it is based on incomplete records from the suddenly interrupted study.[11] He emphasizes the tangibles that the Revolution brought to the former slum dwellers: secure jobs, a sufficient and balanced diet, excellent health care, and improved housing. A substantial proportion of the men were skilled or semi-skilled workers, and a majority of these were young men who had acquired their skills since the triumph of the Revolution. Unlike the situation in Las Yaguas, where the father was sometimes an inadequate provider and thus may have been a marginal member of the household, he was now virtually assured of employment and a steady income. The result was a more stable household. Only five of seventy-one family households were made up of single women with their children.

If there had been major improvements, serious problems remained. A quarter of the children between six and fourteen years of age had either dropped out of school or never entered. Eight homes were recognized as black-market centres. While gambling in any form was forbidden, at least six homes served as gambling centres, all run by women. Rum was illegally distilled and sold. There was trafficking in marijuana. Most striking was the low level of integration into mass organizations and campaigns. Such was the case for the campaigns to perform voluntary work in agriculture, for the Federation of Cuban Women, and for the neighbourhood organization, the Committees for the Defence of the Revolution (CDR). The three CDRs had experienced a limited degree of success for a year or so after their founding in 1964 but had gradually became inactive. Cursory investigations suggested that the CDRs in the six other housing projects where Las Yaguas residents had been resettled had followed the same pattern.

Butterworth points to both internal and external factors to explain the persistence of such problems. There had been a good deal of inertia in the CDRs, and personal feuds and animosities had inhibited co-operation. We may further surmise that those involved in illegal activities had reason to resist the effective operation of a government-controlled neighbourhood organization. Indeed, much conflict was created within the settlement because of the attempt to enforce rules emanating from the outside in an environment characterized by a relatively high incidence of deviance. One might be led to conclude that a populace reared in the culture of poverty largely persisted in its ways. However, Butterworth also notes that the residents still carried the stigma of having come from Las Yaguas; indeed, the housing development was referred to as 'Las Yaguas made of cement'.[12] They were looked down upon by the people in a middle-class neighbourhood close by.[13] Their children in the primary grades had to put up not only with belittlement from the other pupils but with a school director who maintained that over 90 per cent of the children from 'the Las Yaguas block' − but none of the other pupils − had been diagnosed as mentally retarded or severely disturbed psychologically. The local People's Court held its trials outside the housing development, none of the judges had been selected from the settlement, and the sitting judges expressed a middle-class morality which sharply differentiated them from the residents. Officials at the next higher level of the CDR organization had become disheartened at the lack of progress. As tasks increasingly went undone, they had eventually stopped all communication and co-operation with the local CDRs.[14]

Lewis's general argument, if not his initial perception of reality in post-revolutionary Cuba, may be labelled 'hard-culture' − in contrast to a 'soft-culture' approach which assumes that changed circumstances will elicit quite rapid cultural responses (Hannerz, 1969: 193−5).[15] If adults are capable of modifying their behaviour, if not their values, in response to changing conditions, inter-generational modifications in behaviour and revision of values tend to be more far-reaching. Adolescents measure the cultural traits evolved by previous generations, proffered by their parents and their teachers, against the economic and political situation they face, or more precisely, against their perception of that situation. As each new generation evaluates its cultural heritage in the context of the conditions it confronts, it collectively evolves its own patterns of behaviour and values. Changing perceptions of reality provoke the reworking of the available cultural inventory. Such a model of cultural change seems to provide a better understanding of social process than either a hard-culture approach or structural determinism.

If the critique of the culture of poverty concept was fuelled by concern that a hard-culture approach can serve as justification for the continued neglect of the needs of the poor, criticism was also inspired by a rejection of the rather bleak image it conveys of lower-class life. Negative evaluations of the behaviour patterns of the poor come about in two ways. The poor themselves are usually aware of middle-class values, and frequently aspire to live by them, while in fact following different standards. And middle-class observers tend to perceive lower-class behaviour as inferior. An appreciation of the conditions the poor face helps to understand the gap between ideal and actual behaviour and goes some way toward putting into question such judgements made by outsiders. But a balanced perspective requires more; it has to be based on an appreciation of elements of the subculture of the poor that carry positive connotations by most standards. Recognition of recurrent patterns of mutual aid and of solidary action among the poor merits special attention from such a perspective. Hollnsteiner (1972: 32) reports from a neighbourhood in the lower-class Tondo section of Manila:

Being poor forces a closeness beyond mere sociability, for crises arise frequently enough to encourage strong patterns of neighbouring. Mutual aid consists largely of contributions of food, money, or service upon the death of a household member or the happier celebration of a baptism or marriage. It surfaces again in the borrowing and lending of household items and money, maintaining surveillance over a neighbour's house or children while the mother runs an errand, notifying one another of job openings and (particularly for adolescents) support in the event of a gang fight with rivals from other blocks.

Lomnitz (1974: 146–54; 1977: 131–58, 189–213) argues that the urban poor in Latin America find their ultimate source of livelihood in market exchange, but cannot survive individually: the market fails to provide any security and the poor are not in a position to accumulate savings. They survive by complementing market exchange with a system based on resources of kinship and friendship, which follows the rules of reciprocity, a mode of exchange among equals, imbedded in a fabric of continuing social relationships. She describes such a pattern in Cerrada del Cóndor, a small shanty town in Mexico City. Here the prevalent rural patterns of individualism and mistrust are superseded by powerful tendencies toward integration, mutual assistance, and co-operation. Recent arrivals are housed, sheltered, and fed by their relatives in the shanty town; the men are taught a trade and oriented toward available urban jobs, in direct competition with their city kin. The migrants thus become integrated into local networks of reciprocity. Such clusters of neighbours practise continuous exchanges of goods and services on an equal footing. They are made up of three or four — less frequently two, five, or six — nuclear families, and nearly all nuclear families belong to a cluster. Ideally, each cluster is composed of neighbours related through kinship, but a third of the clusters were partly or totally based on friendship. Ties within the clusters are reinforced through godfather relationships (*compadrazgo*) and through drinking companionship among men (*cuatismo*). The exchange is underpinned by a strong ideology of assistance:

The duty of assistance is endowed with every positive moral quality; it is the ethical justification for network relations. Any direct or indirect refusal of help within a network is judged in the harshest possible terms and gives rise to disparaging gossip. People are constantly watching for signs of change in the economic status of all members of the network. Envy and gossip are the twin mechanisms used for keeping the others in line. Any show of selfishness or excessive desire for privacy will set the grapevine buzzing. There will be righteous comments, and eventually someone will find a way to set the errant person straight. (Lomnitz, 1974: 151)

Patterns of mutual aid are common among the urban poor and appear as an effective adaptation to their circumstances. A more profound change in their condition requires solidary action. Indeed, in many Third World cities great numbers of the apparently powerless have grasped a measure of power through collective action: they have organized as squatters. To this and other forms of political responses to poverty I shall now turn.

7

POLITICAL RESPONSES TO POVERTY

A wide gap in income and wealth, power, and status separates the élite from the mass of the population in most Third World countires, and the middle class is frequently quite small. The majority of the urban population have a standard of living so low as to be inconceivable to the average citizen of an industrialized country. While most urbanites are better off than the rural masses, there are some who have no shelter, others who can barely clothe themselves. Malnutrition is common. For many the quest for food, for themselves, for their children, is a daily struggle for survival.

The urban masses cope with their condition in a variety of ways. In the last chapter we saw how the urban poor secure the help of neighbours, friends, and kin in the recurrent crises which turn so rapidly into emergencies for those who live at subsistence or close to it. But government officials loom large in a variety of contexts, as a threat or a potential resource. Policemen and tax collectors have to be evaded, trade licences and building permits are required, government employment or welfare assistance has to be applied for, public services may be secured.

Government leaders appear less than responsive to the needs of the masses. Most are preoccupied with maintaining the support of the armed forces and encouraging the investment of indigenous and foreign capital. They have to operate within the limits set by foreign powers who offer investments, buy exports, supply raw materials and spare parts, and wield the ultimate threat of subversion and military intervention. In this concert of the powerful the voices of the mass of the population usually remain muted. Many regimes have done away with the complications of elections altogether. In some countries they have become a farce: in the Ivory Coast 99.98 per cent of those registered were reported to have voted in the 1970 national elections, and 99.89 per cent of the votes supposedly went to the single candidates of the one and only part (M. A. Cohen 1974: 179–80). Elsewhere elections take the form of a plebiscite for a one-party regime.

Even where elections offer a choice, and where the ballot is secret, one party is frequently well entrenched and apparently assured of re-election. Such a party may receive widespread electoral support because areas voting for opposition candidates face neglect from the government or even outright retribution; this was a common pattern in Nigeria while civilian rule lasted in the 1960s. Patron-client relationships such as charactetize the Partido Revolucionario Institucional in Mexico operate in a less crass manner. Once a working relationship has been established with a patron, his clients have good reason to vote for, and to persuade their followers to vote for, the local list which renews their patron's mandate; voting in opposition candidates would entail depriving oneself of local representatives who have access to government agencies.

In other countries parties do effectively compete for electoral support, but they are not mass-based. They become active in low-income neighbourhoods primarily at election time when they offer limited material rewards to groups and individuals in exchange for votes. Anthony and Elizabeth Leeds (1976) describe such a pattern in Brazil, and I shall return to their account. Wirsing (1976) reports on municipal elections in Nagpur, India, in 1969. Many candidates had provided patronage in the past and were well positioned to transmit long-term benefits to their constituents, but as election day approached short-term tactics became more prominent. The voters' choice was restricted through the kidnapping of political rivals, paid withdrawals of opposing candidates, and the setting up of bogus candidacies; voters were intimidated, for example through administrators controlling the employment or the housing privileges of low-ranking government employees; and votes were bought:

For many of the urban poor, the campaign period is a time when the market value of their support appears to soar and when the clever seller may turn the value of his vote or the votes of his followers to good advantage. The poor are wined and dined, wooed with gifts and bribed with cash. There are free haircuts, free saris, free mutton dinners, free entertainment, and plenty of free intoxicants. (Wirsing, 1976: 195)

If the circumstances vary, the outcome is similar throughout most of the Third World: the masses are rarely able to make significant inputs through an electoral process. This is particularly the case for rural populations. Where they do participate in elections their vote is frequently controlled by local élites through patronage or outright coercion. Powell (1980: 202), in a comprehensive review of rural voting patterns, concludes that there are hints almost everywhere, when one penetrates beneath the surface of political behaviour in rural areas, of a style of politics that can be labelled a 'rural mafia' system. The rural masses are thus usually without a voice, and their fate is neglect. They may rebel because land has been taken away from them, taxes have been raised, or the prices paid for their crops have been lowered, but such upheavals tend to be isolated and rarely constitute an effective threat to the élites in the cities. The country at large is affected when peasants withdraw from the market and revert to subsistence farming, as happened in Senegal in the late 1960s. But the most serious consequence of the neglect of the rural masses is the stream of rural–urban migrants who cannot be absorbed into the urban economy productively and who put severe pressure on urban resources. They swell the ranks of the urban masses strategically poised at the centres of local, regional, and national decision-making. They people the nightmares of conservatives and the daydreams of the radical Left:

All over the world, often long in advance of effective industrialization, the un-skilled poor are streaming away from subsistence agriculture to exchange the squalor of rural poverty for the even deeper miseries of the shanty-towns, *favelas*, and *bidonvilles* that, year by year, grow inexorably on the fringes of the developing cities.

And they, too, are the core of local despair and disaffection – filling the *Jeunesses* movements of the Congo, swelling the urban mobs of Rio, voting Communist in the ghastly alleys of Calcutta, everywhere undermining the all too frail structure of public order and thus retarding the economic development that can alone help their plight. Unchecked, disregarded, left to grow and fester, there is here enough explosive material to produce in the world at large the pattern of a bitter class conflict finding to an increasing degree a racial bias, erupting in guerrilla warfare, and threatening, ultimately, the security even of the comfortable West. (Ward, 1964: 191–2)

The statement, by a Third World specialist soon to be appointed to the Albert Schweitzer Chair of International Economic Development at Columbia University in New York, was published in August 1964.[1] Earlier that year the military had toppled President João Goulart of Brazil after he had launched a campaign for broad structural and political reforms. It established a regime of repression. During the following decade there was little evidence of the urban masses threatening a regime anywhere in the Third World. Only in 1978 did mass demonstrations and strikes challenge the rule of the Shah of Iran, and the towns of Nicaragua rise to the call of the Sandinistas to topple Anastasio Somoza. Up to that point governments everywhere had shown themselves in effective control. That more and more countries came under military rule seemed to escape the attention of those social scientists who now swung to another extreme position: urban masses were described as conservative in outlook, ignorant of the political system, and apathetic in public affairs.[2]

Exploring five distinct patterns of political integration and conflict in the urban arena, we shall see how misleading any generalizations about the political stance of the masses are bound to be.[3] The urban masses are neither radical nor apathetic. Their behaviour, the attitudes that underlie it, and ultimately even their values have to be understood in terms of the economic, social, and political realities they face._The masses are frequently hostile to the more powerful and affluent. In varying degrees they have some understanding of the mechanisms that create and perpetuate the inequality they so acutely experience, but they have to get on with the daily struggle for survival. They evolve a design for living that takes the existing situation as a given to be coped with and only rarely defines it as a contingency to be challenged (Portes and Walton, 1976: 72).[4] The recurrent theme in the interplay between the masses and those who control the state and dominate economic decision is that the leverage of the masses is usually narrowly circumscribed. The quest to break these constraints remains the preoccupation of a few visionaries; only rarely are historical constel-lations such as to provide an opportunity for them to lead the masses in an effective challenge to the established order.

The Politics of Co-optation

In any country public officials allocate a variety of resources and enforce a range of sanctions. The proportion of resources they control tends to be large in Third World countries. Government is a major employer; in many places such employment extends beyond public administration to public or semi-public corporations in charge of major sectors of the economy. Governments frequently control prices, e.g. for agricultural products that have to be sold to government agencies, or for food sold in urban markets. They allocate scarce resources such as credit and foreign exchange. They attempt to collect an assortment of indirect and direct taxes. A wide range of activities, from building permits to trade licences, are usually subject to government regulation. The scope for sanctions is extended in those many Third World countries in which civil rights are limited or non-existent. Penal sanctions can be particularly severe where prison conditions are harsh and the death sentence is common.

Many Third World governments are less than effective in their exercise of control and sanctions. Myrdal (1970: 208–52) coined the phrase 'soft state' to illuminate the fact that laws and government regulations are more prone to be flouted in Third World countries than in most industrialized countries:[5]

The term 'soft state' is understood to comprise all the various types of social indiscipline which manifest themselves by: deficiencies in legislation and in particular law observance and enforcement, a widespread disobedience by public officials on various levels to rules and directives handed down to them, and often their collusion with powerful persons and groups of persons whose conduct they should regulate. Within the concept of the soft state belongs also corruption . . . These several patterns of behaviour are interrelated in the sense that they permit or even provoke each other in circular causation having cumulative effects. (Mydral, 1970: 208)

The soft state reinforces inequality. Those who control state power directly, or who have the economic resources to gain access to it, find opportunities for large-scale gains and can evade sanctions. For the mass of the population the allocation of such resources as are not pre-empted by a privileged minority appears quite arbitrary. There are only a few jobs for the many work seekers who have limited qualifications; satisfactory schooling, subsidized housing, adequate medical care, trade licences — these are available only for some of the many who require them. Impersonal rules meant to govern the allocation of such resources remain a dead letter. The mass of the population has little leverage in dealing with the élite and its representatives who control these resources, whether it be managers in private firms or government officials. Not only do they have few legal claims, but those claims may be unavailing. Such a situation may be challenged through collective action, and in subsequent sections of this chapter I shall explore four forms the action may take. Or individuals may try to deal with the sytem as best they can. Cultivating a patron — a person in a position to further one's career and to assist in crises — is a promising approach.

Four characteristics of clientelism stand out. The patron–client relationship is a relationship between two individuals, a dyad. The relationship is reciprocal; in exchange for the patron's help, the client gives political support and contributes to the patron's status. This exchange is not based on legal or contractual requirements but is an informal understanding; where the two have a legal or contractual relationship, e.g. employer and employee, the patron–client exchange introduces additional elements. Finally, the relationship is profoundly unequal: not only does the patron have greater power, more economic resources, and higher status, but he usually has numerous clients and the leverage any one of them can exert on the patron is therefore narrowly circumscribed.

I follow Landé (1977: xxi–xxii)' in emphasizing that patron–client relationships are addenda to formal institutions. The fulfilment of institutionalized requirements does not establish the special patron–client bond. To take our example, meeting what are established expectations of employees in general cannot constitute the basis for patronage. Where the employer provides more benefits to some of his employees, e.g. assurance of permanent employment, and they reciprocate by performing according to norms of loyalty beyond what is expected of employees in general, these acts constitute special favours: the patron–client addendum to the institutionalized employer–employee relationship. The point helps to highlight the fact that the scope for clientelism is a function of the lack of impersonal rules for the allocation of resources. To pursue our example, if job tenure were institutionalized, if it were a function of universalistic criteria such as qualifications, performance, and/or seniority, if it were not a special favour at the whim of the employer, then it could not be a source of patronage.

Complementary to the instrumental content of patron–client relationships, there are usually affective elements. Kinship, common origin, shared experiences, can be the source of genuine affective ties; mutual appreciation constitutes an affective reward. Sometimes a fictive kinship relationship is established. The *compadrazgo* system in Latin America and the Philippines is frequently used in such fashion. The client asks his actual or potential patron to act as godfather at his child's baptism, and the two men thereby become *compadres*.

The owner of a small firm who is a patron to some of his workers or the mayor of a small municipality has ultimate control over the resources he provides to his clients. In contrast, many patrons are themselves clients to higher-placed patrons. Thus, in large urban systems the poor man's patron frequently finds himself in the role of broker: he has to obtain many of the benefits for his clients through a patron of his own, and what his clients offer him in return – e.g. their votes – goes to a higher-placed patron with whom they do not interact directly. There is a pyramidal structure, where those at the intermediary levels are both patron and client, they are mediators between levels of social organization in a complex order (Michaelson, 1976: 282). Patron–client relationships do not necessarily have to be repeated at the different levels of interaction. But the typical case appears to be for clientelist patterns to prevail throughout the hierarchy of social strata. The lack of impersonal rules and collective action characterizes the entire society, and clientelism is an all-pervading part of its political culture.

Clientelism takes different forms, but it has a long tradition in many societies. In Mali patron–client relationships were found between urban merchants and peasants, and between long-established citizens of a town and both newcomers to the town and peasants, in pre-colonial times. Hopkins (1972: 142-5) shows how a similar system developed in the years following the imposition of colonial rule. It was now three-tiered, involving petitioner, grantor, and an intermediary broker. The relationship between the petitioner and the broker was often expressed in terms of the traditional link between merchant and farmer. After Independence the brokers were usually people who held positions in the ruling party. Grantors might hold party positions, but the essential qualification was that they were in administrative positions that gave them some degree of control over admissions to schools, recruitment for jobs, assignments of building lots, and so on.

In Lebanon the origin and some of the persisting pecularities of patronage can be traced to a feudal past. To a large measure, much of the country's socio-political history may be viewed as the history of various groups and communities seeking to secure patronage: client groups in search of protection, security, and vital benefits, and patrons seeking to extend the scope of their clientage (Khalaf, 1977). With the advent of electoral politics success at parliamentary elections became the prerequisite for gaining access to governmental patronage.[6] The political system was dominated by locally powerful leaders called *zu'ama* (plural of *za'im*), who in the cities developed sophisticated machines to recruit a clientèle. Johnson (1977: 209) describes the patronage they dispensed:

The *za'im* maintains his support in two important ways: first, by being regularly returned to office, so that he can influence the administration and continuously provide his clients with governmental services; and secondly, by being a successful businessman, so that he can use his commercial and financial contacts to give his clients employment, contracts and capital. Depending on the wealth and influence of his clients, the *za'im* provides public works contracts, governmental concessions, employment in the government and private sectors, promotion within the professions and civil service, free or cheap education and medical treatment in government or charitable institutions, and even protection from the law. In order to survive electoral defeats and periods in opposition, the *za'im* must himself be rich or have access to other people's wealth, so as to buy the support of the electorate as well as the acquiescence of ministers and officials responsible for particular governmental services. Although election to the Assembly is of considerable advantage, it is not always essential, and a *za'im* can survive temporary periods of opposition and political weakness by using the credit he has built up in the past.

The clients were expected to offer in exchange consistent political loyalty, which used to take the form of voting for the *za'im* and his allies in parliamentary elections, but the clientèle could be required to support the *za'im* in other political conflicts as well. Clients publicly demonstrated their loyalty: on feast days, they visited their *za'im* to extend the compliments of the season; and when a *za'im* returned from a journey, they usually turned out to welcome him home.

The most important part of the *za'im*'s apparatus was a core of strong-arm neighbourhood leaders, the *qabadayat*. The *qabaday* recruited a following on the basis of his reputation as a man of the people, as a helper of the weak and the poor, as a protector of the quarter and its inhabitants, and, most important, as a man who was prepared to defend his claims to leadership by force. The *qabaday* assisted the *za'im* in the allocation of patronage by vetting the loyalty and political reliability of applicants. *Qabadayat* furthermore ensured that clients voted in the way they were instructed. Finally, they organized armed bands of young men to fight for their *za'im* in disputes with other *zu'ama* as well as in the serious battles that rent the country in 1903, 1936, 1958, and again, most devastatingly, since 1975. The civil war in turn has further undermined the Lebanese state, and the position of the *zu'ama* has grown stronger (Joseph, 1982).

The use of the *qabadayat* fragmented the electorate and prevented the emergence of self-conscious, horizontally linked social categories, such as interest groups or classes. By insisting on approach through the *qabaday*, the *za'im* encouraged the individual client to see himself as a member of a particular quarter or clan, and discouraged the formation of other social categories that might threaten the *status quo*. In some cases artificial quarter and clan identifications were created. In complementary fashion, the government put down with considerable severity such industrial action as did occur.

Co-optation plays a key role in maintaining a small élite in power in many other countries, and its manifestations vary widely:

Again, the weakness of the state allowing the emergence of patrons, may have different forms. It has been said, for instance, that whereas the Lebanese state is an association of patrons, the Tunisian state is a machine for the making and unmaking of patrons. There may be a kind of spectrum, ranging from a state which is an association for the protection of a pre-existing patron class, via a state which plays off patrons against each other, to a state which creates and destroys them through temporary allocation of political positions. (Gellner, 1977: 5)

While patrons all but usurped the power of the state in Lebanon, India presents an intermediate position, where considerable public resources are expressly shifted to voluntary associations. Two key arenas are education and housing: most schools, from pre-primary to collegiate, are run by associations heavily dependent on public finance; and cooperative housing societies allocate land and credit. The management of educational and housing resources, heavily subsidized by the government, is thus left to the discretion of voluntary groupings frequently set up along linguistic or caste lines. Many local politicians are active in them, obtaining and dispensing government patronage so as to maximize electoral support. Thus a third of the candidates for municipal councillor in Nagpur in 1969 held executive positions in co-operatives, and a quarter did so in education societies (Wirsing, 1973; Michaelson, 1979).

In Mexico political power is effectively concentrated at the apex of the state, in the hands of the president and his close advisers. Mexico is remarkable in that the government legitimizes itself on the basis of a revolution and justifies social change in the name of revolution yet consistently flouts the officially proclaimed revolutionary goals. Nevertheless, in the regularly scheduled elections the Institutionalized Revolutionary Party, ruling under a variety of 'revolutionary' names since 1928, has never been threatened by any of the other parties. Co-optation throughout the political and administrative system has effectively channelled and scaled down demands and paralysed nearly all potential opposition (Hellman, 1978: 100-22). Eckstein (1977a: 78-102), in a study of three low-income areas in Mexico City, found a range of social and economic associations in addition to political and administrative groups. On their own, residents had organized to deal with the municipal government. They had also joined national groups that deal with municipal authorities, including some that publicly profess a concern with their social welfare and that have grass-roots organizations. However, all these efforts had met with limited success. Eckstein (1977a: 87) explains:

The informal processes that inhibit the political effectiveness of organized residents are rooted in various national institutional arrangements: mainly in the hierarchical nature of national inter- and intragroup relations, the class structure, the personalistic style of Mexican politics, the multiplicity of groups operating nationally along with the containment of overt elite competition, and the government's threat to apply force. They reflect social structural forces closely associated with the state, but not necessarily deliberate efforts of function-aries to regulate local poor. For these reasons political stability can be maintained with little cost, and the state can nationally advance the interests of capital without using brute repression against a major base of political support.

Local leaders are constrained to conform with national political 'rules of the game.' Otherwise they can neither personally advance in politics nor secure benefits for their constituents. The prospects of removal from office also compel local subordinates to conform with the expectations (or their perception of the expectations) of higher-ranking functionaries. Thereby, 'appropriate' local concerns are delimited and heads of local groups are encouraged to be subservient, although they are not necessarily accordingly rewarded.[7]

Eckstein reported that local leaders usually established institutional ties with national political-administrative groups because they felt that their political and economic mobility would be thereby enhanced, and that in doing so they would be more apt to secure social and urban services for the members. On occasion they fashioned covert arrangements with non-local functionaries because they felt that constituents or potential constituents were antagonistic to the idea of being openly associated with the government or the ruling party. Mexico's ostensibly democratic political institutions thus do not serve as means by which urban and rural poor, on the basis of their numerical strength and legitimate political organizations, can effectively advance their own interests. And the Mexican urban poor do not appear any better off than their counterparts in non-democratic Latin American countries.

Cultural Elements in Political Alignments

Glaring contrasts between rich and poor characterize most Third World countries, but the primary alignments are frequently in terms of shared identities of a different order.[8] Three modes of distinguishing 'we' from 'they' stand out: region of origin, religion, and caste. The salient characteristics of such identities are articulated in juxtaposition to the identities of other groups. As they evolve over generations they take on a subconscious dimension (Saberwal, 1981). In much of Africa, and in major parts of Asia, most migrants in the cities and their children categorize themselves and others in terms of region of origin. To refer to such a pattern as 'tribalism' is unfortunate because of the pejorative conno-tations the term 'tribe' has acquired. It is also misleading. Such identities in the urban setting, and their cultural content, usually bear little relationship to traditional societies and their culture. The past provides the raw materials, but they are fashioned in the confrontations of the urban arena. In parts of Africa and Asia adherents of two or even three world religions live within the same city boundaries. At times they have clashed with each other, most dramatically Hindu and Muslim in South Asia. But conflict can also crystallize around internal divisions within a religion, such as the Muslim sects in Syria. Caste is of central importance in the Hindu religion, and for the majority of Indians it remains the primary referent. Determined by birth and supposedly immutable, it also changes its guise according to context.

Recognition of common origin has provided the basis for political alignments in many parts of the world time and again. In Subsaharan Africa the great majority of adult urban dwellers are first-generation townsmen; they spent their early childhood in a culturally more homogeneous rural environment. In town a whole series of potential identities of origin are available to them: their extended family, their home village, the village groups to which it belongs, their 'subtribe', their 'tribe', their 'supertribe', their nation, their race. Some are traditional contexts of common bonds and shared culture, others are newly perceived. I shall refer to such identities of origin and descent as 'ethnic'. The new arrival may discard some of these identities; others he may not yet be ready to recognize. Which ethnic identity is salient to him varies according to his situation, in particular with reference to the categories of people to whom he is opposed. Banton (1965: 145) observed that the migrant to Freetown, Sierra Leone, was involved in a series of oppositions: African versus European, tribesman versus Creole, Temne versus, say, Mende. The three categories – African, tribesman,

Temne — were in a straight hierarchy, and each one could be socially relevant only when the higher-order oppositions did not enter. Such a series of identities of origin may be seen as a nested hierarchy (Leeds, 1973: 23 f.). A set of concentric circles provides a graphic model of the more narrowly or more largely defined ethnic groups that the individual identifies with, recruits his friends from, joins in unions, and supports in formal organizations (Gugler, 1975a: 304).

Specific economic opportunities are frequently monopolized by members of an ethnic group. Two processes are responsible. First, during colonial rule some ethnic groups built up an important lead because of better access to education, because they were recruited into certain occupations (most importantly, as it turned out, the army), because their land offered exceptional opportunities (such as the growing of cocoa), or because they dominated the distribution of major commodities (for example, Hausa control of the long-distance trade in cattle in West Africa). Second, once an ethnic group was established in a privileged position, it wielded considerable influence over the opportunities open to others, and patronage tended to go to kinsmen, fellow villagers, or any 'brother'. Thus on the Copperbelt in what was then Northern Rhodesia, as in most of colonial Africa, the opposition was at one level between white management and black employees. But a lower-order opposition was found within the African Mine Workers' Trade Union, where cleavages followed lines that were also both ethnic and economic: the lines of an emerging class structure tended to coincide with ethnic divisions (Epstein, 1958: 235–40).

The perceived coincidence of ethnic difference and economic opposition may lead to a reaffirmation of cultural distinctiveness and culminate in an ethnic renaissance. Abner Cohen (1969) described such a process among the Hausa people in Ibadan, Nigeria, and concluded:

The situation will be entirely different if the new class cleavages will overlap with tribal groupings, so that within the new system the privileged will tend to be identified with one ethnic group and the under-privileged with another ethnic group. In this situation cultural differences between the two groups will become entrenched, consolidated, and strengthened in order to express the struggle between the two interest groups across the new class lines. Old customs will tend to persist, but within the newly emerging social system they will assume new values and new social significance. A great deal of social change will take place, but it will tend to be effected through the rearrangement of traditional cultural items, rather than through the development of new cultural items, or, more significantly, rather than the borrowing of cultural items from the other tribal groups. Thus to the casual observer it will look as if there is here stagnation, conservatism, or a return to the past, when in fact we are confronted with a new social system in which men articulate their *new roles* in terms of traditional ethnic idioms. (Cohen, 1969: 194)

Language is frequently the key element in delineating common origin.[9] Common language not only facilitates communication, but is the medium of ideology. Take the example of Nigeria. The Ibo Union was founded in Lagos in

1936, a Pan-Yoruba cultural society in London in 1945 – both played a principal role in enlisting popular support for two major Nigerian parties after World War II, parties which were soon identified with the Ibo and Yoruba people respectively. A third party came to represent Northern Nigerian interests. These divisions shaped civilian politics until 1966, underlay the Civil War 1967–70, and continue to be important in Nigerian politics. In the past neither Ibo nor Yoruba had constituted political units. Still, these new structural alignments followed lines of cultural affinity, and in particular of shared language. The various dialects of the Ibo people are clearly distinct from the languages of their neighbours. At the same time there is such variation within Ibo that some dialects are barely intelligible to speakers of others. Significantly, major efforts were made to evolve a standard Ibo speech and script. In addition, certain elements of traditional culture, such as music and dance, were reaffirmed, and a new pride in Ibo identity fostered.

In some cities conflicts arise between indigenous peoples and migrants. In Nigeria this has been the case in Kano (Paden, 1973), Ibadan (Sklar, 1963: 289–320), and Lagos (Baker, 1974), all urban centres established in pre-colonial times. However, such conflicts are exceptional in Subsaharan Africa. Because of the recent origin of most cities and their explosive growth, the urban-born usually constitute a small minority. Even in India, characterized by a greater proportion of old cities, by colonial cities dating back to the nineteenth century, and by comparatively slow urban growth, the lines of ethnic conflict are usually drawn between migrant groups.

People from a city's hinterland and migrants from more distant locations are frequently juxtaposed in conflict. 'Nativism' is a label used to describe such confrontations between 'sons of the soil' and 'outsiders'. The 'native' protagonists are indeed sons of the soil in the sense that they were born in the city's hinterland and are newcomers to the city. They typically argue that their claims to the opportunities in the region's urban centres are prior to those of outsiders who speak a different language and/or hail from distant lands. In federations such as India and Nigeria, state boundaries both reflect cultural diversity and provide a ready framework for assertions of subnational rights. Natives hold that they are committed to the advancement of their region, whereas outsiders are perceived to take an exploitative approach and to remain oriented toward the development of their region of origin. Nativist demands are usually fuelled by resentment against outsiders who had a headstart and are seen to control major parts of the opportunity structure. As Weiner (1978: 293) concluded for India, 'Nativism tends to be associated with a blockage to social mobility for the native population by a culturally distinguishable migrant population.'

Bombay is one of India's most cosmopolitan cities. Its migrants constitute a wide variety of linguistic, religious, and cultural communities which were competing for political power and educational opportunities already in the nineteenth century (Dobbin, 1972: 217–46). Still, Bombay is one of the few Indian cities in which for many residence in the city becomes a dominant element in their identity. Here they call themselves Bombaywallas to signify they belong to, and identify with, a culturally and linguistically heterogeneous city. But once the state of Maharashtra was established, Marathi speakers sought to turn Bombay, the state's premier city, into a Marathi city. They argued that the city belonged to Maharashtra, that native Marathi speakers had special rights within it, and that its residents had to speak Marathi at least as a second language. The Marathi nativists explicitly rejected the residential concept of the Bombaywalla in favour of ethnic identities of origin. Their demands were articulated by a party, the Shiv Sena, which demanded that jobs in the city should not be given to immigrants from other Indian states. Within two years of its founding in 1966 the Shiv Sena became the largest single opposition party in the municipal elections, supported by a majority of the Marathi-speaking people in the city. The Shiv Sena did not gain power in the state government, but the governing Congress Party adopted many of its stands: it put pressure on private employers to recruit Marathi-speaking people rather than other migrants, it gave preference to local people for employment in the state government, and it tacitly supported placing Marathi signs on public and private places. Such political pressures were complemented by physical attacks against businessmen who were not co-operative (Katzenstein, 1979; Weiner, 1978).

Language constitutes a central issue in ethnic conflict in India. Not only does language serve to delineate ethnic groups and provide the vehicle for the affirmation of ethnic identity, but policies that strengthen a particular language and weaken others differentially affect the speakers of different languages. The issue has rarely become as salient in Subsaharan Africa. While nearly all countries in the region are multilingual, most are dependent on a lingua franca which has been introduced by the colonial power. Decisions concerning the use of such a language thus usually do not have ethnic, but rather class implications: the children of the educated élite have a decisive advantage in educational systems that use a foreign language as the medium of instruction from the first years of schooling. In contrast, in multilingual countries in which one or a few indigenous languages predominate, language policy is of major concern to the various language groups. Which language or languages are used at different levels of the educational system shapes the educational opportunities of those more or less fluent and literate in them. The choice of official language affects access to the bureaucracy and, particularly important, circumscribes career opportunities there. The language policies pursued by private firms have similar consequences.

The Struggle for Land

In many Third World cities the most conspicuous political action of the urban masses has been the illegal occupation of land. The urban dweller who can barely make ends meet will try to obtain free shelter. For some people this means no more than space in the open street to lie down and sleep. But more common is the attempt to secure a spot where some kind of shelter can be constructed without paying for the land..The pattern is not unknown in industrialized societies. During the Great Depression squatters set up shanty towns in many US cities which came to be called 'Hoovervilles' in ironic tribute to the then president. More recently, squatting in empty buildings has occurred in several West European countries and the US. Squatting may occur unobtrusively; an individual, a family, or a small group establish themselves undetected, or, when found out, are tolerated by the authorities. More typically, they are liable to forcible eviction by police. In a number of Third World countries, however, the illegal occupation of land has been organized on a scale so large as to persuade the authorities initially to condone it and finally to grant the squatters legal title (chapter 5).

Large-scale seizures of land are carried out rapidly, and usually at night, so as to present the authorities with a *fait accompli*. This is reflected in some of the designations used for squatter settlements: in Mexico they are known as *barrios paracaidistas*, i.e. 'parachute settlements'; in Turkey as *geçekondu*, i.e. 'built overnight'. Such invasions are major operations which require careful planning. A group of people prepares in secret. A site is selected and surveyed where the likelihood of eviction is low because of its ownership, i.e. land owned by the government or the church, or property in dispute, and/or because it holds little interest for anybody but the poor, e.g. land subject to flooding, waste dumps, steep hill-sides. A public holiday or the visit of a foreign dignitary is chosen as an invasion date when the authorities will be reluctant to use force. Finally, contacts are established to secure support from political or religious leaders and to ensure that sympathetic journalists will be present to denounce police excesses. On the agreed night the chosen site is occupied by people numbering in the hundreds and sometimes more than a thousand, plots are marked out, and rudimentary shelters are put up. Usually the squatters project an image of moderation: they fly the national flag on their new huts and name the settlement after a religious or government figure.[10]

The presence and form of squatter movements varies from city to city and depends upon the political context (Leeds, 1969; Gilbert, 1981b). In Peru various military and civilian governments since 1948 have tolerated land invasions, though specific policies toward squatters fluctuated (Collier, 1976). Anthony and Elizabeth Leeds (1976) relate this liberal approach to the fact that the Alianza Popular Revolucionaria Americana (APRA), had a mass base, primarily in rural and urban trade unions. All political action, whether undertaken by any of the other parties, by coalitions, by the bureaucracy, by a civilian or a military executive, or by the Catholic Church, had to cope with APRA's popularity and its covert organizational links in the bureaucracy, the military, the legislature, and elsewhere. In order to circumscribe APRA's popular support, even quite conservative groups saw no alternative but to pursue policies vis-a-vis the squatters that ranged from accommodation to the allocation of substantial resources.

In Brazil the political context is quite different. Parties compete in state and national elections, even after the military coup of 1964, but none of them has a mass base:

Thus, in Brazil, are found an array of parties, none of which has a mass base in the sense of effective, formally organized, local, self-expressive constituencies acting within the operational norms of the party. All the parties both intentionally and unintentionally (perhaps!) follow policies, make choices, and act in such a way that such a mass base cannot or will not develop. Specifically, whether deliberately or not, they act to maintain links to the constituencies through patronal ties alone and even encourage their clients in the masses to operate as lower level or sub-patrons to *their* clients, voters in general . . .

This structure of party organization, of course, defines the rules of the game that must be played *among* parties. For example, aside from each party's elite-class interest *not* to allow an organized mass-base to develop, it is also *constrained* from organizing such a base (which, in the ideal, it could hopefully keep under control) by the threat of the other parties' also organizing a mass base — indeed, by the threat of creating a Chilean kind of party situation, a quite intolerable idea in Brazil. The peculiar congeries of circumstances which, in Peru, allowed an APRA to spring up as a unique mass-based party did not occur in Brazil. Preventive action (e.g., such as after the coup of 1964, the military's smashing the unions, low-ranking military, student, and left-wing clerical movements) is taken expeditiously when such a set of circumstances seems to be developing — usually by a broad elite-party coalition of peculiar bed-fellows who fall out with each other shortly afterwards. Brazil, then, from the point of view of elite-bounded parties, is characterized by a pulsating tension between controlledly mobilizing for votes a mass excluded from real participation and intensifying its exclusion sometimes to the point of almost universal repression. One major feature of the procedure is the maintenance of that fragile bond, the paternalistic politician, who can so easily, too, be withdrawn as a contact route for the proletariats. (Leeds and Leeds 1976: 205)

In this context *favelas* are, for the most part, settled by accretion. The parties deliberately avoid creating, or allowing to be created, overt, public, formal organizations for political ends at the local level. Instead, the local scene is dominated by informal cliques. Clients of the party organization, they are to furnish an ambience of pro-party feeling which will produce votes, but they are not to bring into being an organization that might have an independent basis of power.

The repressive character of Brazilian politics is reflected in major campaigns to eradicate squatter settlements. Since 1962, and particularly between 1969 and 1972, the *favelas* of Rio de Janeiro suffered from sweeping evictions. It is estimated that eighty out of 283 *favelas* were totally or partially destroyed, and that 140,000 people were rehoused.[11] Opposition was squashed forcefully. In 1966, in the *favela* Jardim America, the police confronted about 2,000 people, many of them children, who had received word on the previous day that their homes were to be demolished; to speed up the process and discourage resistance, gunshots were fired randomly into the crowd, and those who seemed to resist were beaten. In 1968 the Federation of Favela Associations in Guanabara held a congress which resolved upon 'rejection of any removal, and the condemnation of the human and financial waste and of the social problems resulting from removal'. The federation immediately mobilized to prevent action against the *favela* Ilha das Dragas. Together with the local Residents' Association it instructed every household to refuse to give information to those in charge of preparing the resettlement. Soon after, the leaders of the federation and of the local association were arrested, held incommunicado for days, and threatened with severe consequences if there were further opposition. Open protest by the federation was effectively ended. And when, in the following year, 7,000 residents of Praia do Pinto refused on their own initiative to be relocated, the *favela* 'accidentally' caught fire. Although residents and neighbours called the fire department, orders had evidently been issued that no help was to be given. Most families were unable to salvage their few possessions, and by morning almost everything had been destroyed. Ominously, the *favela*'s leaders disappeared. Still, by 1977 one million people, one out of every five inhabitants of Rio, were estimated to live in *favelas*, i.e. more not only in absolute numbers but also in relative terms than in 1968 when the major thrust toward eradication was initiated (Perlman, 1976: 200-7; Valladares, 1978b).

Chile was characterized, until the military takeover in 1973, by fierce electoral competition among several mass-based political parties which for the most part were closely connected with sectors of the well-established trade union movement. Squatter settlement took two forms: *callampas*, through accreditive occupation of a particular location; *campamentos*, through organized invasions. The inhabitants of the *callampas*, like their counterparts in Brazil, manipulated the competition among the parties and established patronal ties with bureaucracies and trade unions. If the affiliations of *callampas* thus were heterogeneous, *campamentos* were invariably led by a political party. Indeed, the original invasion was typically encouraged by a party and organized by its leaders.

The extent of the organized illegal occupation of land and its sponsorship was a function of the national political configuration. There was a dramatic change even during the reformist presidency of Eduardo Frei of the Christian Democratic Party. In 1965 a few land invasions sponsored by the Left were violently squashed. With the municipal elections of 1967 there was a sudden rise in invasions and the government responded again by repression. However, in 1969-70, with the advent of the presidential elections, government resistance broke down. Early in 1969 the authorities still opposed invasions forcefully; in March several squatters were killed in Puerto Montt. A large invasion in January 1970 initially met with strong resistance but was ultimately successful. Thenceforward repression diminished as the campaign got under way. After the indignation caused by its treatment of squatters in Puente Alto in July 1970, the government abandoned all recourse to force. When Salvador Allende, leader of the left coalition Unidad Popular, was elected president on 4 September 1970, the period until his inauguration on 3 November was marked by indecision on the part of the authorities; this encouraged many new invasions, which led to the establishment of *campamentos* of a variety of political tendencies. However, once Unidad Popular had been established in authority, it was the Christian Democratic Party rather than the Left that encouraged land invasions and even extended the movement to the occupation of recently built apartments (Collectif Chili, 1972: 39–41).

The difference in strategy between parties in and out of government can be seen, at one level, as the responsibility of those in authority to maintain law and order, i.e. the respect of private property and the application of planning, building, and health regulations. However, there is also the fact that those in power have a wide array of resources available to attract the vote of the poorly housed. The government allocates low-cost housing and site-and-services plots, it controls the issue of land titles to squatters; it grants planning and building permits; it establishes and maintains urban infrastructure; it may even offer building materials to squatters and employ them to build their own housing, as was the case in Chile under the Unidad Popular government. The opposition, in contrast, cannot offer any of these resources. To sponsor the illegal occupation of unused land or buildings constitutes an alternative approach towards gaining popular support. If such actions undermine the authority of the ruling party, so much the better.

The politics of squatter settlements vary from country to country, and change within a country over time. They are also articulated differently by various squatter settlements in a given country at a particular political juncture.[12] A survey of twenty-five *campamentos* in Chile in 1971, the first year of the Unidad Popular government, reported major variations in form and extent of political activity. The key variables appeared to be, on the one hand, the social composition of a given *campamento*, i.e. the extent to which common workers, élite workers,[13] and *lumpenproletariat* were represented, and on the other hand, the political line pursued by its outside sponsors (Collectif Chili, 1972). Presumably there was some interaction between these two variables because a party would tend to sponsor social strata close to it in their attempts to secure land and amenities.

Squatter settlements composed primarily of blue-collar workers in low-paying industries and sponsored by the Movimiento de Izquierda Revolucionaria (MIR) were the most politicized and radical. The radical commitment of MIR was clearly established. A student organization founded in 1965, it had remained underground during the Frei period, and acted as a leftist opposition to the Allende government for the first two years before joining it. That common workers should have been most receptive to radical mobilization may be understood in terms of their interests: they had more to gain from revolutionary change than élite workers, however defined. And may be related to their political culture: unlike the *lumpenproletariat*, they had had experience, in the trade unions, with organized political struggle.

Radical transformation in the context of squatter settlements meant both, alternative institutions within the settlements and revolutionary changes in the national political structure. Internally, the most dramatic change was the emergence of autonomous organs of judicial control in a few *campamentos*. With them came new definitions of what was considered unacceptable behaviour and a search for integrative forms of punishment. Non-participation at meetings or poor direction of an assembly called for an accounting; particular attention was directed toward resolving conflicts within families. Drunkenness was a target of social control: those who arrived drunk at a *campamento*'s entrance would be detained, and in some, alcohol was banned altogether. Sanctions ranged from self-criticism, study of revolutionary texts, physical punishment, internment, and fines to expulsion from the *campamento*. But the most used were reprimands and the settlement of quarrels and reconciliation of those involved (Collectif Chili, 1972: 43–5). Handelman (1975: 40, 42) emphasizes the significance of these developments:

Because the *campamento* is somewhat removed from the existing socio-political order and lacks basic municipal services, its inhabitants develop their own civic institutions to deal with a variety of daily problems – maintenance of law and order, criminal justice, housing, local administration, and the like. For the most part the police, welfare agencies, courts, and government bureaucracies of both Frei and Allende's civilian administrations did not operate within the *campamentos*. Consequently, the marginal communities created new alternative institutional forms in some of these areas that offered the basis for greater mass participation and political consciousness in the society at large. Thus, the settlements may well have contained the seeds of a new, mass-based social order . . .

Had the Chilean military coup not terminated such *campamento* organizations, their political implications might ultimately have been quite significant. In effect, some *campamentos* had created a small-scale state within a state. Locally controlled courts, work brigades, and other administrative agencies offered an opportunity for active political participation that is normally far beyond the reach of the urban poor in the developing world.

The radicalized *campamentos* made demands beyond the initial quest for land. They occupied hospitals to press for health services, they occupied administrative offices to protest delays, they participated in mass demonstrations (Collectif Chili, 1972: 49–50). When the truckers went on strike in 1972, the *pobladores* opened up the highways and organized supplies. They established committees to control distribution, forged links with factories, and eventually obtained food directly from the rural areas. In 1973, when the recognition spread that a military coup was imminent, the squatter settlements made preparations to resist it.[14]

On 11 September 1973 the military acted in concert. The few loyalists within the armed forces were rapidly neutralized. The Moncada, the presidential palace, defended by a handful of faithful with submachine guns, succumbed to an assault by tanks and planes. Salvador Allende, who led the resistance, was killed.

With him died the promise that socialism could be established in Latin America in a peaceful transition, through the electoral process. Pockets of resistance at some factories were crushed by military might. Mass arrests, systematic torture, and random killings established a regime of terror. In what has come to be known as the *Pinochetazo* 30,000 people are said to have been killed, an estimated 150,000 arrests were made, and more than 100,000 Chileans went into exile (Henfrey and Sorj, 1977: 189). The armed underground struggle, threatened by groups of the Left such as MIR, never took form. A particularly brutal military regime had established its variety of law and order.[15]

The Force of Organized Labour

One classic answer to the oppression of the masses is for the workers of the world to unite to create a just order. Such solidarity must appear as a far-distant goal at a time when workers in the industralized countries jealously watch the industrialization process elsewhere, resisting both investments in Third World countries and imports of manufactured goods from there. Workers in Third World countries have to rely by and large on their own resources, whether it be to ameliorate their condition or to radically transform their society. They may chant 'The International', but the chorus in distant countries is rarely heard.

In contrast, the resources and options available to business interests and governments are much less circumscribed by national boundaries. Multinational corporations can choose their location and secure advantageous conditions for their investments by playing host governments off against each other. Most governments have easy access to external resources to counter any popular threats to their rule, whether it be development of the mass media they control, equipment for army and police, or training: the Brazilian authorities sent torture experts to instruct Pinochet's men in Chile.

Generations of workers have laboured in the textile mills of India, down the gold mines of South Africa, on the docks of Brazil since the nineteenth century. By now nearly all Third World countries have a history of worker protest. There is also growing awareness of revolutionary changes wrought in some countries, of reforms achieved by workers in many others. Consciousness of both, historical precedent and actual condition, is facilitated by rising levels of educational experience.[16] The wide gap in living conditions separating the labouring masses from local élites, foreign advisers, and tourists is less and less taken for granted. Still, the emergence of a broad, class-conscious movement of workers is very much the exception in Third World countries. Such movements are usually aborted by governments responsive to pressures from workers in strategic positions. Time and again potentially powerful sectors of the labour force are induced to behave as vested-interest groups, concerned to preserve and improve their privileges rather than to express solidarity with the great numbers of less privileged workers (Bromley and Gerry, 1979: 9).[17]

Industrial action in Third World countries tends to have immediate political implications. Not only is a substantial proportion of the labour force employed in the public bureaucracy, but in most Third World countries public bodies have full or partial control of the utilities, of mining, and of major industries. Thus the public sector is frequently the foremost large-scale employer. In addition, the government is often closely involved in setting wages and establishing working conditions in the private sector. In this situation the grievances of wage earners are directed towards the government and its leaders; they are expressed in a political form, and the state cannot appear in the role of arbitrator between wage earners and their employers.

Any country's economy is immediately dependent on the sustained labour of its working force, but the leverage different sectors of the labour force can exert varies greatly. On the one hand, unskilled workers can be easily replaced by eager recruits from the unemployed and underemployed masses. On the other hand, many skills are in short supply. At the same time, underdeveloped economies tend to be heavily dependent on the effective operation of a few key sectors. A strike by railroad or dock workers brings the entire economy to a halt in many a country; a work stoppage by mineworkers can threaten a foreign exchange crisis. Those who operate such crucial economic resources, and whose skills are not easily replaced, can thus exert very real political power.

The proportion of the labour force employed in large-scale enterprises in mining, transport, and industry is typically small, but the workers in any one such enterprise constitute a compact mass more difficult to manipulate than workers in small or medium-sized firms where they are usually closely controlled by a paternalistic employer. Indeed, the very numbers of workers can become menacing, as in the Indian and Pakistani *gherao*, (workers blockading in an office a manager or group of managers). And threats of mass dismissals lack plausibility because large numbers of skilled workers are difficult to replace at short notice.[18] Further, conflict is frequently not limited to one plant. Many issues, e.g. minimum wages, compulsory contributions to retirement funds, social-security benefits, transcend the boundaries of the individual firm. They affect workers in general and tend to bring them into conflict with political authorities. Once substantial numbers of workers are aroused, they pose a very real threat of mass riots in which elements of the urban poor can be expected to join.

The task of organizing industrial workers is facilitated by their concentration in the factory, in industrial estates, and in residential communities. In Karachi labour protest has been based on both place of employment and residence. In 1961 the decision to call a general strike was reached at a meeting of about 10,000 workers on a hilltop between the main industrial area and the neighbouring workers' colonies. The 1972 strike showed a high degree of co-ordination between industrial and residential areas. The worker's colonies, where the police hesitated to venture, provided a haven for the strike leaders. The factories were efficiently *gherao*ed, often by work-shifts: the shift going home would bring the news from the industrial front and the shift going to the sites would take back directives from the leadership (Shaheed, 1979: 187, 198). Sandbrook and Arn (1977: 57) conclude from their survey of political attitudes in two residential areas in the Accra–Tema conurbation that the emergence of a working-class orientation is encouraged among workers who live in 'occupational communities', where – owing to a concentration of the similarly employed, their insulation from moderating outside influences, and their particular schedules occasioned by shift-work – workmates interact both on and off the job to create and reinforce common images of the world.

Labour organizers face the threats of repression and the blandishments of co-optation. Trade-union leaders are prominent among political prisoners in Third World countries; they have suffered tortures and met violent death. Many have compromised their vision of a more just society. Some have done so simply to reap the benefits promised them individually, but others chose to compromise so as to obtain benefits for limited sectors of labour. The classic case occurred during the Mexican revolution when the 'Red Batallions' of urban workers supported Venustiano Carranza, the representative of the middle class, against the disinherited Indians of rural Mexico led by Emiliano Zapata. Substantial benefits accrued to urban workers in Uruguay when they gave their loyalty to José Batlle at the beginning of this century, to urban workers in Brazil when they were wooed by Getúlio Vargas from 1937 on, to urban workers in Argentina when they provided the mass following of Juan and Eva Perón from the mid-1940s.[19]

Where organized labour has not established a political alliance with the ruling élite, there is frequently tacit collusion, as Joshi and Joshi (1976: 172) phrase it for India, among government, big business, and trade unions. In capital-intensive industries the share of labour costs is low, and employers are more concerned to minimize labour turnover and absenteeism among trained workers, and to avoid strikes that entail huge losses in output and may lead to sabotage of valuable equipment and violence against managerial personnel. Employers also need to be careful about their public image, especially if they represent foreign or minority capital. Governments in turn are acutely aware of the crucial contribution certain sectors of labour make to the economy and the disruptive potential of massed urban labour. Elements of urban labour thus wield power that is translated into wages, working conditions, and job security that are governed by legislation and/or collective bargaining. I have already referred to them, in chapter 3, as a 'protected' work force. They appear privileged *vis-à-vis* the rest of urban labour in nearly every Third World country.[20] Authoritarian regimes can constitute a counterweight to the power of the protected work force. Indeed, its position appears to have weakened in many countries. Between 1956 and 1972 real wages in the manufacturing sector lagged behind the growth of GDP per capita in fourteen out of twenty-seven Third World countries (Webb, 1977).

The internal stratification of labour is usually codified by social-security legislation which is partial and unequal. In Latin America only a small portion of the economically active population was covered by such legislation as late as the 1960s: countries such as Brazil, Colombia, Guatemala, and Mexico provided coverage for less than 30 per cent of their economically active population, while at the other extreme Cuba provided total coverage, and Chile about 70 per cent coverage (Rosenberg and Malloy, 1978: 160).[21] The history of social-security legislation in the region is instructive:

Social security coverage in general evolved on a piecemeal, group-by-group basis. The usual sequence in the evolution was: the military and public functionaries; workers in critical infrastructure activities; workers in important urban services; and industrial workers. By and large, the quality of coverage was positively correlated with the sequence of coverage. Both the sequence and quality of coverage were determined by the power of groups to pose a threat to the existing sociopolitical systems and the administrative logic of the contractual type of social insurance schemes developed within the region. As a result, the great mass of rural workers and urban marginals were either ignored or received coverage of an inferior quality. The upshot was the incremental evolution of social security systems that were both highly fragmented and unequally stratified in terms of the quality of programs. Even among late adopters, which had more unified administrative structures, coverage was extended on a piecemeal and unequal group-by-group basis.

The corporatist structures of 'representational participation' were an important factor accounting for the fragmentation and inequality of the social security systems. These structures, which were often a part of a general corporatist approach to labor relations, reflected the goal of established elites to undercut the emergence of a broad, class-conscious movement of workers. In the social security area these structures both encouraged and permitted discrete groupings to pursue their own particularistic advantage at the expense of other groups. (Rosenberg and Malloy, 1978: 168)

The degree of protection enjoyed by sectors of the labour force varies from country to country. According to Roberts (1978: 134), state regulation of the economy in Brazil has depressed wages to such an extent that there is relatively little difference between the wages of unskilled and semi-skilled workers in the large-scale sector and those in the small-scale sector. He relates this to the influence of a strong internal and foreign-linked bourgeoisie. Roberts describes Peru, in contrast, as an 'enclave' country where the national bourgeoisie was weak, and the state under nationalist pressures imposed strict labour regulations on the predominantly foreign-controlled large-scale enterprises. The workers in such firms enjoy much better conditions than their counterparts in the informal sector. The parallel with the difference in government response to squatter settlements in these two countries, which I discussed earlier, is striking.

Where an electoral process operates, trade unions tend to be attached to political parties. Indeed, multi-party competition is often mirrored in a proliferation of trade unions hostile to one another. Although the connection with political parties resembles the tendency of squatter movement to come under party control, industrial workers have greater leverage than squatters. Their unions, if allowed to operate freely, are not easily manipulated. In India unions are started by party functionaries. Once established, they are linked to parties both through trade-union federations — which are informally tied to parties through their leaders — and directly through important union officials who are members of the sponsoring party and union cadres who are also the local party cadres. Every union is referred to by the name of the party to which it owes allegiance, and union and party collaborate closely in strikes, elections, agitations, and meetings. Intra-party struggles and shifting party alliances are reflected in conflict within unions and changes in union coalitions. Through prolonged membership the rank and file develop loyalties to the sponsoring party. Yet the unions have a logic and momentum of their own, and the political commitment of the workers, and even of the union leaders holding high offices in the party, is vitally influenced by their perception of union interests. Thus when the Congress Party and its national trade-union federation branded the *gherao* movement as unconstitutional, the unions associated with them in different parts of West Bengal nevertheless organized *gherao* and other violent protest movements. Rather than adhering to the more conservative ideology of the Congress Party, they responded to the fact that the establishment of a leftist United Front government in the state had cut them off from sources of patronage. In contrast, when the major Marxist union moved to support the United Front government, stopped all agitations, and began to collaborate with management, it lost much of its support (Sengupta, 1977; Chatterji, 1980: 147-58; Ramaswamy, 1973).

The primacy of union over party was demonstrated in the case of the Chilean mine workers. They supported the Left while it was in opposition, but when the Unidad Popular government came to power they increasingly transferred their electoral support toward the parties of the centre and the right. Zapata ([1975] 1979) infers that the miners' political radicalism was not ideological, but was instead connected to a search for political support for economic goals. This pattern was highlighted when the workers at the El Teniente copper mine went on strike against the Allende government in April 1973 and substantial numbers stayed on strike until June in spite of the 'workers' government' being already severely threatened by pressures from foreign powers, Chilean capital interests, sectors of the middle class, and the military.

The Urban Bases of Revolutions

Chinese Communists, led by Zhou Enlai, were driven from Shanghai in April 1927. A Communist commune established in Canton in December of that year was short-lived. The attempt to base a socialist revolution on the urban proletariat had failed. The Communist Party moved to build up peasant support through land and tax reforms in the areas it controlled, and from guerrilla origins it raised peasant armies which were victorious in a civil war fought on conventional lines.

Mao Zedong, an early advocate of the rural strategy, was to declare the establishment of the People's Republic of China in Beijing on 1 October 1949. The Chinese experience demonstrated, or so it seemed, that Third World revolutions would have to be based on the peasantry. The rural-based guerrilla movements in Indonesia, Vietnam, Algeria, Mozambique, Angola, and Guinea-Bissau reinforced this point of view (Moore, 1966; Skocpol, 1979). However, the struggle in these countries was directed foremost against a colonial regime. I propose to distinguish such wars of national liberation from revolutionary movements challenging a national government for control. I shall argue that contemporary revolutions are largely urban in character.[22]

National wars of liberation have invariably been fought in predominantly rural countries. More than 80 per cent of the country's population lived in rural areas when the Dutch abandoned Indonesia in 1949, the French left Indochina in 1954, the Portuguese granted independence to Guinea-Bissau, Mozambique, and Angola in 1974–5. Algeria was a more urbanized country, but still about two-thirds rural, when the French finally made peace in 1962. In every case the colonial power was challenged by a rural-based guerrilla movement which curtailed the production, processing, and transport of crops for export, thus striking at the very backbone of the colonial economy. If the colonial regime's capability to extract agricultural surplus was thus impaired, it invariably continued to control the cities effectively and withdrew of its own accord, and at a time of its choosing, even if precipitately in the case of the French after their defeat at Dien Bien Phu. The benefits to be derived from maintaining the colonial presence had been reduced, and the expeditionary force, the metropolitan government, and/or powerful sectors of public opinion were led to weigh the costs of protracted warfare. The colonial power eventually accepted that its interests would be better served by a harmonious relationship with a formally independent country. Indeed, most colonies were granted independence before any armed resistance emerged.

Essential characteristics of the revolutionary movement are that it employs extra-legal means in challenging a national government and that elements outside the government and the security forces play the principal role: it is 'popular' in the sense that it bases itself outside the ruling élite. Revolutionary movements have seized power in four countries since the establishment of the People's Republic of China. A brief look at the cases of Bolivia, Iran, and Nicaragua will show that these were essentially urban struggles. The case of Cuba is more ambiguous.

If Ernesto 'Che' Guevara inspired revolutionaries throughout the Third World, he exalted rural guerrillas in his *Guerrilla Warfare*. The argument of the primacy of the rural guerrilla *foco* was further developed by Debray (1967). The austere, difficult, and dangerous life experienced by the Cuban *guerrilleros*, and their encounter with rural poverty, profoundly marked Fidel Castro, Che Guevara, and their fellow fighters, many of whom came similarly from the urban middle class. The fact that it was Castro and a nucleus of his comrades from the Sierra

Maestra who seized control of the destiny of Cuba gave additional weight to their experience. But a closer look at the Cuban revolution reveals a more complex picture. First of all, the urban underground provided the lifeline for the rural guerrillas. An estimated 60 to 80 per cent of their recruits came from the urban areas as did arms, information, money, and even food. And it was through urban contacts that the *guerrilleros* gained national and international recognition.[23] Second, the urban underground carried out a wide range of violent actions and sustained most of the casualites. More than 5,000 bombings were reported in 1957 and 1958. Havana's international airport was burned. The Argentinian racing driver, Juan Fangio, was kidnapped and kept prisoner for two days, attracting worldwide attention. The underground in Cienfuegos collaborated with the conspirators of the naval uprising there in 1957. The most spectacular action was carried out by the Directorio Revolucionario, the student organization, when it stormed the presidential palace on 13 March 1957, but failed in its attempt to kill the dictator.[24] In comparison, there were probably never more than 300 *guerrilleros* in the Sierra Maestra at one time. This was the case even during the largest army offensive, in the summer of 1958, when forty of their number fell. Finally, when the regime collapsed, rebel troops were too few to seize power. It was the urban underground that policed the streets and took over the administrative machinery. And it was a general strike that signified mass support for the rebels and discouraged attempts to establish a conservative successor regime (Karol, 1970: 164–80; Thomas, [1971] 1977: 256–63 and *passim*).

The Bolivian revolution may be seen compressed into three days of intensive fighting when the government was overthrown in 1952. Or it may be traced back to its roots in organized labour and disaffected elements of the middle class. The artisan–labour movement had reached a degree of national coherence at the beginning of the Great Depression. During World War II organized labour had become politicized and radicalized as its leadership shifted to the tin miners. In an uneasy alliance with the labour movement, the Movimiento Nacionalista Revolucionario (MNR) became from 1946 on increasingly the rallying point of middle-class opposition committed to revolution. The first major joint effort of the MNR and the labour movement occurred in 1949 when a nationwide revolt exploded. Rebel forces seized control of every provincial capital and mining camp but failed in La Paz. Loyal government troops used the capital as a base and succeeded in suppressing the rebels, province by province. The 1952 insurrection was launched in La Paz by Los Grupos de Honor and the national police, whose commanding officer had agreed to join the MNR in a coup. The Groups of Honour were paramilitary cells, their composition was mainly lower-middle class: artisans, less well-organized workers of small factories, and elements of the *clase popular*. When the insurrection appeared to be doomed, the police general sought asylum in a foreign embassy. However, armed workers from the mines and factories joined the fight in several provincial centres, turned the tide in La Paz, and cut off possible reinforcements for the capital. What had started out as a coup with limited civil participation, ended with Victor Paz Estenssoro, the leader of the MNR, presiding over a government which included three labour ministers, i.e. official representatives of the labour Left. Whichever way the Bolivian revolution is delineated, there was no involvement of rural elements until after the overthrow of the government (Malloy, 1970: 103-6, 127-50, 157, 167-8).

The success of the anti-Shah revolution is the more remarkable for the odds it faced. Iran had a well-established government and enjoyed an economic boom. The Shah boasted a large modern army which was extremely well equipped. SAVAK, the secret police, had established a reign of terror: tens of thousands had been arrested and savagely tortured, hundreds had been executed. Many dissidents had gone into exile, and great numbers of young people had refused to return after completing their studies abroad.

Some elements in the anti-Shah movement stand out, though it is too early to assess their relative contribution to its success. Most conspicious were the street demonstrations. On 8 January 1978 theological students in the holy city of Qom staged a sit-in. It was broken up by security forces, an action which quickly provoked retaliation, and the security forces started shooting. In two days of disturbances dozens were killed, according to one estimate, at least seventy persons, by another. In February the Tabriz demonstration of sympathy and solidarity to commemorate those killed in Qom turned rapidly into a vehement protest against the Shah. The local Azarbaijani police refused to intervene; troops were called in and responded violently. The demonstration was transformed into a riot, spearheaded, it is said, by recent poor migrants and radical students. An estimated 100 persons were killed. A pattern evolved as demonstrators took to the streets again and again to commemorate the victims of earlier confrontations and to face troops who were shooting to kill. Over 3,000 are believed to have died in the first eleven months of 1978.

A second key element in the overthrow of the Shah was worker protest. Strikes did not gather momentum until mid-September. By the end of October oil production had dropped by nearly three-quarters; and many factories were forced to go on short time or to close for lack of energy supplies. The drying up of oil exports threatened to create foreign-exchange problems. By early November all public services — transport, telecommunications, ports, and fuel supplies — were paralysed or nearly so. Strikes at major banks affected import credits; strikes at customs halted industrial production by shutting off raw materials and spare parts.

A third factor was that large sectors of the middle class, and especially the university students, had become increasingly disaffected over the years. Several guerrilla groups sprang from the student milieu abroad and at home, but their impact was effectively circumscribed by SAVAK, and their significance was primarily symbolic until very late in the struggle (Graham, 1979: 214-15, 220, 224, 233, 237, Bill, 1978). Central to our argument is that neither a rural guerrilla movement nor the rural masses played any role in the Iranian revolution.

In Nicaragua the junction of an organized guerrilla force with an urban insurrection appears to have been crucial to the overthrow of the Somoza regime. In 1975, splits had developed among the Sandinistas over strategy: whether to concentrate on rural guerrilla warfare or on organizing among urban workers, whether to give priority to military action or political activity. In 1978 spontaneous urban insurrections confronted them with the alternative to stop such tactics or to lead them. They launched uprisings in five cities but eventually had to retreat into the hills. They returned in June 1979 to spearhead insurrections in the major towns, while a general strike paralyzed the country. Within six weeks the dictator was put to flight (Chavarría, 1982).

Each of these revolutionary movements was largely urban in character. Even where rural guerrillas played a prominent role, in Cuba and Nicaragua, their leadership, a large proportion of their fellow combatants, and much of their material support were drawn from the urban milieu. It was in the cities that all the confrontations took place in Bolivia and Iran, that the decisive battles were fought in Nicaragua, and that the Cuban *guerrilleros* found crucial support to establish their regime. Urban workers determined the outcome in the battle for the control of La Paz, paralysed the economy in Iran and Nicaragua, and thwarted efforts to snatch the fruits of victory from the hands of the *guerrilleros* who had put the Cuban dictator to flight.

How to explain the urban character of contemporary revolutions? The four revolutionary struggles successful in the 1950s and 1970s were carried out in countries that varied greatly in their level of urbanization. Little more than a fifth of the population lived in cities in Bolivia at the time of the revolution, slightly less than half in Iran and Nicaragua, somewhat more than half in Cuba. The importance of urban elements in the revolutions of the latter three countries may be seen as a function of their high level of urbanization. In such a perspective the rapid urban growth experienced by most Third World countries can be taken to presage the age of urban revolutions. As Abraham Guillén ([1966] 1973: 238), the intellectual mentor of urban guerrillas in Uruguay and beyond, put it:[25]

Strategically, in the case of a popular revolution in a country in which the highest percentage of the population is urban, the center of operations of the revolutionary war should be in the city. Operations should consist of scattered surprise attacks by quick and mobile units superior in arms and numbers at designated points, but avoiding barricades in order not to attract the enemy's attention at one place. The units will then attack with the greatest part of their strength the enemy's least fortified or weakest links in the city . . . The revolution's potential is where the population is.

The demographic observation reflects an economic reality: the surplus is increasingly produced in the urban sector. Even in largely rural Bolivia it was tin mining rather than agriculture that constituted the core element in the national economy. The state's ability to extract agricultural surplus is no longer crucial to its very operation. Rather, it is the urban economy that finances the state apparatus. The extreme example is Imperial Iran, which filled its coffers with petro-dollars while importing food. Because the state is dependent on the urban economy, there are limits to repression in the urban context. Managers, professionals, skilled workers, and even semi-skilled workers in great numbers cannot be replaced at short notice. To imprison them for any length of time, to push them into exile, or to kill them entails severe economic losses. This means not only a reduction in the resources available to the state but also a deterioration in living conditions for the population at large that is likely to foster discontent.

Difficulties in extracting surplus provide powerful motivation for colonial powers to reconsider the merits of their direct control over distant lands. For national governments and their supporters the situation is quite different. For one thing, they can appropriate surplus via the money-printing press, though inflation has its political costs. For another, many governments can count on foreign assistance to tide them over a crisis. If patron countries find it in their interest, they may provide substantial economic and/or military support for many years. Even a bankrupt government is unlikely to abdicate of its own accord. It may fall victim to shifts within its political base, or it may be toppled by sections of the army dissatisfied with the lack of resources. But confronted with a revolutionary movement, the ruling group will desperately cling to power. If a national war of liberation threatens the tentacles of empire, a revolutionary movement attacks the very existence of political and economic élites. And while members of the élite can make provision to live out their days in comfort in exile, much of the indigenous middle class, unlike colonial civil servants, has nowhere to go. The level of resistance of the élite and the middle class tends accordingly to be high.[26] The MNR, it is true, could effectively appeal to a large part of a middle class which had been deeply divided ever since Bolivia's humiliating defeat in the Chaco War. In Cuba large sectors of the middle class had been hostile to Batista since 1952, when, after three popularly elected administrations, ·he seized power in a *coup d'état*, and elements of the middle class in Iran and Nicaragua had been similarly alienated from autocratic rulers. But in these three countries it was only when the revolutionary movement made life in the cities insecure and brought the economy to a halt that a full-scale withdrawal of support from the government took place. And only when they had thus been quite isolated did Batista, the Shah, and Somoza flee their countries.

Colonial governments withdrew in spite of their success in maintaining control of the cities; this was even the case in Algeria, where the French effectively destroyed the large terrorist organization in Algiers. But loss of control over rural areas is not a sufficient condition to persuade a national government to relinquish power to a revolutionary movement. For such a movement to succeed it must confront the government in its urban location. Control over the capital city is usually of crucial importance, as the abortive revolution of 1949 demonstrated in Bolivia.

The city seems to hold specific attractions for guerrilla activity. For the students and professionals who invariably predominate among the guerrillas in the early stages, and frequently longer, the city constitutes familiar terrain: they know it and their presence does not attract undue attention. Furthermore, while most guerrillas in rural areas are outsiders, even if they are of rural origin, the urban guerrilla can maintain the cover of a conventional life until he/she arouses the suspicions of the authorities. Finally, the urban crowd promises the guerrilla anonymity. But systematic torture revealed the urban guerrillas' vulnerability to security leaks because of their dependency on safe houses which, once uncovered, can be rapidly investigated by vastly superior armed forces. A circle was established as torture – at the beginning often of quite haphazardly arrested people – provided information that led to the capture of participants or sympathizers who under torture provided further information. Torture served also to deter recruits to the ranks of the guerrillas and their sympathizers.[27]

Rural areas can shield small mobile guerrilla units. But the transition from rural guerrilla activity to peasant army faces impossible odds. The circumstances in which the Chinese Communists were able to control entire provinces and to build up their armies were unique. There was no government exercising hegemonic power over China, and the country's vastnesses inhibited the establishment of such power. The Japanese invasion further undermined any effort at central government, gained the Communist forces recognition as nationalists fighting the invader, and at times forced a truce on the Communists' opponents. Today governments everywhere can rapidly dispatch army units across an entire country. Any attempt to move beyond the guerrilla stage in rural areas has to reckon with the immense firepower, the high mobility, and the efficient communications system that are the hallmark of a modern army.[28] Governments have shown little hesitation in razing rural settlements and relocating peasants to counter rural-based challenges.

A national government is unlikely to surrender to a revolutionary movement unless it is confronted in its urban location by forces it can no longer contain. Such forces are most unlikely to be constituted of a peasant army. They must be established in an urban insurrection, as shown in Bolivia, in Iran, and most dramatically in Nicaragua. Urban insurgency confronts governments with difficult choices. No government has yet responded by relocating urban populations on any scale. And if heavy arms are used in re-establishing control over a city, or major parts of it, the destruction wrought is bound to be huge and support of the government will be alienated. Somoza, though, went so far as to order the destruction of entire small towns and of neighbourhoods in Managua held by the Sandinistas.

Against heavy odds guerrillas have maintained their presence in a number of countries for many years. They face the even more difficult task of mobilizing an urban mass movement that will confront the firepower of a modern army.[29] Power and privilege are centred in the city; it is in the city that they are effectively challenged.

8

URBAN AND REGIONAL SYSTEMS:
A SUITABLE CASE FOR TREATMENT?

One of the common features of policy statements throughout the Third World is the frequency with which politicians and planners have averred that something must be done about the growth of cities and the increasing levels of regional inequality. The city is devouring national resources at the expense of the country-side and the farmer; centralization is destroying the dynamism of the provincial city; there is urban bias, metropolitan bias, rural underdevelopment; development is required in the poorest regions. Despite repeated statements of intent, however, there are few examples, outside the socialist countries, of any real determination to develop the rural areas, to decentralize industry, to control the rapid growth of metropolitan areas, and still less to reduce poverty in the poorest regions.

This chapter asks whether and in what ways urban settlement systems are distorted. Do too many people live in cities or in urban areas that have grown too large? Has urban bias in development policy distorted the pattern of national development? Is there a case for arguing that Third World cities are becoming unmanageable and that their growth must be slowed? In short, are the arguments relating to 'distorted' settlement systems valid, and, if they are valid, what can be done to modify current trends? I also consider the kinds of policies that have been introduced to treat urban and regional imbalances and comment upon their effectiveness. In general, I am unimpressed by the spatial policies of most Third World countries and question the usefulness of most kinds of spatial policy as a means of reducing poverty and narrowing personal income disparities. Can a spatial strategy, in fact, achieve anything if fundamental social and economic reforms are absent? Is it only political changes and modifications in develop-mental style that can cure those imbalances? Is spatial policy necessary if such reforms take place?

Although asking such broad questions, I am trying hard not to overgeneralize. General statements about the appropriate treatment of urban bias, over-urbanization, and regional imbalance are often highly misleading. Too often policies useful in one country at one specific time are turned into panacea for all countries at all times. Rarely do the authors of such panaceas caution that what is good for one society may well be irrelevant for another; what is good in terms of settlement policy for India is unlikely to be terribly relevant to the problems of Hong Kong; Brazil's national settlement strategy is likely to be more than an ocean apart from that of most West African states; China's policies may be of academic interest to the decentralizers in India, but they can scarcely be contem-plated in policy terms, given the different political systems. In short, generalizations are of only limited use; 'instant solutions' taken from the latest vogue generalization have wrought havoc in the planning field. Let nothing that may be said here contribute to such instant planning; the generalizations made in this chapter are intended for thought, not to be introduced in evangelistic glee.

Forms of Regional, Spatial, and Urban Imbalance

Urban Bias

Most of the social sciences have contributed to the extensive literature on the appropriate balance between urban and rural development. During the 1950s many economists were involved in a long debate about the correct allocation of investment between agriculture and industry. Authors such as Papanek (1954) and Johnston and Mellor (1961) favoured agricultural development, arguing that the agricultural sector must be made more productive in order to provide the necessary surplus for industrial and urban development. Without such a surplus inadequate funds would be available for industrial and urban growth and no market would develop for urban products and services. Counterposed to this argument was the idea that industrial and urban growth were prerequisites for a more modern and productive agricultural sector. Surplus rural labour needed to be absorbed into more productive urban activities, thereby permitting the introduction of more modern and capital-intensive agricultural practices and encouraging the diffusion of modern ideas and institutions into the traditional rural areas (Currie, 1965). Linked to this debate were various controversies over the balance of advantages associated with balanced growth (Nurkse, 1952), a 'big push' towards industrialization (Rosenstein-Rodan, 1943; Prebisch, 1950), or a programme of balanced imbalances (Hirschman, 1958).

Meanwhile, some demographers and sociologists were arguing that most Third World countries were suffering from 'over-urbanization' (Davis and Hertz, 1954; UNESCO, 1957). Statistical studies showed that a much larger proportion of the populations of Third World countries were employed in non-agricultural activities, and especially in services, than had been the case in the developed countries at similar levels of urbanization. This finding was interpreted as evidence that rural–urban migration had taken place despite the lack of adequate numbers of productive industrial jobs in the urban areas. Over-urbanization 'explained' why urban misery coexisted with rural poverty. Such views were countered by charges that the definitions of over-urbanization were invalid. Sovani (1964: 117) called them 'chimerical and so unusable' and others pointed out that even if it were valid to compare the present experiences of the developing countries with those of the now developed countries in the past, no policy conclusion could be drawn from such comparisons (Brookfield, 1973; McGee, 1971). The over-urbanization concept was also attacked by the pro-urban lobby which argued that the city was the historical centre of innovation and change. Pirenne (1925) and Mumford (1938) had shown that historically the city had been the climax of civilization and the stimulus to further development. Friedmann (1968) argued that urbanization should be adopted as a deliberate strategy for change, without it meaningful development would be held back.

Parallel debates may well have taken place in socialist countries relating to the correct interpretation of Marx's ideas about the elimination of differences between town and country and about the revolutionary potential of the urban proletariat and the peasantry. In the Soviet Union the collectivization of the peasantry under Stalin effectively resolved the issue in favour of urban-industrial development. In China the different revolutionary experience and the lower levels of urban development encouraged an anti-urban stance (Frolic, 1976: 158). In Kampuchea Phnom Penh and the other major cities were evacuated in 1975 both in an effort to avert starvation and to increase the chances of establishing an equitable, self-sufficient, and socialist country.

Throughout the world, at an academic level and more importantly in major political circles, the debate continues. The advocates of both the rural and the urban sectors remain convinced that most of the failures of capitalist or of communist society may be attributed to the excessive allocation of resources to the other sector. Thus Jakobson and Prakesh (1974: 279) complain that 'the prevailing world-wide attitude among politicians of all persuasions is anti-urban, and in particular anti-big city', while Lipton (1977) argues that the major developmental issue in the Third World today is the need to stem 'urban bias'.

Lipton's argument is currently so influential that it is worth examining in more detail. He argues that power in most Third World countries is held by urban groups who distort the allocation of resources in their favour thereby worsening inequality and slowing development.

The most important conflict in the poor countries of the world today is not between capital and labour. Nor is it between foreign and the national interests. It is between the rural classes and the urban classes. The rural sector contains most of the poverty, and most of the low cost sources of potential advance; but the urban sector contains most of the articulateness, organization and power. So the urban classes have been able to 'win' most of the rounds of the struggle with the countryside; but in doing they have made the development process slow and unfair.

In consequence, 'a shift of resources to the rural sector . . . is often, perhaps usually, the overriding developmental task.' He is not without support. For example, Gugler (1982: 187) argues 'there would appear to be an approach that promises a more efficient allocation of labor between the rural and the urban sector as well as a reduction in the extreme inequalities that characterize most Third World countries. It will aim at improving rural living standards by channelling productive resources to the rural areas and/or by directing a larger share of income to them.' Similarly Lefeber (1978: 22) notes that 'the required policies are known. The problem is to break through the deadlock caused by dominance of congruent urban class interests.'

But is the urban/rural dichotomy too simple? Does it ev\
described? Lipton's thesis covers most Third World countries, \
Asia, and Latin America, even though most of the evidence he pre\
from South Asia. Clearly, it is unlikely that any simple generalizat\
importance will apply equally well in all parts of the Third World. I\
interesting that several strands of evidence suggest that urban bias may v
inappropriate term even to describe the situation in India. For a start, it is
possible that during the 1960s it was the urban poor who suffered deterioration
in their standards of living rather than the rural poor. Dandekar and Rath (1971:
33) point out that between 1960-1 and 1967-8 private consumer expenditure of
the bottom 20 per cent of rural Indians remained steady while that of the
bottom quintile of the urban poor deteriorated. In addition, Byres (1974) has
pointed out that the limited net marketed surplus flowing from the agricultural
to the industrial sector in the 1950s and 1960s was hardly consistent with an
acute case of urban bias, and Mitra (1977) and Byres have shown that during
much of the 1950s and 1960s the terms of trade moved against the cities. It is
also pertinent to point out that the rate of urban growth in India has been very
slow by Third World standards, increasing only from 17.3 per cent of the population in 1951 to 19.9 per cent in 1971.

If there are certain empirical difficulties for application of the urban-bias
thesis to India there are also alternative interpretations of the Indian scene. Thus
Ashish Bose (1973: 20) argues that 'the lack of an urban lobby in the Indian
Parliament and in the state legislatures is responsible for the continued neglect
of problems of urban development.' And if this interpretation is difficult to
reconcile with urban bias, Byres' (1974: 252) conclusion is still more contra-
dictory: 'the most important contradiction in the Indian socio-economic system
in coming decades is that posed by an urban bourgeoisie intent upon industrialization but frustrated by a strong and increasingly powerful class of rich peasants
and small and medium landlords, on their way to becoming capitalists and
exercising growing political power.'

If urban bias is not universally accepted by students of India, where might it
apply? It is most likely to be relevant to those countries in which urbanization
has been very rapid, as in Africa or in Latin America. But even in countries in
which urban growth has been rapid, would everyone agree that urban bias has
been the explanation? In Uganda, for example, the proportion of the total
population living in urban areas increased from 5 to 10 per cent between 1960
and 1975, a rate surpassed by few Third World nations (World Bank, 1979:
164). Yet, despite this finding, Muench (1978) argues firmly against the idea of
urban bias. He points out that the urban poor have suffered considerable neglect
in Kampala as a result of politically inspired regional policies which have favoured
provincial élites in the name of greater regional equality.

Of course, there are many countries in the world where urban–rural disparities
are too wide, having been brought about by policies that have clearly favoured the

urban areas at the expense of the rural groups. But the generalization can be applied too broadly and, like all generalizations based on a dichotomy, it is likely to ignore other important processes that contribute to the same socio-economic pattern. A particular danger with the urban-bias thesis is that it portrays most power conflicts in Third World countries as arising 'primarily from where people live (rural versus urban areas) rather than, say, from the economic sectors in which they derive a livelihood (industry versus agriculture) or from their position in the class hierarchy' (Griffin, 1978: 108). In fact much of the developmental literature has pointed out that many of the difficulties Lipton portrays stem not from urban bias but from policies that favour some rural groups at the expense of others. Thus Lefeber (1978: 8) points to a common situation, in which rich agriculturalists support, or at least do not oppose, policies that keep agricultural prices down so as to reduce the cost of urban food. Such a policy is less biased against rural areas than against the small and medium-sized farmer who is unable to benefit from other government policies such as export credit, loans, and subsidies in the same way as the large farmer. The large farmer supports urban bias in one set of policies so as to benefit from rural bias in another set. In such circumstances, it is more appropriate to analyse the problems of the poor farmer in class terms than in terms of urban bias.[1] As Griffin has said 'Lipton has tried to explain too much, indeed virtually everything, in terms of urban bias. In the end it becomes a brilliant obsession.'

A more limited and less simplified generalization might find wider support. Bias in the allocation of resources in most Third World countries is typically directed against the poor. They lack access to critical resources such as land, water, and credit and receive little for their labour or their products. This bias applies to all poor people, but because most of the Third World poor live in the rural areas there appears to be a measure of urban bias. The discrimination is not against the rural areas, but against the poor of those areas. It is normal for the larger, commercial farmers to prosper even in areas such as Asia, where the evidence suggests that conditions for large numbers of the rural poor are deteriorating (Friedmann and Douglass, 1976; Griffin and Khan, 1978). Here lies the paradox of the green revolution; increasing agricultural production allied with increasing poverty. Those who have resources such as land and water increase their production while those who lack resources suffer as a consequence of the changes occurring about them (falling prices due to increased agricultural production by the big producers, higher fertilizer costs, rising costs of land, increasing mechanization, reduced access to water, etc.). But it is also important to remember that the urban poor are not well treated in most Third World countries. Low incomes, under-employment, and poor housing, infrastructure, and services are the lot of millions of families. If they generally fare better than their poor rural cousins, it is by little compared to the neglect they suffer compared to their richer urban neighbours.

As a consequence of these processes it may well be true that there is a net transfer of resources to urban areas.[2] Indeed, it would be most surprising in a rapidly urbanizing world if that were not the case. But are the evils of Third World countries due to the speed of urban growth, or is urban growth a symptom of other processes? In any case is the transfer of resources to urban areas at the expense of rural areas always undesirable? If higher productivity and greater welfare can be achieved in urban areas through a relative concentration of resources is that not development? Should such a situation be described as urban bias? It is surely better, and surely follows Lipton's meaning more closely, to apply the term only when an excessive allocation of resources to the urban areas reduces economic growth and distorts the distribution of income. Thus, if agriculture is neglected because funds are being invested in urban areas fuelling land speculation, government bureaucracy and the import of luxury consumption goods, we might conclude legitimately that urban bias is the problem. Unfortunately, while such a situation may appear to obtain in many Third World nations, it is not easy to measure accurately. Obviously cost-benefit analysis and other forms of economic appraisal can approximate the returns on urban versus rural investment, but great care needs to be taken given the artificiality of prices and foreign exchange rates in so many Third World countries.

But even if we can measure the degree of urban bias by noting that funds are being directed into urban investment at rates of return far lower than those available in rural projects, even if we can show that urban programmes are less equitable than rural programmes, the fundamental issue comes down not to the desirability of urban versus rural development but to the power to interpret that desirability. In short, who makes the decisions, who holds power, and how do they use that power? Even if we agree with Lipton that rural areas should receive higher priority in decision-making, how can that change be achieved? And if it is achieved, would the outcome be an improvement? If the Chinese have improved welfare through an anti-urban development path, have the Kampucheans? Brazilians poured money into the Amazon region, but did they improve welfare? Merely posing these issues demonstrates that urban bias is not unlike the jabberwocky. As Alice said, 'it seems very pretty but it's rather hard to understand!'

Closely linked to the idea of urban bias is the belief that rural development has been distorted by the pattern of urban growth. Specifically, it has been argued that there is an absence of towns at the base of the urban system in most Third World countries. As a result of a distorted development process, new central places are required to service the rural areas and to reinvigorate agricultural development. Johnson (1970) has noted that there is one central place for every sixteen villages in Europe compared with one for every 157 villages in the Middle East. This gap in the urban-size distribution lowers agricultural productivity because there is nowhere to sell the produce and no opportunities for buying consumer goods which might stimulate farmers to increase production. Johnson also sees the small city as a means of providing services for the rural areas. At one level, Johnson is clearly right. Distant market centres do make the selling of agricultural produce more difficult and encourage the emergence of exploitative middlemen. But, the creation of new centres is at best a partial remedy, for marketing difficulties and exploitative middlemen are endemic in most poor countries simply because of the absence of good transportation, storage facilities, and credit. The poor farmer can neither move his produce to the city nor store it until prices improve. Similarly, the development of new urban centres may provide health and education services, but cannot guarantee their use. More often than not the cost of health provision is a greater barrier to attendance at clinics than is distance; new urban centres would only be effective if services and drugs were free. In my opinion, it is likely that Johnson's gap in the urban system is less a cause than a consequence of lower agricultural productivity; central places fail to emerge because farmers have low purchasing power. While the establishment of new central places would no doubt be of some assistance, it is difficult to see it as the major plank of a development programme or to agree with Johnson's principal conclusion that 'the raising of average incomes in under-developed countries will require town-building programmes' (p. 177).

Such a programme can be supported only if it goes hand in hand with a more radical change in development policy. This is what Friedmann and Douglass (1976: 372) suggest in their argument for agropolitan development. In Asia the countryside should be transformed by 'introducing and adapting elements of urbanism to a specific rural setting. This means: instead of encouraging the drift of rural people to cities by investing in cities, encouraging them to remain where they are by investing in rural districts and to transmute existing settlements into a hybrid form we call agropolis or city in the fields.' The spatial planning component in this strategy is the agropolis, designed '. . . to have a total population of between 15,000 and 60,000' and to permit the desired mix of local production, democracy, and cultural integration. The agropolitan district is self-reliant, self-financing, and self-governing; its political autonomy is limited only by the 'concurrent needs of all other districts and the combined needs of the larger community of which they form part' (Friedmann and Weaver, 1979: 203). The ultimate aim of this strategy is to reduce severely the power of transnational corporations over local areas. Equal access to the bases of social power allows the local community to express a rightful territorial interest. 'The territorial interest, then, becomes in every case controlling over subordinate, including corporate, decisions' (p. 204). In these circumstances, the territorial interest is the equivalent to the local societal interest. I shall return to this radical suggestion on pp. 174–5.

Distortions in the Urban-regional System

If many observers believe that too many resources are devoted to urban areas to the detriment of the countryside, there is also no shortage of politicians and planners complaining of excessive spatial concentration within the urban-regional system. Indeed, the literature on regional development is full of statements about 'excessive' regional inequalities, 'over-developed' metropolises, 'over-centralized' population distributions and 'unbalanced' settlement systems. Sometimes these distortions are blamed upon the inefficient or the inequitable model of development being pursued in a particular country, sometimes they themselves are seen to be a source of distortions. Not infrequently, such arguments are emphasized through ugly physical analogies; most commonly, the 'neglected periphery' and the 'booming metropolis' are depicted in terms of a shrunken body with a swollen head. The swollen head has grown on the basis of resources that should have nourished the body. The head is variously described as over-large, the victim of an enormous influx of untutored rural migrants, the centre of crime, social deprivation, and inequalities. Similarly, the shrunken body is the subject of emotional diagnosis; provincial politicians complain about centralization and its draining effect on regional dynamism; local services are inadequate because national governments provide insufficient resources; employment opportunities are limited because most of the highly productive industry is concentrated in the major city; most skilled manpower leaves the provincial cities for the metropolis.

In certain countries there is some truth in this analogy, but in general it is an over-simplified picture of reality; like all analogies, it must be used carefully. In anatomy a misshapen body can be diagnosed easily by comparison with the size and shape of the average human body; there may be marginal cases, but on the whole the norm is so prevalent that the dwarf or the giant stand out. But in the realm of human settlement systems what is the norm? There is no typical urban system against which the swollen head and shrunken body can be so easily compared. If there is no norm, then can we be sure that the exception is an exception? If there is no norm, can we be sure there is anything wrong with the presumed exception? The misshapen human body is exceptional because there are so many healthy bodies around with which to compare it; among human settlements it is probably more accurate to depict the misshapen as the norm. After all, more nations have primate cities than have non-primate centres, there are more countries with wide regional disparities than with equitable regional distributions of income. In short, we are comparing the urban system with an ideal; the body is misshapen only when compared to the ideal, but that ideal is not likely to be accepted by everyone with the same readiness. Few people agree on the best distribution of urban settlement; different ideologies and developmental goals lead to the recommendation of different ideal types. Equity and efficiency considerations may well indicate different urban forms, proponents of the free market are likely to recommend different urban distributions than socialists.

In addition to this normative problem the debates about human settlement systems frequently confuse a number of related but diagnostically distinct issues. Confusion over these issues often leads to policy recommendations that can do nothing to resolve more fundamental problems. Contributing to these confusions are the way we use the terms 'centralization' and 'urban primacy', the belief that there may be an optimum city size and the failure to distinguish between the welfare of places and the welfare of people. I wish to examine these confusions briefly before going on to discuss the circumstances in which it may be justifiable to speak of distortions in the national settlement system.

Centralization is a much abused term. The essential problem is that it is used interchangeably both in a functional and in a geographical sense. Thus the centralization of power may mean that the president of the country makes all major decisions and laws in the country; power is centralized hierarchically in a functional sense. But the same term may be used to describe the power the capital city exerts over the rest of the country; all the main foci of power are located within that city. Clearly, the two senses of the phrase are related. If the all-powerful president favours the capital city at the expense of the rest of the nation, centralization is an appropriate term. But, power may be centralized in the hands of a president whose decisions may lead to some measure of geographical decentralization. This distinction is particularly important, given that the term 'centralization' is frequently applied to variables other than power; it is used also to describe the location of industry or population or government revenues. In such cases centralization of one variable may be linked weakly to another. Thus the Venezuelan State is highly centralized because three-quarters of ordinary government revenues come from oil controlled by the central government; but the production of petroleum is certainly not centralized; production occurs in two major regions located far from the national capital; Caracas has no oil. In the USSR power is strongly centralized but policies have for long attempted to disperse population and economic activity more equally across the country.

In this chapter I shall use the terms *spatial concentration* or *spatial dispersal/ deconcentration* to describe the geographical distribution of any variable, whether it be government revenues, power, industry, or population (Fig. 8.1). The concentration of power in the hands of a central government (as opposed to second-tier (regional) or third-tier (municipal) governments) or in the hands of a president (rather than the legislature or the people) will be described as *functional centralization*. Only when the two phenomena occur together do we employ the term *centralization*. This terminology will prevent us falling into traps such as that of describing as decentralization the establishment of branch industries in the periphery (spatial deconcentration) when power clearly remains in the head offices of the capital city.

The meaning and the implications of the term 'urban primacy' are also much abused. As I observed in chapter 2, the issue of urban size should be distinguished from that of a distortion of the national city size distribution. For while very large primate cities exist (Mexico City, Buenos Aires, and Bangkok), some primate cities are very small (Lomé, Asunción, Kathmandu, and Banjul) and certain large cities are not at all primate (São Paulo, Bogotá, and Calcutta). If we fail to distinguish between the size of the city and its position in the national city-size distribution we shall confuse discussion of different kinds of problem. Thus it is pointless to complain of urban diseconomies in Kathmandu or Lomé when neither city has more than 200,000 people. If the problem is that the city has grown larger than others in the nation because it has received most governmental revenues or controlled the benefits of foreign trade, we need to separate that problem from the issue of urban diseconomies.

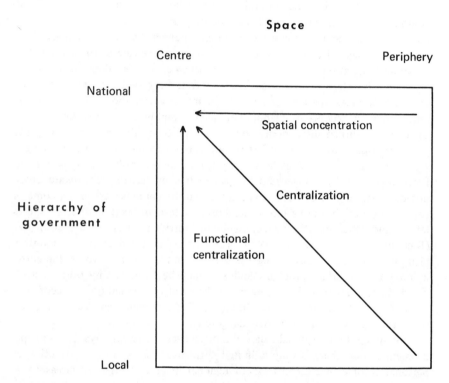

Space

Centre   Periphery

National

Spatial concentration

Centralization

Hierarchy of
government

Functional
centralization

Local

8.1. Forms of the centralization of power

The issue of an imbalance in the urban-size distribution raises a major problem which was alluded to earlier. To measure an imbalance we need to have a norm. But what is the norm against which to measure primacy when, as chapter 2 demonstrated, most nations have primate city distributions? Is the city-size distribution 'primate' when the largest city is three times or when it is twenty times the size of the second city? Should we measure primacy in economic and social terms or only in demographic terms?[3] The difficulty is that we lack an adequate general indicator of urban imbalance.[4] As a consequence, the desirable balance between cities remains in the minds of the politician, planner, or academic;

value judgements and political commitments are as important in the recommendation of spatial deconcentration and decentralization as technical criteria. Indeed, as I shall argue below, where major changes have occurred in the national settlement system, they have been normally the result of major changes in the political and developmental model.

Similar difficulties relate to the idea that major cities have become too large, or even that they have exceeded the maximum population at which all cities become inefficient and/or inequitable. Such a judgement normally rests on the assumption that urban diseconomies – for example, pollution or traffic congestion – have become so severe that the only answer is to deconcentrate both population and economic activity. Such an argument has several failings. First, it does not recognize that diseconomies are only one side of the argument; if urban agglomerations generate still greater urban economies, then the balance of economic advantage rests with spatial concentration. Second, even if diseconomies exceed economies, the best policy may be to reorganize the way the city is run rather than to deconcentrate population and employment. Thus the best way to reduce an urban diseconomy such as traffic congestion may be to improve public transport, to cut the use of private cars, or to introduce parking meters. Air pollution can be reduced by the physical removal of polluting industries, but it can also be cut by fining errant companies. In short, urban problems are caused not only by size; more often than not urban diseconomies are an outcome of the rate of growth, the pattern of land use, the level of taxation or urban speculation, and other specific characteristics of individual cities rather than of size (Richardson, 1977; Townroe, 1979). Like the reputed finding that the monthly birthrate in Sweden rises during the seasonal in-migration of storks, the correlation between urban problems and size may be explained by other factors. Third, it assumes that the geographical dispersal of population and economic activity is both possible and without negative consequences. As pp. 176–81 show, such assumptions may prove dangerous.

Finally, the term 'regional balance' is often used in suspect ways. The principal problem is that there is only a limited correlation between the distribution of personal income and the pattern of regional income. Thus it is unreasonable to argue that a spatial deconcentration programme will automatically improve the distribution of personal income. Although equality of personal income guarantees regional income equality, the converse does not hold. Acute personal income inequality is consistent with total regional equality when the distributions of personal income and average per capita incomes are the same in every region but wide intraregional and interpersonal differences exist. Despite frequent exhortations to the contrary, observers frequently fail to distinguish between 'place' welfare and 'people' welfare. A region may be rich without its inhabitants participating equally in that wealth, another region may be poor but contain rich people. These points are easily illustrated by consideration of the case of India. In India measures of interregional disparity compare favourably with distributions in other nations, even though differences between urban and rural areas within regions and between income groups in those regions are very wide (Majmudar, 1977; Mathur, 1976).

Failure to distinguish between place and personal welfare encourages the adoption of regional programmes favouring particular regional groups. It also allows such a programme to pass as a measure to achieve greater equity rather than as a further source of interpersonal disparity. The convergence in regional incomes which occurred in the 1960s in Brazil, largely as a result of regional policies, failed to improve the situation of poorer groups in the poorest part of the country (Gilbert and Goodman, 1976). The upper-income groups in the north-east merely improved their position in comparison with the more prosperous groups in the richer south-east; an increase in regional prosperity brought an increase in personal welfare for some, but not for others. The term 'regional disparities' is dangerous if not supplemented by other measures of welfare for different income groups.

Having pointed out some of the principal errors that have appeared in discussions about national settlement systems and about regional income disparities, I wish to consider some of the more serious arguments put forward in support of, and contrary to, particular kinds of spatial policy. Such arguments may be broadly categorized into those recommending (i) some kind of employment deconcentration programme; (ii) continued but better planned metropolitan eXpansion; (iii) neglect of the spatial problematic in favour of other kinds of policy change.

(i) *Employment deconcentration*   Employment deconcentration from the major cities is the most common spatial policy. It may take the form of discouraging new economic activities from being located in the largest centres either through negative controls or through incentives to location in other parts of the country, it may seek to relocate existing economic activities to smaller cities, it may deconcentrate government activity, it may stimulate the expansion of smaller cities, it may even involve the construction of new cities. What all these approaches have in common is the general wish to control the growth of the largest cities, usually located in the most prosperous regions, and to stimulate the expansion of urban centres in peripheral areas. The transfer of economic activities from rich regions to poor is seen to serve several functions; it reduces the problems of the centre; it reactivates the provincial cities; it reduces regional disparity; and it helps lower-income groups in the provinces. Spatial deconcentration is seen to benefit both national and regional interests and is compatible with national economic growth.

Such economic deconcentration strategies often take the form of a 'growth centre' policy; a concept which holds a venerable place in the regional development literature (Friedmann, 1966; Darwent, 1969; Kuklinski, 1972; Moseley, 1975). At its simplest, the growth-centre notion conceives of an urban complex containing a series of industrial enterprises focused on a dynamic growth industry.

The growth industry stimulates the emergence of ancillary companies whose presence lowers its own operation costs. Specialized services and a skilled labour force emerge which help to maintain inter-regional competitiveness and generate new activities. As an agent of regional development, the growth centre serves a double function. It prevents the dissipation of agglomeration economies while achieving a more equitable distribution of economic activity: in Rodwin's (1961) words it permits 'concentrated decentralization'. In addition, it provides a focus for the development of the centre's hinterland. Industries that consume agricultural products will create a market for the region's farmers, as will the growing concentration of urban inhabitants. And in a traditional or conservative region the growth centre will perform an innovative role; it will encourage the spread of new ideas, techniques, machines, and products (Berry, 1972).

   The more intelligent regional analysts always accepted that the effects of a 'growth centre' strategy would be limited. Such an approach might reduce income inequalities and lighten the deepest pockets of poverty, but it would not remove them. Premissed on the assumption that, rightly or wrongly, industrialization was the archetypal national development policy, it was an incrementalist strategy which promised to improve the regional distribution of activity by raising urban efficiency and thereby increasing the opportunities for improving social services, employment, and productivity. It was also an opportunistic strategy in the sense that the less developed countries had scarcely begun the transformations required by the development process (Friedmann, 1966). As Lewis (1962: 183) said of India, 'so much of the total locational outcome is yet to be settled that the question at issue virtually comes down to this: what will the territorial disposition of demand be in the Indian economy of 1970 and 1980?' Decisions about the future distribution of demand might recommend a policy of regional development and the stimulation of growth centres.

   This argument has been strongly attacked by Friedmann and Weaver (1979: 187), who have blamed the growth centre for accentuating unequal and inequitable patterns of development in less developed countries. 'With the growth centre doctrine as its principal tool, spatial development planning became the handmaiden of transnational capital.' The espousal of polarized development in the growth-centre doctrine allowed transnational corporations to dominate Third World nations. In the sense that the growth-centre notion is closely linked to the idea of industrialization and urban growth, this is a correct interpretation. But it is too simple to claim that there is any close convergence of interests between the practice of growth-centre planning and the interests of transnational corporations. For example, growth-centre planning may be compatible with industrial development but experience shows that transnational corporations are less than keen to be decentralized from national capitals to growth centres in the periphery. Similarly, if growth centres are so well attuned to the ideology of transnational corporations, why do so many communist and socialist countries employ the same regional planning terminology and practice? Regional development in the USSR and Poland clearly differs in important respects from that in capitalist economies; nevertheless it is still clearly based on growth-centre strategy.[5] In the Third World Tanzania has clearly embraced the growth-centre strategy as a means of achieving greater regional balance and reducing urban bias. Given such examples, is the form of regional development in most Third World countries a consequence of the belief in growth centres or the nature of the society in which those centres are introduced? To my mind, the trouble with the growth-centre strategy is not its underlying ideology but rather the blandness of the notion. Indeed, as I have argued elsewhere, the idea is so flaccid that Marxist and right-wing regimes use the tool with equal facility (Gilbert, 1970).

The learned literature has described as 'growth centres' everything from villages of 5,000 people to the world's largest metropolis. Industrial areas, administrative centres, university cities, and sleepy market towns have all been labelled growth centres. As a result, the growth centre has been used as the intellectual rationale of every spatial strategy from Dodoma to the continued growth of Mexico City.[6] It has been used in one form or another in Tanzania, Brazil, Poland, Chile, China, and India. Its blandness has allowed it to be the handmaiden of whatever regime found it useful. It is not the regional approach that is the villian, but the development model which limits and dictates that manner of its use.

The problem with most growth-centre strategies is that they fail to perform the multiple functions with which they were entrusted. They failed normally because such aims were too ambitious given the resources made available or because the spatial strategy was not supported by complementary sectoral policies. The blandness of the growth-centre notion has encouraged its rhetorical use in the least felicitous circumstances. But despite its inherent weaknesses and the consequent dangers, the growth-centre strategy should not be totally discarded. There are countries (Mexico and Venezuela perhaps) in which it is advisable to deconcentrate activities from major cities because topography, deficiencies in water supply, or pollution problems make continued expansion of the major cities undesirable; there are nations whose resources in poor or resource-rich areas may be best developed through some kind of urban-industrial programme; there are countries in which decentralization and employment deconcentration may be encouraged through a growth-centre strategy. Certainly no general case for employment deconcentration in Third World countries can be made, but as a limited contribution to certain kinds of economic, social, and political problems, it can sometimes be recommended. If the growth centre has been grossly misused by planners and politicians, it does not follow that the approach is useless. Where employment deconcentration and regional development based on industrial and urban expansion are to be recommended, the growth-centre approach may be appropriate. Most approaches have their uses if responsibly applied and if backed with adequate resources.

(ii) *More efficient and equitable metropolitan expansion*   If a case can be made that employment deconcentration has its uses, there can be little doubt that the need for such a strategy has been frequently exaggerated in many countries. Some of the more simplistic arguments have already been dismissed but in addition an argument that has gradually regained strength during the last few years is that policies to restructure the national settlement system are unnecessary. This argument is supported on the basis of three kinds of evidence, first, that regional polarization is a natural process in the path of national development and early state intervention will slow the pace of economic expansion; second, that metropolitan cities are rarely as inefficient or as inequitable as is often claimed, and, third, that solution of metropolitan problems is achieved more effectively through improved metropolitan planning than through employment deconcentration.

The argument that regional polarization is a natural corollary of the early stages of economic expansion finds intellectual and empirical support in the work of Kuznets (1966) and Williamson (1965). Both used historical data for developed countries and cross-section analysis to support the proposition that there is a long-term trend towards the equalization of personal (Kuznets) and regional (Williamson) incomes. Williamson found that in the ten countries for which temporal data were available, regional income disparities first increased and then declined as a more mature economic system evolved. More recently, Richardson (1977) has noted strong signs of what he has called 'polarization reversal' in the urban system; in South Korea, Brazil, and Colombia population and economic activity may have begun to deconcentrate spontaneously.[7]

The implication of these findings is that government intervention and deconcentration is unnecessary because regional balance will occur naturally. Some economists have taken this point further to argue that government intervention in the distribution of economic activity is likely to waste scarce capital resources and thereby slow the rate of national economic growth. Thus in the longer term the country will be less able to redistribute income and remedy the problems of poverty. Regional balance and urban deconcentration should be left until a nation has achieved a higher level of development. The argument has been well put by a strong advocate of regional *laissez-faire* (Mera, 1976: 271): 'There is a fundamental conflict between high economic growth and decentralization of population. If a high rate of economic growth is to be achieved, further concentration of population into a few large metropolitan areas cannot be avoided.'

This view is supported by the finding that large cities are often more efficient and innovative than other urban centres. 'In brief, there is no basis for the belief that primacy or over-urbanization *per se* is detrimental to the efficiency goal of economic development. There are good grounds for believing in increasing returns to urban size' (Alonso, 1969: 4). Several writers have sought to demonstrate that there is no 'optimum' size of city beyond which further growth is undesirable and that, in general, large cities are more efficient and even more equitable than smaller urban centres. This argument is based upon evidence from Brazil, India, Sweden, and the United States which shows that industrial productivity is highest in the largest cities even when allowance is made for differences in capital per worker and size of enterprise (Richardson, 1973; Rocca, 1970); upon information from Japan, West Germany, Mexico, and the Soviet Union which shows that households are much better off in metropolitan areas; even when due allowance is made for higher living costs and for intervening variables such as age, colour, sex, and education (Hoch, 1972); on data which show that the per capita costs of social overhead capital tend to fall with increasing city size, or at least fail to rise (Richardson, 1973); and upon data from the United States which point to greater equality of incomes in metropolitan areas than elsewhere (Richardson, 1973). The sum of this evidence supports the view that urban economies exceed urban diseconomies even in today's largest cities and that there is no prima-facie case in favour of deconcentration.

Several writers go further and argue that even where there are signs of urban diseconomies, spatial deconcentration is not the answer; the fact that urban diseconomies such as crime, pollution, or traffic congestion tend to rise with city size can normally be explained by intervening variables (Alonso, 1971: 6; Richardson, 1973: 3). The fact that crime rates are so high in New York says more about the organization of, and the society in, that city than it does about urban centres of 10 million people. The most appropriate solution to such diseconomies, they believe, is to improve the organization and administration of the city, not deconcentration. Crime is better handled by a more efficient police force than by deconcentration; traffic congestion better controlled by higher car taxes or by parking meters than by migration control. The implicit policy recommendation stemming from these arguments is that the growth of large cities should rarely be discouraged.

Such a recommendation is not uncontroversial and the evidence on which it is based has been criticized on numerous grounds.

First, the tendency for regional income levels to converge is much weaker in contemporary less developed countries than it was in the now developed nations. As Gilbert and Goodman (1976: 119–22) have argued, convergence is likely to be weak because: today's poor countries may never reach the levels of per capita income at which regional convergence begins; regional disparities in less developed countries today are much greater than those characteristic of developed countries in the past; and convergence depends on effective government intervention and many governments show little sign of interest or ability to remedy regional inequalities. They conclude 'There is no reason to assume that the processes which have led to convergence in the United States and other developed countries will function automatically and effectively in the less developed nations.' If the process of development is different in the less developed countries, then the pattern shown by cross-section studies is an unreliable guide to likely tendencies in the spatial distribution of resources and wealth.

Second, the efficiency of the larger cities has recently been called into question

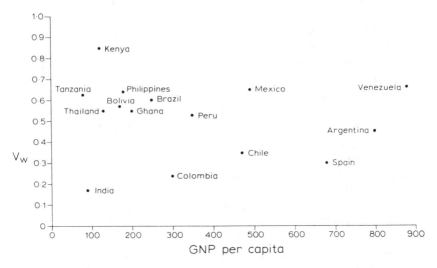

8.2. Levels of regional income disparity in Third World nations

(Johnston, 1976; Borukhov, 1975; Ternent, 1976). Gilbert (1976) argues that evidence of higher productivity in the largest cities should not be attributed only to agglomeration economies, for such 'economies' may derive from better urban infrastructure or higher-quality labour. In the latter case, it may be argued that higher productivity in the largest cities is to some degree achieved at the cost of lower productivity in smaller cities; if equivalent infrastructure or labour were available in medium-sized centres then the productivity of those centres might well rise. In addition, high productivity among private firms in large cities may be apparent because private companies are often subsidized indirectly by the state. If firms had to bear the full externality costs they impose, the higher productivity of large cities might well be less pronounced. If the firms were forced to pay some share of the diseconomies they create they might find the large city less attractive and many would transfer the higher productivity enterprises to intermediate cities. This process would reduce the apparent differential in industrial productivity between the smaller and the larger cities.

The higher productivity of the larger cities may also be peculiar to developed countries. While some data for Brazil support the large city case (Rocca, 1970), other evidence for Brazil (Boisier, 1973) and for Colombia (Ternent, 1976) suggests that productivity is higher outside the major cities. At the present time, however, there is just too little evidence to draw any reasonable conclusion; most of the work on urban economies and diseconomies has been carried out in developed countries. While Richardson (1976) contends that large cities are likely to prove relatively still more efficient in Third World countries than in the developed, the case remains to be proven.

Doubt has also been cast on the argument that diseconomies in large cities are caused by intervening variables, viz. 'all large cities are locations for social problems, but not necessarily the same set of social problems, and their incidence in the big cities is higher merely because cities as a focus of civilization mirror society at large, perhaps in a magnified form' (Richardson, 1973: 3). While this is correct, it is clear that major cities not only draw attention to societal problems but frequently accentuate them. Crime rates rise in large cities not only because of the more obvious concentrations of poor and wealthy, but also because it is more difficult to catch criminals. Traffic congestion is greater in metropolitan cities not only because there are more cars per capita, but also because transport problems are more complex. Solutions to such problems need to be larger, more expensive, and more radical than the solutions required in small cities. The solutions, however, may be very difficult to apply in most Third World metropolises.

Even if urban economies outweigh the diseconomies in large cities in less developed countries, are the overall benefits equitably distributed? It can be argued that urban diseconomies most affect the lower-income groups, who are least able to escape them. Middle- and upper-income groups have the resources and knowledge to change their residential areas, command better public services, and influence political decisions, whereas the poor do not. Industrial zones are designated to keep pollution and lorries out of the high-income areas. The worst consequences of traffic congestion are inflicted on the middle- and lower-income groups living between the city centre and the more affluent housing areas. Urban renewal schemes rarely displace the rich but often dislocate low-income communities with inadequate consideration for the problems of the poor (Batley, forthcoming). Similarly, distribution of the benefits in metropolitan areas rarely favours the poor. In most cities there is a clear demarcation line between the high-income and the low-income areas. Public roads, telephone, water, and electricity services in the high income areas are superior, and where the public sector cannot provide adequate services, as in health and education, wealthy groups can resort to the private sector. The operation of the land and housing markets guarantee that the wealthy gain most from uncontrolled speculation.

Finally, it is obvious that the worst consequences of metropolitan expansion can be avoided by better urban planning. Critics and advocates of continued metropolitan expansion can agree that better planning is necessary. Nevertheless, it is by no means certain that better planning is possible. All around the less developed world urban plans abound with little sign of effective implementation. Shibli (1974: 115) states that 'since 1947, the Karachi metropolitan area has not been planned systematically. The government did make an effort to prepare a plan, but did not provide the institutional, legal, and financial tools for the plan to be implemented.' In Jamaica 'as in so many countries, the ability to plan exceeds the administrative ability to deliver on announced proposals' (Trowbridge, 1973: 20). Summarizing a study of thirteen nations, the Ford Foundation's International Urbanization Survey (1972: 21) notes that 'urban management in the developing countries is an ad hoc adaptation to circumstances always in danger of failure to adapt quickly enough to meet the pressure of those same circumstances.'

It can be argued that the absence of effective and equitable metropolitan planning is due to the fact that local politics are manipulated by important interest groups. Any attempt to raise taxes is immediately crushed, changes in zoning are made illicitly with the aid of bribes, major construction programmes are launched to cure problems that could be resolved in much cheaper ways. A glance at the attempts to give governments greater control over their urban areas supports the idea that real-estate interests are a powerful political lobby; such interests prosper because of the rising land values which bring chaos to other groups in the metropolitan areas. Effective planning is dependent on the political power balance and that balance has seldom favoured either equitable or even efficient metropolitan planning. The result of this situation, in the view of the Ford Foundation, is that 'as of 1972, the world has coped with its urban problems in its usual muddle-through way, and the cities are not as intolerable – nor ungovernable – as it is fashionable to say .... We do think, however, that the worst is yet to come' (p. 31).

Even if major differences exist about the desirability of spatial deconcentration and the possibility of good metropolitan planning, most writers agree on certain issues. First, the concept of an optimum size of city is redundant. Since city organization is at least as critical as size, and the nature of metropolitan economies varies considerably across the globe, no single size of city can be optimal. If a case is to be made in favour of deconcentration it has to be on the basis that certain goals can be achieved more cheaply, efficiently, or equitably in a more deconcentrated settlement system. Second, whether or not deconcentration is favoured, more effective and fairer urban planning is a necessity in the large cities because there is no sign even in China or Cuba that metropolitan growth can be stemmed for very long. Such planning requires the implementation of policies unpopular with certain influential urban groups; a slowing in the growth of car ownership or at least severe constraints on car use within urban areas, the development of cheap forms of public transport, controls on pollution, and the introduction of effective land-use policies and land taxes. Urban politicians and vested-interest groups have to accept the modifications in the way large cities operate. Planning needs to be more effective both to maintain economic efficiency and to help the urban poor. Better planning is a necessity, not an unnecessary adornment to urban administration.

Third, each city requires different kinds of reforms. Some large cities have special problems which increase urban diseconomies; Caracas is located in a narrow valley and its region lacks water; Mexico City suffers from subsidence of the centre, from water shortages, and from atmospheric conditions which exacerbate air pollution. Where it is more difficult to avoid urban diseconomies deconcentration may be a strong contender for political consideration on efficiency grounds alone. In other cases it may be quite unnecessary and may dissipate developmental potential.

Fourth, more should be done to compensate the sufferers of noise, pollution, and congestion. If large cities do indeed generate vital urban economies, companies will remain even if they are forced to pay the costs they impose on other city dwellers. Should firms decide to move because of the increased charges, then some of the arguments for decentralization will have been demonstrated to practical effect.

(iii) *The irrelevance of the spatial problematic* There is a body of thought to which I shall return, which argues that deconcentration is irrelevant to the problems of society. Such an argument is implicit in some of the work just reviewed. Many economists clearly believe that the main focus of development efforts should not be distorted by the unnecessary expenditure of time and effort on urban deconcentration. This argument was especially persuasive in the 1950s. More recently, however, an echo of this argument has been taken up by the Left. Rather than serving to remedy some of the faults of society, urban deconcentration and regional development policies serve to mystify the issue of what is really wrong with society. As Geisse and Coraggio (1972: 58) put it 'the centralization − decentralization [*sic*] dichotomy tends to distract attention from the really important problem in Latin America. That is the necessity of permitting vigorous social restructuring and participation of all members of society in the benefits of economic growth, controlled and propelled by endogenous forces.' In similar vein, Singer (1975: 436) accuses those who wish to slow large city growth as attacking 'the consequences rather than the contradictions of capitalist development. Such misplaced criticism recommends solutions such as the control of urbanization, control of population, industrialization with less advanced (intermediate) techniques − [which] are utopian and tend to divert attention from the real problems of development.'

Moreover, treatment of the regional problem can make the social situation worse and actually create greater inequalities between social groups. Thus Geisse and Coraggio (1972: 46) point to the fact that in some Latin American countries the difference in income between social groups in the metropolitan areas are as great as the differences between regions. In addition, since more poor people live in metropolitan areas in Argentina, Chile, or Uruguay than in the peripheral regions of those countries and are more socially aware than their provincial counterparts, dispersal policies are as likely to magnify as to reduce personal income disparities. While the argument has much greater force in the southern cone of Latin America than in most other Third World countries, the point is well taken. Regional dispersal policies can serve either to reduce personal income inequality or to increase it.

The Practice of Spatial Deconcentration

If we take the number of deconcentration and regional development programmes as our criterion, there can be little doubt of the popularity of spatial planning in the Third World. During the 1960s and 1970s different froms of spatial planning swept Africa, Asia, and Latin America (Stöhr, 1975; Utria, 1972; UNCRD, 1976; UNRISD, 1971; Funnell, 1976). Such policies ranged widely in both form and effectiveness, but may be divided into three general categories: (1) polices that aimed at transforming the rural economy and thereby slowing the rate of urban expansion; (2) policies that aimed at limiting the growth of large cities through the control of migration; and (3) policies that tried to slow the growth of the largest cities by stimulating the growth of intermediate cities or by establishing new urban centres. Sometimes, of course, the three kinds of policy were used together.

Transforming the Rural Economy

Any policy that transforms the rural economy affects the pace and form of urban development. Policies such as the redistribution of land to the poor may reduce urban/rural income disparities and slow urban growth by raising agricultural incomes. Other rural programmes, of course, may have the opposite effect; the green revolution and other efforts to raise agricultural productivity through incentives to commercial agriculture have accentuated landlessness and probably stimulated, rather than reduced, the flow of city bound migrants (Griffin and Ghose, 1979; Griffin and Khan, 1978; Kalmanovitz, 1977). Because of the variety of rural policies and their divergent effects I shall concentrate here on two major countries which have adopted very different approaches. The two sets of programmes, in Brazil and China, are interesting because of their scale and because they employ different technologies, favour different social groups, and follow economic and social models at opposite ends of the political spectrum. Brazilian efforts to colonize the Amazon have embraced the capitalist ethic and used the transnational corporation as the main agent of change. The Chinese have used rural development to accelerate the introduction of socialism in an already populated countryside. The comparison is not intended to demonstrate the superiority of one mode of production over another, indeed such a comparison would be futile given the dangers of generalizing about two such vast and very different nations. What the comparison does demonstrate, however, is that regional development programmes cannot be separated from national development models. The programmes form an integral part of the process of national change and can be understood only in those terms. What the experiences also show is that the achievement of any regional goal is dependent on the resources and support given the programme. Whatever the differences between China and Brazil in their regional approaches, both have channelled resources into certain non-urban areas.

The Brazilian frontier programme has gone through several phases and variations.[8] It has included, under the broadest definition, the building of Brasília, the construction of 10,000 miles of roads including the Belém–Brasília highway and the *Transamazónica*, the setting up of regional agencies for this vast area, and the encouragement through huge tax incentives of private investment in the region. The programme has been effective in opening up a huge area for development; directly or indirectly, it has encouraged the migration of several million people into the states of Goîas, Mato Grosso, Pará, and Amazonas; large deposits of newly discovered minerals are now being extracted; huge timber and cattle ranches have been established; Manaus has been turned into a booming free-trade zone through tax reductions (Katzman, 1977; Kleinpenning, 1978; Brazil, 1976). As an example to the world of the speed with which a committed government in alliance with big business can act, there can be no doubt that the Brazilian experience has been impressive.

On the other hand, major questions must be asked about the success of the Brazilian exercise in terms of its effects on the poor, on the indigenous population, and on the environment. Major queries also can be posed about the benefits that the programme will produce for the majority of Brazilians. At one stage, between 1970 and 1974, a major aim of the Amazon programme was the resettlement of poor families from the north-east. The drought of 1970 had convinced the military government of the need to encourage familes without land in the arid parts of the north-east to move west to open up the land along the sides of the new roads. In the absence of land reform in the north-east, land colonization was seen as the best possibility for alleviating the poverty of so many *nordestinos.* Unfortunately, the chance offered the poor was very much against the odds; the settlers received little advice or credit and were provided with insufficient infrastructural support to develop their land. By mid-1975 only a few thousand had been settled compared to the planned 100,000 (Katzman, 1977: 81). Apart from the construction of the roads, too little was spent on the Amazon programme. Having failed to take their 'chance', the small settlers were deemed to have little future in the region and emphasis shifted to the large company as colonizer. These companies were offered the chance of reducing their income-tax liabilities by an amount equal to the sum they invested in the Amazon region, up to half of their total tax bill. In addition, tax exemptions or deductions and the waiving of import duties on equipment were granted. These incentives led to the creation of vast cattle ranches, huge timber projects, and the opening of major mining areas. The Amazon programme had always contained a resource-development objective, but now it was dominant. The opening of the Amazon was now to help to resuscitate the slowing Brazilian economic miracle; the poor of the north-east, and indeed the indigenous Amazon population, were conveniently forgotten. If the Brazilian miracle was more notable for its economic growth rate than its ability to redistribute income, then the Amazon programme became part of that miracle.[9] If agriculture and mining have boomed, it has been to the benefit of a few large companies and at the cost of further increasing Brazil's huge mortgage with the world's bankers: Brazil's per capita foreign debt is one of the highest in the world and in 1980 the country was expected to borrow

16 billion dollars (*Guardian*, 22 May 1980). In spatial terms, the programme has led to the partial settlement of the area but is has not markedly slowed the growth of Brazil's major cities. São Paulo and Rio de Janeiro have continued to expand rapidly, stimulated in part by the profits from the Amazon being reinvested in commercial and construction activities. As a spatial deconcentration policy it has been only a partial success. As to the environmental effects, comments vary from the critical to the cataclysmic; Goodland and Irwin (1975) and Davis (1977) have pointed out that once cleared, the Amazon forest rapidly suffers from soil erosion and leaching. Calder (1974) has even argued that continued clearance of the *selva* will change the world's climate, raising the temperature of the globe with dire consequences. Similarly critical have been the comments on the treatment afforded to the Brazilian Indians who have been issued the command 'integrate or perish'. Spectacular the Amazon programme may well be, but it demonstrates most of the faults of uncontrolled capitalist development; it generates economic growth, without improving the extreme maldistribution of wealth and income. As a spatial programme it clearly demonstrates the paramount importance of the style of national development on the formulation of subsidiary policies.

The last point can be drawn equally from the Chinese experience. The anti-urban, pro-rural policies adopted since 1949 say more about Chinese socialism than about rural development or spatial policies *per se*. The range of policies that have been adopted have not just focused on locational elements, but have sought to modify the nature of the whole economic and social system. Whatever the effect of explicit spatial policies, implicit spatial policies would have had a dramatic effect. The combination of birth control, the redistribution of land from private landlords to the peasantry, state ownership of most economic activities, and limits on improving urban living conditions would have had a favourable effect on the rural population even without explicit spatial policies. The Chinese experience is undoubtedly interesting as an example of a spatial policy, but it would be absurd to classify it as the outcome of only such a policy.

It would also be erroneous to overemphasize the rural dimension. Clearly, the distinguishing features of the Chinese experience have been the attempts to control the growth of cities, to increase self-reliance in the countryside, and to open up the western part of the country through resource development. But the Chinese have not closed the cities or neglected the urban economic base; there has been a programme of rural industrialization but industry has continued to locate in major cities or in nearby satellite towns. The populations of the cities have been controlled, but even Shanghai has not lost population (Thompson, 1979: 301). Many new cities have been established in the metropolitan regions and in the newly developed resource areas (Murphey, 1976: 324).

Anti-urban bias has been manifest in numerous ways. First, real industrial wages have been kept stable and, as a result, the terms of trade have moved in favour of agriculture and against industry (Lardy, 1978: 178). Even given my earlier reservation about the Indian terms of trade, this represents a major exception to the pattern in most Third World countries. Second, the Chinese have attempted to increase economic self-sufficiency among their rural communes. As far as possible communes have been encouraged to set up industrial plants to produce for their own needs – a deliberate attempt to limit the geographical areas of the markets of urban industries. Regions are encouraged to develop their own resources so as to reduce transport flows and to commit local people to the drive for national development. The mobilization of resources that would otherwise be wasted is one of the most interesting elements in the Chinese experience. Third, the Chinese have tried to change cultural values in favour of the rural areas. Urban bureaucrats and youths have been 'sent down' to the countryside either for short- or long-term stays. Controls have restricted the movement of people to the urban areas.

The outcome of these policies has been impressive in many respects. Perhaps the most notable achievement has been that all members of Chinese society have received an adequate minimum income protecting them from malnutrition and guaranteeing access to basic essentials. If the standard of living in China remains low, there can be little comparison with the lot of the average Chinese before the revolution nor any doubt that the distribution of income is much more equitable. This, together with the elimination of starvation and exploitation, is the main achievement of China, which compares well against the experiences of any other Third World country. These achievements have led to many calls that the world should learn from China and such calls should be rightly heard. At the same time, there is a danger that whatever lessons China may offer other countries, implementation may be difficult (Green, 1978; Dore, 1978; Lardy, 1978). But before commenting further on transferability, it is sensible to detail some of the problems the Chinese have faced in their policies; there can be little doubt that some of the consequences of the Chinese experience have been both unexpected and unwanted.

China has not managed to eliminate inter-regional or rural–urban disparities. In 1957, the last date for which reliable figures for agricultural and industrial incomes can be calculated, the difference in the provincial incomes of Shanghai and Honan was of the order of eight times. At that time regional inequalities compared badly to most developed countries but were not atypical for most Third World countries (table 2.1). Lardy's (1978) estimates suggest, however, that there has been a consistent, if slow, convergence in regional income levels since 1957: a trend less than typical for most Third World countries (Gilbert and Goodman, 1976). Urban–rural disparities remain, even if they have been softened, and the levels of wages, consumption, and services continue to be much higher in the cities (Murphey, 1976: 327). This contrast, together with the 'indefinable glitter of urban life', has attracted migrants to the urban areas. Frolic (1976: 154) argues that despite totalitarian controls, 'planners simply have been unable to limit the population of their largest cities, or to effectively control population movement.' Both he and Murphey anticipate that urban–rural differences may widen and that in the future greater emphasis upon industrialization and modernization may weaken the current anti-urban stance. China continues to be a very rural nation but it may be at a stage where industrial and urban development will become more important. In such circumstances, Chinese cities 'will not be like other cities, and there will be less of a split between them and their rural surroundings than in most of the rest of the world, but they will not conform either to the perfect model which the Maoist ideal has created in men's minds' (Murphey, 1976: 328).

Nevertheless major changes have been made in the distributions of population and economic activity in China since ↘1949. The reorientation of the space economy has been motivated largely by the desire to reduce regional and personal income inequalities and to increase self sufficiency, but it should not be forgotten that the Chinese programmes, like those of the Brazilians, have also been influenced by geo-politics. The uneasy relationship with the Soviet Union has encouraged economic deconcentration and self-sufficiency for strategic reasons. Nor should it be forgotten that the policy of rural bias and deconcentration has not been entirely successful in economic terms. Lardy (1978) notes that the Chinese have accepted that people should come before per capita income growth but queries whether the same goals might not have been achieved more effectively through modified policies.

Finally, it is important to emphasize that while China has achieved a considerable level of economic deconcentration, political centralization remains strongly entrenched. China is a highly centralized nation; all policy initiatives come from the top down and local needs are regularly sacrificed to national priorities. What has been achieved in China is local self-sufficiency rather than local independence. The country is therefore some way from the ideal balance that Friedman and Weaver (1979) advocate between territorial and functional needs. Within China there is an incipient totalitarianism which could prove disastrous if the political machine should fall into the wrong hands (Morawetz, 1979).

China has adopted ambitious and highly innovative spatial policies as part of a unique social and economic experiment. For this reason it is rightly recommended as an example to other Third world nations where equity and self-sufficiency rank low in the order of national priorities. But it would be erroneous to portray the Chinese experience as an unconditional success or to suggest that the example can be easily transferred. Perhaps the most important lesson to be learned from China is that it is very much a special case due to its size, its history, and its revolution. Its recent experience is very different not only from other Third World countries but also from other Communist nations. As Frolic (1976) points out, it is not by chance that the urban policies of China and the Soviet Union differ so markedly; urban bias in the Soviet Union contrasting strongly with rural bias in China. If China's experience is relevant and useful to countries in other parts of the world, it would be wrong to ignore both the problems that it has faced and the difficulties that transferring the experience might bring.

Migration Control

Many city administrations in the Third World have felt the need to introduce policies to slow the rate of migration from the rural areas. Incapable of supplying the housing or infrastructure required to accommodate the growing population, they have frequently advocated the idea of influx control. In fact very few countries have introduced such a policy and in most places it has had limited success.

By far the best-known experiment in migration control has been in China. Beginning with the Great Leap Forward (1957–8) and accelerated during the Cultural Revolution (1966–8), millions of young and unemployed people were 'sent down' to the countryside for short or long stays (Murphey, 1976: 316). Since 1968 8 million young people have been exhorted to move to the rural areas both as a means of reducing pressure on the urban areas and as a means of lessening the cultural gap between urban and rural areas (Thompson, 1979: 305). While this policy has had an important effect upon urban growth, it has probably had less influence than the combination of improved rural conditions and the regular controls over migration available to the Chinese authorities. In a society where housing, work, and even food are allocated by the state, the movement of families can be easily controlled. Acquiring permission to travel in China has been likened to the process by which a soldier in a developed western country applies for a two-week pass. As a result, China has been one of the few countries in the world that has managed to slow the rate of urban expansion and even to reverse it.

In Kampuchea, of course, migration policy was still more drastic. Within hours of the arrival in Phnom Penh of a new government in April 1975, the city was being evacuated. By the end of the month the cities of Ream, Poipet, and Pailin had received similar treatment. Urban dwellers were simply directed to rural areas where they were to be absorbed. The rationale behind this policy was a mixture of the strategic and the Utopian. The fear of starvation in the refugee-swollen cities was clearly of importance, as was the possible threat of a counter revolution. But there was also a longer-term aim of increasing the self-reliance of the country, the wish to control the bourgeoisification of middle-class groups and the goal of increasing agricultural production (Shawcross, 1979). Whatever the objectives, however, it is difficult to find support for such a policy in Kampuchea or indeed anywhere else.

Outside the socialist world, the only nation in which controls on population movement have been effective has been the Republic of South Africa. Unless they have a job, Africans are not permitted to live in urban areas and even those with jobs have to work in the city for fifteen years before they are permitted to bring their families. The Republic's policy has long been one of permitting Africans residence in the cities only when their labour was required (Wilson, 1972). For an African the loss of his job means that he is forced to move to his respective 'Homeland' unless he manages to avoid the authorities. Clearly, there are many people who are living illegally in Soweto or Crossroads, but there can be little doubt that the policy has severely limited the movement of Black Africans to the city. However unfair the policy may be, it has limited the growth of the major cities: Johannesburg's African population, for example, increased annually by only 2 per cent between 1960 and 1970 (Fair and Davies, 1976: 155).

Elsewhere controls on population movement have been rather less effective. In Indonesia, the governor of Jakarta limited migration by decree in 1970. All rural–urban migrants were required to obtain six-month permits by depositing a sum equivalent to twice the cost of their bus fare home. If after six months a job had been obtained, the deposit was returned. In addition to this policy, attempts were made to limit employment in the so-called formal sector: the number of tricycle taxis in the city was severely limited, an activity which employed a quarter of a million people in 1972 (Simmons, 1978: 15). The only real effects of this policy have been to make life for the poor much harder and to increase the possibility of corruption. It has done little to limit population expansion. Similarly, in Tanzania efforts to persuade the unemployed to leave Dar es Salaam and return to their rural homes met with little success.

In general, migration control does not recommend itself as a suitable policy in most Third World countries. It can be effectively applied only where there is an efficient authoritarian government or where a genuine rural development programme reduces the differences between urban and rural living standards. In many cases its effect is likely to be harmful to the poor; in most countries it will have little effect beyond increasing the scope for corruption.

Employment Deconcentration

By far the most common response to urban and regional imbalances is a programme to limit growth of the larger cities and to stimulate the economies of medium-sized centres. The prime candidate for inclusion in such a programme is invariably the industrial sector. Existing or new companies are persuaded to locate their plants in peripheral regions through a combination of tax incentives, the provision of infrastructure, the construction of industrial estates, and occasionally compulsion. In general, however, the stick has been used much less than the carrot; most governments have feared that too strong a programme of deconcentration would dissuade foreign companies from investing in the country, would lower efficiency in the industrial sector, or would offend important national business interests. Hence, few governments have compelled companies to move from the larger cities or even required that new companies should locate in peripheral regions. Even where some measure of compulsion has been used, as in Chile, Colombia, and Venezuela, the measure has been leavened by various incentives or confined to specific kinds of industries (UNCRD, 1976; Stöhr, 1975; Gilbert, 1974a; Townroe, 1979).

Various incentives have been used to attract industries to new locations. The Mexican border programme encouraged North American companies to take advantage of cheap Mexican labour and assemble products across the border for re-export to the United States. In Brazil major tax incentives attracted numerous companies to the principal cities of the poverty-striken north-east. Experience shows that provided the incentives are sufficiently attractive, manufacturing companies will locate in a wide variety of 'undesirable' locations. But such incentives have to be gauged carefully, since industry tends to favour those areas that are closest to their preferred locations. Thus, in north-east Brazil new industry was located only in the three largest cities and in Peru new industrial estates attracted companies only to the most prosperous and attractive city, Arequipa (Gilbert, 1974a). In India the second and third development plans led to the establishment of 486 industrial estates throughout the country, but only estates close to the largest cities prospered; since 1963 most estates have been set up near the major cities. Manufacturers can be persuaded to locate in lower priority centres, but usually the incentives are inadequate, too widely spread, or constantly change as governments re-evaluate both their programmes and their commitment to industrial dispersal. As a consequence, few programmes have been wholly effective in shifting the location of industrial activity and many dispersal strategies have been declared redundant. As Jakobson and Prakesh (1974: 263) note, 'Indian planners today admit that the decentralization efforts have failed, that the aggregation of industry of all scales has continued in the large cities and that regional disparities have increased rather than decreased.'

In some countries, however, industry has been encouraged to move away from the largest cities. The issue here is whether such deconcentration has had a positive effect on the poorer regions. In some cases, such as the banishment of the Chilean car industry to Arica in the far north of that elongated country, the results were little less than ludicrous. Cross-movements of parts and finished vehicles from the major industrial centre and major market in Santiago to the assembly plants in Arica were grossly inefficient (Johnson, 1967; Gwynne, 1978). More often industrial dispersal has increased regional output, but created few jobs. Indeed, deconcentration programmes have tended to suffer the same difficulty as national industralization programmes: capital-intensive technology has created few local jobs and little demand for local inputs. Thus the Mexican border programme and the Brazilian 34/18 tax incentive scheme have had very little effect on local poverty (Baerresen, 1971; Goodman, 1972). The industry that has been established has failed to stimulate local enterprise or the surrounding regions in the way suggested by growth-centre theory. Indeed the effects on areas surrounding growth centres have been uniformly discouraging. Studies of the regions around Kuala Lumpur (Robinson and Salih, 1971), Medellín (Gilbert, 1975), and Ciudad Guayana (Travieso, 1972) have found that either as a result of weak 'spread' effects and/or substantial 'backwash' effects, the regions beyond the immediate vicinity of the growth centres receive little in the way of positive economic or social benefits. Large-scale industrialization within a growth centre is a poor means of developing a poor region in the absence of fundamental changes in the agricultural economy, the marketing system, and the pattern of land holding. Industrial deconcentration may serve to reduce pressure on the metropolitan areas, but unless accompanied by other, often more radical, programmes brings little benefit to poorer regions.

The Building of New Cities

⎰The most direct, and often most dramatic, form of spatial-deconcentration policy has been the construction of new cities. New cities have performed a variety of spatial functions: as satellite centres to accommodate the growing population of a near-by metropolitan city; to house the population engaged in the development of a major new mineral resource; or to function as a new political capital. ⎱

Many satellite cities have been built along the lines of the British new towns. Efforts have been made to attract industry so as to provide jobs for the displaced populations and to prevent the emergence of 'dormitory suburbs'. Often such programmes have been a response to some special problem which has made metropolitan growth difficult to manage. Thus the partition of India led to a flood of migrants into Karachi which stimulated the construction of two satellite cities, Korangi and North Karachi (UNRISD, 1971). In other cases the aim has been to avoid perceived diseconomies associated with metropolitan expansion. In Venezuela new cities are being established in the Tuy Valley as a means of deconcentrating employment and population from Caracas' narrow valleys. In China Greater Shanghai now has over sixty satellites with populations rising to 60,000 people (Thompson, 1979: 305). Occasionally, too, new cities serve more debatable goals, as for instance in South Africa.[11]

New cities have often been associated with the development of mineral resource programmes. In Venezuela the widely publicized Ciudad Guayana project is part of an ambitious programme to develop the iron-ore, bauxite, and hydro-electric potential of the region (Friedmann, 1966; Rodwin, 1969). Today the city has a population of some 300,000, the Guri dam supplies 38 per cent of Venezuela's electricity, the steel works 79 per cent of its steel, and the aluminium plant all of its aluminium. Whether such a spectacular example of modern urban and industrial expansion has been an effective way of spending Venezuela's oil reserves is debatable given the social conditions in the city, the lack of stimulus afforded the surrounding region, and the limited numbers of jobs created (CEU, 1977; Travieso, 1972; Izaguirre, 1977). Nevertheless, whatever the criticisms, the plan has had a major impact on the spatial organization of the Venezuelan economy.

Similarly spectacular new cities have been built in several countries as new national or provincial capitals. Brasília, Islamabad, and Ankara were all built to serve as examples of the new future facing their nations. Their architecture and urban design reflected this goal; if Brasília was to serve as a national symbol nothing should be spared in its construction and nothing permitted to destroy the image created by Oscar Niemeyer (Epstein, 1973). Chandigarh, the new capital of the Indian Punjab, commissioned Le Corbusier to produce a city evocative of India's future; a future offering the poorest the means of living a dignified life (Sarin, 1979: 136-7). Such capitals represented a break with the past and with existing metropolitan centres which had dominated national life. They promised a new direction for development, located inland, away from the coast which had dominated previous political and economic history. More recently, several African nations have begun to construct new capitals. In Nigeria a new federal capital is being built in the more sparsely populated central area of the country to provide greater balance between the three major ethnic groups and the rest of the population and to reduce the dominance of Lagos. Nonakchott in Mauritania, Lilongwe in Malawi, and Dodoma in Tanzania are other examples in new nations striving to redress regional imbalances or to establish a new national identity through the construction of capital cities.

Dramatic though many of these new cities are, and despite the imaginative and optimistic philosophies underlying their construction, few have been totally effective. In few parts of the Third World has their growth radically altered the national settlement system. As the Ford Foundation (1972: 9) note, '. . . in a time span of some 20 years, they have a combined population of little more than one million – together, they comprise a city roughly equivalent to Recife or Bangalore.' Nor has their development slowed the growth of metropolitan São Paulo, Caracas, or Karachi; all expand as rapidly and as chaotically as ever. The governments of Brazil and Pakistan may now be physically located in new capitals, but the old power centres still exert considerable political influence. Nor do the new cities live up to their ideals of creating new lifestyles for their inhabitants. More often they have created artificially divided twin cities. Ciudad Guayana contains the planned city and the next-door unplanned city of Puerto Ordaz where most of the poor live. Brasília has experienced a series of conflicts between the planners, who have tried to exclude the spontaneous settlements from the urban area, and the poor who wish to live and work in the city (Epstein, 1973). Nor, of course, have most new cities been cheap to build. Vast sums have been spent on some of these cities which can never be repeated in those or many other countries. It is possible that these capitals have served their nations in other ways; increasing national integration, evoking national pride, and breaking economic and sentimental attachments to the past. But set against these advantages is their cost and the limited effect they have had in helping the poor.

Models of Development and Spatial Policies

The Failure of Decentralization and National Settlement Strategies

If the standard of judgement is that an adequate spatial policy should help the poor in the poorer regions and organize the distribution of settlement so as to help lower-income groups, few explicit spatial policies have been effective. Metropolitan areas have been allowed to develop in ways which have favoured the higher-income groups and created problems suffered at least proportionately by the poor; regional programmes have either served to boost national economic growth rates or have been pushed less than wholeheartedly.

Regional policies have normally been embraced enthusiastically only when they have promised to accelerate national economic growth. Perhaps the example *par excellence* is the Guayana programme in Venezuela. Publicized widely as an example to the Third World of how to implement both an urban planning and a regional development policy in a poor country, the Guayana programme was first a national growth strategy and only second an urban and regional policy. Although a regional and social dimension was explicit in the adoption of the programme, its primary appeal to the national government lay in the economic potential of the region's rich iron, bauxite, and water resources. Had there been another explanation, then the regional agencies set up in other parts of Venezuela would have been given greater support than they were (Friedmann, 1966). The continued flow of resources into the Guayana and the rapid demise of regional development programmes in other parts of the country can be explained only in terms of the former's contribution to national growth and the lack of similar potential in the rest of the country. Similar experiences are common throughout the Third World. Major regional development projects have been adopted *only* when their principal contribution was likely to accrue to the nation as a whole.

The corollary of this argument is that when urban and regional policy goals have conflicted with the paradigm of national economic growth, the latter has been the winner. Government after government has established regional programmes espousing goals of greater equity and regional balance. Almost invariably these policies have been counteracted by national programmes that have tended to accentuate regional disparities and encourage the growth of major urban areas. Of course, the introduction of regional programme may have reduced the level of spatial concentration that would have resulted from the national programme alone. But in general the weakness of regional and deconcentration programmes suggest that they were never priorities and never intended to achieve a real balance (Boisier, 1979).

The growth-before-distribution ethos also pervades the formulation of regional-development programmes even when politics have dictated that a genuine policy of deconcentration be espoused. Thus, in the Brazilian north-east resources have been channelled for redistributive reasons away from the south-east. New industrial employment has been created in the main cities of the north-east and the programme has helped to raise the regional product of the area. Such a programme was not motivated originally by national growth objectives. The locational inefficiency involved in locating industry so far from the country's main markets and supply areas was not negligible and without considerable incentives private industry would not have responded to the programme. But while the aims of the policy clearly did not reflect the national growth ethos, the method of implementation did. Industrial expansion for large companies was certainly not slowed by the enormous tax reliefs offered under the 34/18 mechanism. No change was invoked in the capital-intensive nature of Brazilian industry because of the failure to offer stronger incentives to labour-intensive companies (Goodman, 1972). Nothing was done to redistribute land or to introduce other social measures alien to the national growth strategy. The inevitable corollary has been that while the regional product increased, intra-regional disparities widened. Whether measured in terms of urban–rural differentials or in terms of the income shares of rich and poor, the latter have seen little improvement in their economic or social situation. There is also some evidence to suggest that real per capita incomes of the poor in several cities actually declined during the 1960s despite the programme (Gilbert and Goodman, 1976). In the north-east certain elements of the programme helped the poor, but the benefits were undermined by the lack of an equity component and by the regional effects of national policies concerned with the control of inflation and hence wage levels.[12] Stabilization policies throughout Latin America have tended to hurt numerous groups, including the poor in peripheral regions.

If nothing else, regional policies have served to maintain, and sometimes even to increase, the share of poor regions in per capita national product. In this sense the arguments of the early Frank (1967) model which argued that rural area, national metropolis, and world 'metropole' were linked in an exploitative relationship which led inevitably to the impoverishment of the periphery was too simple. Most peripheral economies are growing either because of the forces of the market or through help from the regional policies of the national government. The problem is that while the poor regions may benefit from regional policies, the poor of those regions benefit insufficiently. Too often the benefits go to industrial and large-scale agricultural groups in the region. A reduction in inter-regional disparities is accompanied by growth in intra-regional disparities and personal inequalities.

What I am arguing is that major regional programmes and indeed programmes for planning the major cities are essential but in themselves are insufficient. As many writers are now suggesting, it is the nature of the development model or style that is critical (Dunham, 1979; Friedmann and Weaver, 1979; Stöhr and Tödtling, 1977). If that model is consistently failing to create sufficient jobs or to redistribute income, then there is little that specific regional policies can do to resolve regional problems. In this one sense the experience of certain European countries is illustrative. Most have now introduced regional policies to remedy their spatial inequalities and to limit the growth of their major cities. In most European nations regional inequalities are tiny by comparison with those of Third World nations. But the connection between regional policy and the reduction of regional income disparities should be viewed with extreme care. It would seem most likely that social policies have been of greater importance than regional. In Britain regional disparities would have continued to be much larger had it not been for the introduction of free public education and health programmes, pensions for the old, grants for retraining, and unemployment benefits. In Europe regional policy was introduced into generally more equitable social systems than exist in the Third World. In the latter not only are existing inequalities extreme, but no real effort seems to have been made in most countries to reduce them (Cornelius, 1975). The continual search for methods to raise per capita income more rapidly is tending to perpetuate existing inequalities. In this context, regional development and decentralization policies are bound to be ineffective. To bring about more balanced regional development and a fairer share of wealth requires much more than regional policy, it requires a national commitment to a much modified development programme in which equality occupies a much more dominant position.

The Promise of Alternative Approaches

The degree to which alternative approaches favouring equity, or even the protection of non-renewable resources can be introduced is clearly a matter of politics. While some developed capitalist countries such as Sweden or Britain have achieved a measure of personal equality, there are few Third World capitalist nations that are improving the distribution of income or raising the standard of living of the poor. Similarly, there are few signs of success in modifying the spatial structure or the national settlement system. Reacting to this unfavourable experience, the literature on regional development and national settlement systems is increasingly arguing that some kind of radical change is required in the capitalist-development model. It is not sufficient to introduce new kinds of spatial or urban policy because the operation of the capitalist system will undermine those policies. Socialism is required to improve the living standards of the poor. Only under socialism is it possible to modify successfully the urban structure, redress the imbalance between urban and rural areas, remove the worst regional disparities, and develop agricultural potential in a non-exploitative fashion. Only by removing some of the power of the transnational corporations and the 'comprador' bourgeoisie can true change take place.[13]

The example of China is clearly foremost in many minds. I have already examined some of the implications of that experience and suggested that socialism does not offer a prescribed policy and attitude towards urban development. This point is perhaps best illustrated in the different attitudes towards urban development taken by Marx, Lenin, Stalin, Mao, and Castro. Marx's view of the peasant attitudes was hardly flattering and his formula for revolution and future progress was linked integrally with urban and industrial development. Of course, as a European he was the child of an urban civilization. While his attitude did not change as the result of a brief study of India, greater experience in the Third World might have modified his views (Marx, 1853). By contrast, Mao Zedong and indeed Castro favoured rural development. In part their attitudes were influenced by the source of their revolutionary support. If Marx and Lenin felt that revolution could come only from the industrial proletariat who were subject to the full contradictions of capitalism, both Mao and Castro came to power as the result of rural support. Whether, of course, this is the most appropriate criterion on which to formulate national development policy as opposed to stimulating revolution is another issue. But these examples demonstrate that the theory and practice of socialism have few clear lessons with respect to spatial development.

Similarly, socialism in practice has not always resolved the problems that afflict poor nations. While some may rightly question whether all Communist countries are socialist, it is instructive to observe that few Communist nations have managed to remove the worst forms of regional inequality. As Fuchs and Demko (1979: 304) have pointed out for Europe,

judged from various perspectives – regional contrasts, urban–rural and urban–urban comparisons, and intra-urban distinctions – the socialist states studied exhibit marked spatial inequalities. The persistence of these inequalities can be explained in terms of the priority placed on efficiency or military security as opposed to equity in industrial location decisions, the favouring of investment in 'productive sectors' rather than social infrastructure, a desire to defer urbanization costs as reflected in constraints on urban growth, the growing scale requirements of service and human welfare facilities, and the continuation of substantial differences in income for various occupation groups.

As we have already seen, regional disparities are still evident in China, even if there is a tendency towards regional convergence in that country. But the point is clear. If regional inequality is a problem in peripheral capitalist nations it is likely to continue to be an issue under a socialist regime. If socialism is able to reduce personal income disparities, then regional disparities will diminish, but anything vaguely resembling complete personal and regional equality seems unlikely under many forms of socialism.

Another issue that a consideration of socialist and Communist experience raises is whether it is possible to slow urban growth. We have seen that the Chinese have adopted an anti-urban strategy, whereas European Communist states have permitted urban growth even if they have controlled metropolitan expansion. The decisive question is whether or not urban growth is inevitable. The Chinese have certainly accepted that Shanghai and its satellite cities serve an important function. If their growth has been limited, it has certainly not been stopped. Similarly, Cuban experience suggests that having slowed the growth of Havana until rural conditions were improved, the national capital and other major cities have once again begun to expand. Now that China seems likely to accept a path of development more dependent on advanced technology and manufacturing, will the anti-urban bias hold with the same intensity? Clearly, China will not suddenly accept the uncontrolled urban growth so typical of capitalist Third World nations, but as Frolic (1976: 159) notes, 'until she industrializes more rapidly, it is too early to say whether she has found a permanent solution to problems of urbanization and modernization.'

Finally, socialist experience is ambivalent on an increasingly important issue in the development debate; the appropriate attitude to the physical environment. The saving of energy and the conservation of renewable resources seem of increasing importance in the modern world even if decision-makers are still scarcely recognizing the policy choices involved. In China policy seems to satisfy the seemingly sensible dictum of Brookfield (1979: 120) that 'to the several objective functions of "development" another must be added: to make the best use of natural and human resources where they are to be found.' The experience of the Soviet Union is almost the complete reverse; no improvement on the worst record of developed capitalist countries can be found there. The devastation of the forest reserves, the virgin land programme, and policies towards pollution hardly point to a viable socialist policy towards the environment. The Soviet Union has acted rather like Brazil; natural resources are something to be exploited to maximize economic growth. The distributive aims of the two countries may differ, but the goal of economic expansion has been predominant.

This last point is perhaps fundamental. Friedmann and Weaver (1979) have suggested that a more rural-based policy is essential for Africa and Asia. Implicitly, they have recommended socialism as the way of achieving such a programme. They may well be right, but socialism is not of itself enough; there must also be a commitment to reducing the large-scale corporative element in decision-making. In this their plea for the reassertion of the territorial criterion over the functional makes sense. It has been the imposition of developmental models on national and international space which has created so many of the problems of urban and rural development, inequality, and environmental waste. Such imposition has been integral to the capitalist model in the sense that transnational corporations have been encouraged to exploit the world's resources and permitted to dominate the markets and productive systems of the Third World. But socialist experience, at least in Europe, does not offer an alternative. The crisis in those nations is at least as great as that in capitalist countries in part because those regimes are equally dependent on centralized, corporative decision processes.

If, as they most assuredly have, the spatial policies in peripheral capitalist nations have failed because of the nature of the development models being applied, then alternatives must be sought. Unfortunately, at first sight there is no simple alternative available. Socialism offers differences and in terms of equity many improvements, but it clearly lacks certain fundamental ingredients which are essential if the problems of poverty in the world are to be resolved. The only undeniable lesson of socialism is that it demonstrates that changes in such key issues are not made by technicians on the basis of objective studies. Rather, they stem from political decisions made initially by a majority of the population.

NOTES

CHAPTER 1

1. Certain cities on the east coast of Africa, such as Dar es Salaam, were founded by Arabs. In addition, there was an indigenous urban culture among the Baganda who established Kampala.
2. Cuba did not gain its independence until 1902.
3. 'By primary urban generation I mean that essentially independent emergence of urban forms through the restructuring of a society that was previously at a folk level of integration and which was subject to no or negligible stimulus from already existing societies. . . . I would suggest that lower Mesopotamia, the Nile valley, the Indus valley, the North China Plain, Meso-America, and the Central Andes be treated as regions of primary urban generation. Regions where the diffusion of traits from already urbanized societies can be shown to have either initiated and/or significantly accelerated the transformation from folk to urban society . . . I shall designate as regions of secondary urban generation' Wheatley (1970: 395).
4. See chapter 2 for an explanation of log-linear city-size systems.
5. For a discussion of the validity of these arguments see chapter 8.

CHAPTER 2

1. There must clearly be some reservation about the first figure for Indonesia.
2. According to Auerbach (1913), Zipf (1941), and Stewart (1958), all city-size distributions tend to a pattern described statistically by the log-normal or Pareto distributions. Zipf went further and argued that where the value of q in the equation Rank of city i = constant times the population of city i to the power of $-q$ ($R_i = K P_i^{-q}$) equals unity, the city-size distribution has reached maturity. While there are many reasons for questioning the wisdom of Zipf's judgement, most national city-size distributions do record values ranging from 0.8 to 1.2 (Richardson, 1973). It also represents a useful rule of thumb according to which the largest city should be twice the size of the second, three times the size of the third, and four times the size of the fourth. Thus we can define normality on the four-city index is 0.48 (i.e. 1.0 divided by the sum of 1.0 = 0.5 + 0.33 + 0.25). If we include cases in which the largest city is up to 25 per cent larger or smaller than in the mature case, we have upper and lower limits of non-primacy. Similarly, if we define high primacy as a condition where the largest city is more than twice the anticipated size we have the following limiting values:

	Four-city index
High primacy	0.65 to 1.00
Primacy	0.54 to 0.65
Non primacy	0.41 to 0.54
Low primacy	0.00 to 0.41

The flimsy basis for this definition is obvious. In addition, the four-city index is arbitrary in the sense that it excludes most of the rank-size distribution and the use of population as the sole indicator excludes other demographic and economic variables. Similarly, the basis of our standard, the rank-size rule of Zipf, is of doubtful theoretical value, once being described by Christaller (1966: 59) as 'a most incredible law'. Its only virtues are computational simplicity and wide usage.

3. High primacy is especially common in Latin America and the Caribbean where 15 out of 22 countries fall into that category compared to 6 out of 26 in Africa, 6 out of 27 in Asia, and 5 out of 24 in Europe. These data support earlier arguments by Browning (1972) and Morse (1971). High primacy is also more common among countries with small populations (Mehta, 1964; Davis, 1962; Linsky, 1965). Of the fifteen countries with less than 4 million inhabitants, in my calculations all but two are primate and nine are high primate.

4. This aspect was recognized by Friedmann in his later writing, most notably in Friedmann (1972-3).

CHAPTER 3

1. For analyses of the incorporation of rural populations, see Pearse (1970) on Latin America, and Gugler and Flanagan (1978a: 180-3) on West Africa.
2. In some cases attention initially focused on inappropriate means, e.g. the cargo cults in Melanesia.
3. Even socialist countries, while reducing income inequality within the urban and rural sectors respectively, appear to find it difficult to deal with inter-sector inequality. In China personal consumption has been estimated at $244 per capita in urban as against $111 per capita in rural areas in 1979. The ratio of 2.2 is quite similar to that of other developing countries in Asia. Despite a commitment to reducing the urban–rural gap, urban per capita incomes are estimated to have increased in 1957-79 at an annual average real rate of 2.9 per cent, but rural incomes at only 1.6 per cent. The gap in personal income is accompanied by a large gap in collective consumption. The quality of education and health facilities in particular is much higher in urban areas (World Bank, 1981: 52-7).
4. Lipton (1977: 146-53, 430-4) provides data on rural–urban differentials in wages, incomes, and expenditures for nineteen developing countries and discusses the shortcomings of such data.
5. Sources for Table 3.2: Death to the age of two for Latin American countries and infant mortality for Cuba from studies prepared by Hugo Behm and his associates, published by the Centro Latinomericano de Demografía, San José, Costa Rica, between 1976 and 1980. Infant mortality for Bangladesh, Colombia, Guyana, Indonesia, Jamacia, Jordan, Kenya, Mexico, Panama, Peru, Senegal, and Sri Lanka from the World Fertility Survey as reported by Eduardo E. Arriaga (1980) 'Direct estimates of infant mortality differentials from birth histories', paper presented to the World Fertility Survey Conference, London; Wariara Mbugua (1981) personal communication; Irma O. García y Garma (1981) 'Determinants of infant and childhood mortality in Mexico', paper presented to the Committee for International Coordination of National Research in Demography; République du Sénégal, Direction de la Statistique and Institut International de la Statistique (1981) *Enquête Senégalaise sur la fécondité 1978*, vol. 1. Dominique Tabutin (1976) *Mortalité infantile et juvénile en Algérie*, Travaux et Documents 77, Presses Universitaires de France, République de Dahomey [Benin] (1964) *Enquête démographique au Dahomey 1961: Résultas définitifs*, INSEE. Diana Oya Sawyer (1981) 'Effects of industrialization and urbanization on mortality in the developing countries: The case of Brazil', in *International Population Conference: Solicited Papers*, vol. 2, International Union for the Scientific Study of Population, pages 255-70. M. Lafarge (1964) *Enquête démographique en République Centrafricaine 1959-1960: Résultats définitifs*, INSEE. World Bank (1981) *China: Socialist economic development, Annex B: Population, health and nutrition* (World Bank East Asia and Pacific Regional Office); and Ding Chen (1980) 'The economic development of China,' *Scientific American* 243(3), 152-65. République Gabonasie, Service de Statistique (1965) *Recensement et enquête démographiques 1960-1961, Ensemble du Gabon: Résultats définitifs*, INSEE. S. K. Gaisie and K. T. de Graft-Johnson (1976) *The population of Ghana*, CICRED. *Survey on infant and child mortality, 1979: A preliminary report* (Government of India, Office of the Registrar General). Djamchid Behnam and Mehdi Amani (1974) *La population de l'Iran*, CICRED. *Results of vital statistics survey 1976*, Central Statistical Organization. Iraq. Abel Z. Massalee (1974) *The population of Liberia*, Republic of Liberia, Ministry of Planning and Economic Affairs. Charles Hirschman and Edward Tan Kah Joo (1971) *Evaluation of mortality data in the vital statistics of West Malaysia*, Department of Statistics, Kuala Lumpur, Malaysia, République du Mali, Service de la Statistique, *Enquête démographique au Mali 1960-1961*, INSEE. Baddou Tajeddine (1974) *La population du Maroc*, CICRED. Adelamar M. Alcantara (1975) *Differential mortality among population sub-groups*, Population Institute Research Note 63, University of the Philippines System, Manila. Lee-Jay Cho (1973) *The demographic*

situation in the Republic of Korea, Paper 29, East–West Population Institute. Abdul-Aziz Mohamed Farah (1981) 'Child mortality and its correlates in Sudan', Ph.D. dissertation in Demography, University of Pennsylvania. K. E. Vaidyanathan (1976) *Estimation of infant and child mortality in Syria from the 1970 census data*, Syrian Population Studies Series 10, Centre for Population Studies, Damascus. Howard R. Hogan and Shiraz Jiwani (1976) 'Differential mortality', in *The demography of Tanzania: An analysis of the 1973 national demographic survey of Tanzania*, vol 6. Bureau of Statistics, Ministry of Finance and Planning, and Bureau of Resource Assessment and Land Use Planning, University of Dar es Salaam, pp. 211–25. John Knodel and Apichat Chamratrithirong (1978) *Infant and child mortality in Thailand: Levels, trends, and differentials as derived through indirect estimation techniques*, Paper 57, East–West Population Institute. Service de la Statistique Generale, République Togolaise, *Enquête démographique 1961: Résultats définitifs*, vol. 2.

6. For an extensive review of the literature on internal migration in Africa, Asia, and Latin America, see Simmons, Diaz-Briquets, and Laquian (1977); for a general review of the migration literature that focuses on theory construction, Shaw (1975); for a comprehensive bibliography of recent literature on labour migration in Latin America, Lowder (1978).

7. Yap (1977) provides a critical review of the econometric studies that have come to dominate research since the later 1960s.

8. See, e.g., Songre, Sawadogo, and Sanogoh (1974: 389–90) on migration from Upper Volta.

9. Once migrants are established in town they can generally be expected to attract new migrants from their home area, to initiate 'chain migration'. However, the concept of 'migrant stock', i.e. the number of migrants of common origin living at a given destination, suffers from a severe disability as an explanatory variable for subsequent migration, since people may continue to migrate from the same origin to the same destination for the very reasons that induced the initial migration (Shaw, 1975: 83–5).

   Chain migration encourages direct moves, even over large distances, in contrast to 'stage migration', i.e. migrants moving from their place of birth to one or several intermediary destinations before reaching their final destination. There is intuitive appeal to the notion that rural emigrants go first to small towns and, after spending an adaptation period there, move on to metropolitan areas. Or the concept of stage migration may be stretched to span two generations: the first makes it to the local town, the second into the city. However, at present we lack the data to substantiate the view that stage migration is a significant mode of rural–urban migration in Africa, Asia, or Latin America (Simmons et al., 1977: 29, 58, 95).

10. To some extent, of course, the immigrants encountered in an urban sample constitute a selection. The least successful are most likely to have returned to their homes. This option is not always available, but it is certainly important in Subsaharan Africa and India.

11. As recently as 1979 policies of the US government had the effect of 'setting aside' 20 million acres of land so as to avoid production of grain in excess of what could be sold at price levels considered acceptable.

12. For an account of subsequent modifications of the model, see Todaro (1976: 36–45). Recently Harris and Sabot (1982) have proposed a generalized model of migration and job search in the context of wage dispersion and imperfect information, of which the Harris–Todaro model is a special case.

13. Some collective-bargaining agreements in India provide for the preferential recruitment of offspring of retiring workers (Ramaswamy, 1979: 376 n. 7). In China it has been customary in some places and some lines of work for a child to be able to succeed a retiring parent in his/her job, and this practice has been more generally encouraged in the period since 1976 (Whyte, n.d.b: 50 n. 24).

14. If there is any 'law' of migration that holds generally it is that migration of selective in terms of age. Most types of migration recruit disproportionately among young adults. The effect is sufficiently strong to mask those types of migration that recruit

primarily from other age groups, most notably retirement migration. Shaw (1975: 133) thus concludes his review with the proposition: 'The propensity to migrate varies inversely with age. Persons in their late teens, twenties and early thirties are more migratory than those in other age groups. The greatest propensity to migrate is observed for those in the age group 20–29 years.'

15. Oceania and Asia also reported a preponderance of men over women in rural areas, a reflection of higher mortality rates for women, but it was considerably less pronounced than in the urban areas.

16. Averages can mask exceptions such as the Philippines in the context of Asia. However, data for twenty Latin American countries show that in each of them a higher proportion of the female than of the male population lived in urban areas in the 1970s (Centro Latinoamericano de Demografía, 1981).

17. I am indebted to Francine van de Walle for this observation.

18. Inasmuch as the efforts of the Chinese regime to raise the age at marriage are successful in the rural areas, young women there are becoming similarly potentially mobile. Whether they move to urban areas will depend on the extent to which urban as against rural opportunities are open to them.

19. Lower urban sex ratios after the age of fifty, relative to rural ratios, in Latin America may be taken as evidence for such a movement. However, they can also be a function of increases in the sex ratios of successive urban cohorts. Indeed, the only time series available for a Latin American country, Mexico, shows a steady increase in the urban sex ratio from 1920 to 1970. This trend holds when the effect of the severe male losses during the civil war is controlled for (United Nations, 1980: 114–18). It indicates a decline in the share of migrants and/or higher sex ratios in the more recent migration streams.

20. One attendant serious problem is the spread of venereal diseases in urban areas and their transmission to the countryside.

21. One solution is for migrants to establish a farm within commuting distance from their place of work. Typically the urban agglomeration provides a ready market for garden produce, but it is frequently difficult for outsiders to gain access to land. Such constraints do not obtain around Kampala, where substantial numbers of those employed in the city have established farms (Gugler, 1975b).

22. Goldstein (1978) reviews the literature on various forms of temporary migration in Asia, and in particular in South-East Asia. He emphasizes that return migration, and in particular circular migration, is much more common than the standard studies based on census data reveal.

23. Perrings' (1979: 130–1, 39, 236) detailed account of the labour policies pursued by the mining companies on both sides of the border suggests that even before 1940 they were not as divergent as is commonly assumed. Some of the most obvious dissimilarities in labour utilization can be accounted for by the fact that the wages of skilled workers recruited from Europe for Katanga were higher than those of their counterparts who came from the South African mines, while the wages of African workers were lower in Katanga.

24. Some employers intent on establishing a stable labour force adapt to this pattern by offering generous leave provisions.

25. Migrants can maintain a pattern of circular migration where they do not face competition from established urban workers. In a country such as India the construction industry is labour-intensive to an extreme degree. Large numbers of unskilled workers are recruited, through middlemen, from rural areas on a temporary basis. They work at wages so low and in conditions to miserable that they are unacceptable to urban workers (Bellwinkel, 1973).

26. In some areas the visiting pattern is reversed as wives visit their spouse in town. Frequently they come on extended visits, a form of circular migration in reverse. Weisner (1973) provides a fine description and analysis of families thus operating two households, one in Nairobi, the other in the rural area. Also, children may stay with their father to take advantage of better educational facilities in the city.

27. This song, reported by Saxena (1977: 176), has been translated by C. Saskia Gugler.
28. In Vunamami on the island of New Britain, Papua New Guinea, the rural community was sufficiently affluent in the early 1960s for about half the wage earners, including the better educated, to find local employment. By the age of thirty they returned home to such local employment in order to educate their children locally and to establish a copra and cocoa farm for the future (Salisbury, 1970: 164–71). Such a situation is exceptional, but it serves to highlight how rural opportunities in employment and in cash crops shape the economic context in which the decision whether to return or not is made.
29. R. E. Johnson (1979: 29–30, 50, 51, 156) describes the typical Moscow worker of the late nineteenth century as having one foot in the village and one in the factory, but showing little inclination to commit himself irrevocably to either, and suggests that this pattern was related to the communal system of land tenure (which carried the burden of redemption payments imposed when serfdom was abolished in 1861) and the division of a father's holdings among his sons.
30. Rural–urban migration in Latin America is generally presumed to be permanent. However, while there has been a great deal of inquiry into migration in the region, there is virtually no information on the retirement plans of migrants or their actual residence upon retirement. Incidental findings suggest that return migration is significant, in some countries at least. On Mexico see Butterworth (1977: 132), and Feindt and Browning (1972: 159); on Colombia, Simmons and Cardona (1972: 172); on Peru, Laite (1981), Roberts (1976: 122), and Skeldon (1977); and on Venezuela, Pollak-Eltz (1979).

CHAPTER 4

1. Abu-Lughod (1971) has written the millenarian history of Africa's largest metropolis, Cairo.
2. Where corruption plays a role in the procurement of capital goods it will bias the choice of technology towards a more capital-intensive pattern because the more expensive the purchase, the greater the scope for the payoff. In addition, the selection of technically complex equipment reduces the risk of detection because of the greater ease of dissimulating the payoff element in the price (Winston, 1979: 841).
3. For an analysis of the ill-fated attempt to restructure the market for consumer goods in Chile when the Unidad Popular government came to power in 1970, see Griffith-Jones (1978).
4. In India the growth of cities with a population over 100,000 has been a function of the expansion of employment in services and in trade and commerce, rather than in industry, in every decade since 1911 (Mitra et al., 1980: 42–8).
5. Turnham (1970: 197–201) discusses the Indian data in some detail and suggests that applying more generous definitions of unemployment would roughly double the rate reported in his compilation, leaving it still exceptionally low. Berry and Sabot (1978: 1212) put open urban unemployment in India at 3 per cent in 1971, and Krishnamurty (1975) reinforces the impression that it is indeed remarkably limited.
6. Berry (1975) offers a comprehensive discussion of voluntary unemployment and presents data from Colombia suggesting its importance there. His study, as well as that of Sabot (1979: 152–62) in Tanzania, indicated that the pool of unemployed comprised predominantly the young and married women.
7. Squire (1981: 71) summarizes data on rates of unemployment by level of education in ten Third World countries. In eight cases the rate is highest, frequently by a large margin, for those who have had secondary education. However, Kenya, the only African country represented, shows a regular decline in unemployment as level of education increases; this may reflect an educational system only beginning to catch up, in 1970, with manpower requirements. It is noteworthy that unemployment is lower among those with post-secondary than among those with only secondary education in every country, including countries such as the Philippines, Sri Lanka, and India, that are notorious for widespread unemployment among college graduates; presumably college students are in a better position to prepare for their transition into the labour market.

8. Perlman (1976: 80), in her study of squatters in Rio de Janeiro, found that among the migrants the best jobs went to those who could afford to take their time and be selective. When men who came from unskilled urban jobs or agriculture were compared with those who previously had skilled employment, the proportion who secured their first job within a month was higher among the less qualified. Also the proportion who found a job within a month was higher among those who knew no one upon arrival than among those with contacts.

9. Most studies focus on earnings instead, either because the researcher's primary concern is with urban poverty or because earnings data are more easily available and are assumed to reflect productivity.

10. Such underemployment can be a quite stable feature among self-employed who have low overhead costs and are assured of a minimum of customers because of personal ties and/or locational advantages.

11. A comparison with the Japanese permanent employment system springs to mind, but the latter precisely fails to provide for workers outside the major firms, and indeed the substantial proportion of casual workers in these firms. The analogy of the commitment to full employment in socialist countries is more accurate. In pre-revolutionary Cuba most workers in the sugar fields and the sugar mills were unemployed for a major part of the year. Since the Revolution they are offered employment throughout the year, and major efforts have been directed toward absorbing them in productive activities during the off-season. As in family enterprise, the problem becomes to what extent full employment, while desirable on equity grounds, only hides unemployment instead of employing workers to productive ends.

12. More than a million menials work as messengers and guards in the Indian Civil Service. According to one calculation they are on the average usefully employed for 12 minutes a day (Maddison, 1971: 95). If this estimate appears exaggerated, few would deny that there is a good deal of redundancy in this category as well as in other ranks of the bureaucracy in India – as in many other countries.

13. Illegal activities frequently come to be tolerated as necessary to the very survival of a major part of the urban population. The acceptance of urban squatting is the most salient example.

14. The conspicuous use of labour may be argued to be preferable to the conspicuous consumption of imported luxury goods precisely because it provides local employment; in addition it saves usually scarce foreign exchange. Such an argument takes for granted extreme income inequalities and, in the case of female domestics, sex discrimination in the labour market. The image of the nursemaid who fulfils her charge's every whim while her own children suffer from neglect is all too disturbing.

15. A dramatic description of scavenging in São Paulo is provided in de Jesus's (1960) reputedly autobiographical account. Cigarette-butt collecting constitutes a major street occupation in Jakarta (Papanek, 1975: 11).

16. The argument that some of the additions to the urban labour force could be more productively employed in the rural economy, where, furthermore, their subsistence costs would be lower, has been developed elsewhere (Gugler and Flanagan, 1977; Gugler, 1982).

17. A survey of low-income neighbourhoods in Jakarta reported that 29 per cent of households were headed by women; fully a third of these women were prostitutes. Out of their income they supported, on average, nearly two dependents (Papanek, 1975; 7-8).

18. In Brazil 34 per cent of female labour outside agriculture was in domestic service around 1970. A decade earlier the proportion was 36 per cent in Chile, 45 per cent in Colombia, 31 per cent in Peru, and 32 per cent in Venezuela (Elizaga, 1979: 531). In 1970 almost 40 per cent of working women in Chile were employed as maids, washerwomen, or ironing women in individual homes (Mattelart, 1976: 294). In Guatemala no fewer than 40 per cent of the female labour force outside agriculture were domestics in 1973 (Chinchilla, 1977: 53). In Mexico 20 per cent of working women were domestic servants in 1969 (Gonzalez, 1976: 187).

19. Jellinek (1977; 1976) provides a unique account of one woman's constant struggle to maintain an existence as a street trader in Jakarta and shows how her changing fortunes affected the very composition of her household.

20. For descriptions of the condition of child labour in a variety of occupations in Delhi and Bombay, see Pandhe (1979).
21. Such abandoned urban youths in Mexico City are the subject of Luis Buñuel's classic *Los Olvidados*; they have indeed been forgotten not only by their parents but also by social scientists.
22. The amount of research, much of it sponsored by the International Labour Office, and writing on the informal sector in the 1970s is truly remarkable. It is the more extraordinary given the severe shortcomings of the concept. For a discussion of the reasons for the rapid diffusion and official adoption of the formal/informal distinction, see Bromley (1978: 1035-7). A comprehensive review of research and analytical approaches is provided by Moser (1978), a well-annotated bibliography by Sinclair (1978).
23. This probably explains why the Kenya Report arrived at the unusually low estimate that only 20 per cent of the income-earning opportunities in Nairobi in 1969 were provided by the informal sector, while suggesting that the share was much higher in other Kenyan cities and especially in small towns (ILO, 1972; 54).
24. A wide range of studies reviewed by Rempel (1979: 226-31) provides no consistent evidence that recent migrants are disproportionately represented in the informal sector. For barriers to entry into specific opportunities in Bogotá, see Peattie (1975).
25. The crime syndicates in Seoul were able to fully employ shoeshine boys because they controlled exclusive territories. Other investments in their territories included boarding-houses, tearooms, restaurants, and inns of prostitution (Kang and Kang, 1978).
26. Tokman (1978) reviews a number of such studies. Some of these assume that benign relationships between the sectors prevail and emphasize their complementarity; others focus on the subordination of informal-sector activities and argue exploitation. From the latter perspective, the analysis may be cast in terms of the articulation of a petty commodity mode of production with a capitalist mode (Moser, 1978: 1055-60).
27. This intermediate level appears similar to the intermediate sector Steel (1977) delineated in Ghana on the basis of a great deal of empirical work. Steel, in contrast to Quijano, singled out this intermediate sector as the most promising for policies aimed at increasing urban employment.
28. Sabot (1979: 229-48) discusses the policy options on both the supply and the demand side of the labour market with reference to Tanzania.
29. The obstacle of an international boundary, while far from impenetrable, appears to be quite effective in stemming migration. The rapid increase in the productivity of the labour force of Singapore was not diluted by rural-urban migration, a measure of control was exerted over the influx of refugees into Hong Kong, and while the employment boom in the oil-exporting countries has attracted foreign workers, their recruitment is closely regulated.
30. Where a group effectively controls such a niche, its members can maintain a pattern of circular migration as they replace each other on the job. See, e.g., Jellinek (1978) on ice-cream vendors in Jakarta and Stretton (1979: 278) on construction workers in Manila.

CHAPTER 5

1. Cape Coast is relatively well provided by African standards, despite these low figures.
2. A judgement based on 360 interviews in four spontaneous housing areas in Bogotá as part of the project on 'Public intervention, housing and land use in Latin American cities' directed by Alan Gilbert and Peter Ward. Henceforth this project will be referred to as PIHLU.
3. Indeed, in a recent paper Peter Ward and I alternate the terms 'irregular settlement' (his preferred term) and 'spontaneous housing' (mine).
4. Renting is often referred to in work on African and Asian cities, but rarely discussed as a separate theme. Partial exceptions to this generalization are Drakakis-Smith (1981) and Peil (1976; 1981). Information on Bogotá and Mexico City is being prepared by PIHLU and on Bucaramanga in Colombia by Michael Edwards for his doctoral dissertation at University College London.

5. Peil (1981), however, notes that class or ethnic segregation is uncommon in some West African cities, although it is increasing.
6. Numerous examples exist of governments having demolished centrally located low-income housing to allow private enterprise to develop the area. All too often the grounds on which such decisions were taken have been problematic.
7. Statement attributed to Dr Mulder, then Minister of Rural Relations, by the *Guardian Weekly*, 8 Oct. 1978.
8. For example, Castro's Cuba has long been antagonistic to spontaneous housing.
9. APRA is a party which had widespread support among low-income groups in both Lima and the north of Peru.
10. Because of the wealth of the Venezuelan State, considerable compensation is sometimes paid to private landowners whose land has been invaded. Another explanation is that landowners encourage the invasion of part of their land, then press the authorities to authorize and service it, which then raises the value of the rest of their land because it can now be serviced easily.

CHAPTER 6

1. Situational change and biographic change refer to the changes in the behaviour of individuals and may be distinguished from the changes a society undergoes over time, or historical change. For a discussion of this conceptual distinction, an account of its intellectual history, and an application to West Africa see Gugler and Flanagan (1978a: 97-117).
2. Lest responses to a survey be discounted, it may be noted that only a minority reported meeting co-workers off the job and that most of these contacts were described as casual.
3. The close-knit network refers to a situation in which the people with whom an individual associates are known to each other. In the loose-knit network, in contrast, an individual relates to people who remain strangers to each other. Various means to enquire into, and describe, social relationships at the micro-level have been developed in network analysis. For a recent exposition of this conceptual methodology and a review of some key studies, see Hannerz (1980: 163-201).
4. I am emphasizing integration in reaction to an academic tradition and persisting popular stereotypes proclaiming urban 'disintegration'. The next task is to investigate degrees of integration and sources of affinity. A first step in this direction has been taken by Graves and Graves (1980) who distinguish kin-reliance and peer-reliance in a comparative analysis of European, Maori, and Pacific Islands workers in New Zealand.
5. Srole (1978) presents a large set of US data according to which self-reported psychosomatic symptoms are less prevalent in cities than in small towns or rural areas among both men and women. However the scores, while standardized for age, are not adjusted for differences in the socio-economic composition of the different types of communities.
6. Data for the US, Australia, New Zealand, and nine European countries show that there the homicide rate is invariably higher in the major city than in the country at large. In the US a strong and perfectly monotonic relationship obtains between size of urban agglomeration and homicide rate. Each category of city size has a higher homicide rate than all smaller city-size categories. However, the rural homicide rate is as high as the rate of cities that have a population of between 50,000 and 100,000, i.e. it is higher than the rates of smaller towns (Archer et al., 1968: 80, 84 f.).
7. Jocano (1975: 100-22) gives an account of the activities in Manila of gangs of young men who have no steady jobs.
8. Such anonymity by no means characterizes all urban neighbourhoods. In a neighbourhood in the lower-class Tondo section of Manila, the Philippines, the outsider, especially the male intruding into a side street off the main thoroughfare with no clear purpose, runs the risk of being challenged, threatened, or actively molested by local guardians of the area (Hollnsteiner, 1972: 36-7). Similarly, Doshi (1974: 34) describes caste-based neighbourhoods in Ahmedabad, India, where everybody knows everybody else. Any stranger entering the neighbourhood is quickly surrounded by a group of boys and young children who enquire as to his purpose.

9. The critique of the culture of poverty concept, fuelled by concern with its political implications, has been extensive and frequently heated: see Valentine (1968), Valentine et al. (1969), and Leeds (1971).

10. The date of Lewis's first visit incorrectly appeared as 1947 in several of his writings.

11. They consist of tapes, typed interviews, and copies of other materials that had been brought to the US before the Cuban authorities halted the research and confiscated manuscripts, interviews, tapes, photographs, and personal papers. In particular all the completed questionnaires of the housing development study were taken (Butterworth, 1980: xxi).

12. The question to what extent the stigma of having come from a notorious slum was reinforced by racism is not addressed by Butterworth. Two-thirds of the residents were classified as black or mulatto. The significance of race within the housing development is indicated by the fact that among forty-four households heads only five were married across the white/non-white divide (Butterworth, 1980: 24, 55).

13. Another housing development, intended to accommodate poor families, including many squatters, is East Havana. Situated on a beautiful site overlooking Havana Bay, it was built to high standards in the very first years of the revolutionary regime and equipped with diverse social and urban services. Residents interviewed informally in 1975 held that many of the families originally relocated there were unaccustomed to apartment living and had abused the buildings. Whatever the reasons, they had moved away and had been replaced by more educated and well-to-do families (Eckstein, 1977b: 455–6).

14. In the early days of their operation, the CDRs organized nightly vigilance in the housing development. However, in contrast to Lewis's account from Las Yaguas in 1961, the guards in the housing development were not permitted to carry firearms. Although this denial of arms to the guards was not unusual, it was resented and seen as another indication that government officials would never trust former slum dwellers (Butterworth, 1980: 112).

15. There is a striking parallel, in both theoretical orientation and political implications, between the hard-culture approach and the predominant focus on cultural barriers to change in the development literature of the 1950s. Resistance to a substantial redistribution of resources, and the disappointing results of such aid as was niggardly given, inspired approaches that were respectively ethno- and class-centric. In both cases the charge must be made that attention is diverted from the real issue, the exploitation of dominated groups, by blaming the victim (Ryan, 1971).

CHAPTER 7

1. Eckstein (1976) relates these concerns to the Cuban Revolution. She notes that the US government, the Defense Department, and private foundations sponsored a large body of research on the urban poor in Latin America in the 1960s. There was little concern to define and describe urban poverty, but rather a preoccupation with the political implications of poverty. The research subsided in the 1970s, not because urban poverty was on the decline, but because the proposition that the urban poor are not vanguards of revolutionary movements was gaining wide acceptance.

2. In 1972 the World Bank broke with its policy of limiting funding to what were considered productive investments and began supporting urban low-cost settlements on a substantial scale. One is left to wonder whether this reflected a different appraisal of the prospects for urban unrest on the part of key decision-makers.

3. J. M. Nelson (1979) provides a comprehensive review of research on the political role of the urban poor in Third World countries.

4. Lloyd (1979: 76–81) distinguishes an ego-oriented cognitive map from the externalized analytical structure. The individual relates his goals, and his image of routes by which these goals are to be achieved, to his own resources, central among them, especially for the poor, his personal network. In contrast he can also observe his society from the outside as it were, and describe it as an externalized analytical structure.

5. Myrdal (1970: 240-2) recognizes that the US shows traits in the system of law, law observance, and law enforcement that in some respects place it nearer the situation in Third World countries than those of north-western Europe. He lists several interrelated facts to account for the comparatively high level of corruption in the US. Among these, the clustering in the cities of disadvantaged racial and immigrant groups, the rise of machine politics, and the relative lack of integration of the lower classes of a still quite heterogeneous population are pertinent to our analysis here.

6. The following account is based on Johnson (1977).

7. The Mexican student movement of 1968 was co-ordinated by a National Strike Council drawn from the 128 participating schools and headed by a rotating committee whose composition changed weekly. There was thus a large reservoir of leaders rather than a handful of organizers who could be co-opted or repressed (Hellman, 1978: 134-5).

8. A comprehensive survey of such cleavages and their relation to national politics in the major Third World regions is provided by Young (1976).

9. In addition to language, manifold clues allow the urban dweller to gauge the ethnic identity of a stranger: dress and ornaments; cultural modifications of physical appearance such as hairstyle, beard, and facial scars; patterns of speech, even when a lingua franca is used; food and drink preferences; behaviour ranging from minor physical mannerisms to dance. Furthermore, particular occupations as well as residential areas are known to be the more or less exclusive preserve of one or another ethnic group. Singh (1976) provides an account of how such markers identify a person's region of origin, religion, and caste in India. Ease in categorizing encourages the rapid establishment of interaction with group members and the maintenance of distance toward outsiders. Easily discernible characteristics guide participants in communal riots in selecting their victims.

10. The classic account by Mangin (1967) describes the pattern in Peru. A filmed documentary, *Children of the Dust*, depicts the establishment of Ciudad de Dios, City of God, Lima, on Christmas Eve 1954.

11. Valladares (1978a) gives a detailed account of the relocation of squatters in Rio de Janeiro. Her emphasis is on how they managed to manipulate the system.

12. Ray (1969: 63-73), in a comparison of squatter settlements in four cities in Venezuela, shows how the economic, social, and political character of a city determines the *barrio*'s choice of leadership. Cornelius (1975a: 67-72), in his survey of six low-income neighbourhoods – including three squatter settlements – in Mexico City, found huge differences on a wide range of measures of support for the political system. Most of these attitudinal differences could be related to the ways the six communities had been established, to the types of local leaders who had emerged within them, to the kinds of interactions that had occurred between the communities and public officials, and to the absolute level of services and benefits provided by the government to each community. An analytical difficulty arises in so far as the neighbourhoods may be assumed to have attracted people with different outlooks to start with.

13. These élite workers are variously described as white-collar employees, skilled workers, or well-paid workers in more modern industries (Collectif Chili, 1972: 54, 56; Handelman, 1975: 44-5, 55).

14. Nueva la Habana has become the most famous of these militant *campamentos*. On the outskirts of Santiago, it had a population of between 8,000 and 10,000 and was led by MIR. New Havana is the subject of a dissertation by Meunier (1976) who lived there from 1971 until the military coup, of a chronological account by Castelain (1975), of an extensive interview with a MIR organizer (Henfrey and Sorj, 1977: 130-48), and of a documentary filmed late in 1971, *Campamento*. It provided the prime focus for Petras's (1973) study of the squatter movement in Chile and one of the two locals of Spence's (1979) research on neighbourhood courts. According to the latter, the directorate went underground on the morning of the military coup, while some units of the settlement's militia went to Vicuña Mackenna and Puente Alto, areas which resisted for several days. On the night of 11 September the military came to New Havana, took the first sixteen men they found, and shot them immediately in the main square. Over the next days the army, the navy, and the police came in turns; sometimes there were four or five searches a day. Women were raped in front of their

men, and children beaten in front of their parents. Residents were tortured in the settlement itself, one woman had both arms broken. Every morning fresh bodies were found at the entrance of the street between New Havana and the neighbouring *campamento*. And the military renamed the settlement: it was to be known henceforth as 'New Dawn'.

15. Castells (1982) has reviewed the experience of squatter movements in Peru, Chile, and Mexico, and attempted to draw political lessons for the Left.

16. A common identity of origin, religion, or caste can foster worker militancy. Sentiments of community ensure a level of trust and solidarity among workers confronting management. And a shared ideology provides the moral basis for protest as in the articulation of a Muslim critique of Westernization and capitalism in northern Nigeria (Lubeck, 1981).

17. There has been considerable debate whether certain categories of workers have come to constitute a labour aristocracy in the process (Arrighi, 1970; Peace, 1975; Saul, 1975; Jeffries, 1978). The privileges enjoyed by part of the urban labour force became an issue even in China during the early stages of the Cultural Revolution.

18. In some cases unskilled workers derive a measure of security from the fact that they can fall back on farming. Thus when contract workers in Namibia went on strike in 1971-2, they returned to their areas of origin (Moorsom, 1979). In late nineteenth-century Moscow it was the smaller, less mechanized factories whose workers were more closely tied to the village that had the higher rates of labour unrest. These workers not only could return to their villages and their plots of land if dismissed but were united by loyalties of common origin which were a major factor in promoting strikes and other protests (R. E. Johnson, 1979: 159-62).

19. Collier and Collier (1979) offer a comparative analysis of the history of organized labour in Latin America.

20. The very privileges of protected workers demonstrate that the leverage they wield is little affected by the large numbers of unprotected workers and unemployed who very much want to join the protected labour force. Instead, the industrial reserve army depresses the incomes and working conditions of the marginalized labour force (Quijano, 1974: 418; Breman, 1976: 1908).

21. Mesa-Lago (1978) gives a detailed account of the social security systems in Argentina, Chile, Mexico, Peru, and Uruguay and an analysis relating them to the strength of various pressure groups. On Brazil see Malloy (1979), who further discusses the contrast between Latin American countries where social-security schemes were introduced early, i.e. Chile, Uruguay, Argentina, Brazil, Peru, and Cuba, and such late adopters as Mexico, Colombia, Venezuela, and Central America.

22. Welch (1977) has emphasized the importance of the distinction between national wars of liberation and revolutions, and predicted that the African peasantry will not play a revolutionary role in the next several decades.

23. The dependence of rural guerrillas on urban support was highlighted when Che Guevara (1968) found himself without such support in Bolivia.

24. For a chronological listing of actions taken by the urban underground from 1952 to 1959, see Bonachea and San Martín (1974: 338-44). The composition of the first government after the victory of the revolution, in which the urban front was more strongly represented than the rural, may be taken as one indication of the importance of the urban movement (Thomas, [1971] 1977: 283-5).

25. Hodges (1973) provides a biographical account of Guillén, an introduction to his writings, and a discussion of his influence on the armed struggle in Latin America.

26. The position of élites in settler regimes is akin to that of national élites. Their followers tend to be even more committed to resistance than a national middle class: elements of the latter may anticipate accommodation with the new rulers, but for settlers defeat invariably means what they consider exile and destitution.

27. For an account of urban guerrilla warfare in Brazil, Uruguay, and Argentina, and excerpts from a large array of writings by and about the guerrillas, see Kohl and Litt (1974); for a comprehensive annotated bibliography, Russell, Miller, and Hildner (1974); for an outstanding collection of documentary materials on the Tupamaros

in Uruguay, drawn from a wide variety of sources, Mayans (1971). Jan Lindquist produced a unique filmed documentary, *Tupamaros*.

28. Governments, rather than revolutionary movements, are invariably the prime beneficiaries of external support. The US in particular, quite apart from its open intervention in Vietnam and the Dominican Republic, has assisted many governments against their domestic opponents. Not only were foreign governments provided with equipment on a lavish scale but their troops were given training specifically geared to meet the guerrilla challenge. La Escuela de las Américas, located in the Panama Canal Zone, received its name in 1963 when a new curriculum emphasizing training in counter-insurgency and civic action was introduced. More than 20,000 officers and enlisted men, representing every Latin American country except Cuba, were trained there in the 1960s. In addition, small groups of Green Berets, stationed at Southern Command in the Panama Canal Zone, have worked with the troops of every Latin American nation except Mexico, Cuba, and Haiti. Fifty-two such missions, including parachute drops into guerrilla zones, were reported for 1965 alone. In 1966 and 1967 Green Berets assisted the Guatemalan army and suffered several losses at the hands of the guerrillas. In 1967 they set up a camp in Bolivia where they trained 600 raw recruits of the Bolivian army who later that year tracked down Che Guevara and his comrades (Gott, 1971: 450-1, 488-9; Klare, 1972: 301, 306, 379-81; Lartéguy, [1967] 1970: 195-7).

29. The failure of the urban guerrilla movements, while they were operating on a significant scale in Venezuela, Brazil, Uruguay, and Argentina, was precisely their inability to mobilize broad-based support and to gain control of the city streets.

CHAPTER 8

1. For a recent development of this critique see Corbridge (1980).
2. I mean here both the transfer of surplus for investment in urban activities and the movement of skilled and educated personnel to the urban areas.
3. I have only used demographic measures here but clearly the degree of concentration of investment, industry, commerce, construction, etc. is at least as important. The only real justification for using demographic data is that in part they reflect the levels of concentration in economic activity. That is to say, people tend to migrate towards centres where jobs, opportunities and higher incomes are available.
4. See note 2 to chapter 2.
5. Indeed from Poland several academic planners have helped diffuse the growth-centre strategy to capitalist nations in both the developed and the less developed world.
6. Dodoma is the new capital of Tanzania.
7. Polarization reversal is not the same as regional per capita income convergence. The former applies only to population and economic concentration and not to per capita income and welfare indicators.
8. I am including broadly all those policies that have attempted to modify the spatial structure by opening up the frontier. The frontier programme includes, but is broader than, the Amazon region which covers the states of Amazonas, Pará, Acre, Rondônia, Roraima, Amapá, the western part of Maranhão, and the north of Goiás and Mato Grosso.
9. The term often used to describe Brazil's economic experience between 1968 and 1974 when the gross domestic product grew at an average annual rate of 10.1 per cent.
10. These are official figures and therefore exclude illegal immigrants. Nevertheless, the rate of expansion is still likely to be much lower than in the absence of such a policy.
11. See pp. 100-1 for discussion of Cape Town's two new satellite cities.
12. I believe the situation of the poor in the North-East would have been still worse without the programme.
13. A 'comprador' bourgeoisie is one that imitates the bourgeois class of developed countries. Instead of investing in the local economy it expatriates profits, instead of developing industrial activity it imports manufactured products from abroad. The outcome is a distorted, dependent, and unequal pattern of social and economic development. 'Comprador' has been used to describe both colonial and neocolonial élites.

BIBLIOGRAPHY

Abrams, C. (1964) *Man's struggle for shelter in an urbanizing world*, MIT Press.
Abu-Lughod, J. L. (1976) 'Developments in North African urbanism: the process of decolonization', in Berry, B. J. L. (ed.) (1976), 191-212.
— — (1971) *Cairo: 1001 years of the city victorious*, Princeton University Press.
— — and Hay, R. (eds.) (1977) *Third World urbanization*, Maaroufa Press.
Achunine Obi, B. (1977) 'Dynamics and strategies for urban housing and infrastructure in developing countries: a case study – Lagos Metropolitan', Doctoral dissertation, Michigan State University.
Acosta, M. and Hardoy, J. E. (1972) 'Urbanization policies in revolutionary Cuba', *Latin American Urban Research* 2. 167-78.
Agarwal, J. P. (1976) 'Factor proportions in foreign and domestic firms in Indian manufacturing', *Economic Journal* 86. 589-94.
Alonso, W. (1971) 'The economics of urban size', *Papers and Proceedings of the Regional Science Association* 26. 67-83.
— — (1969) 'Urban and regional imbalances in economic development', *Economic Development and Cultural Change* 17. 1-14.
— — (1968) *Industrial location and regional policy in economic development*, Center for Planning and Development Research, University of California.
Amato, P. W. (1970) 'Elitism and settlement patterns in the Latin American city', *Journal of the American Institute of Planners* 36. 96-105.
Amin, S. (1974) *Accumulation on a world scale: a critique of the theory of underdevelopment*, Monthly Review Press.
Anstey, V. (1936) *The economic development of India*, Longman, 3rd edition.
Appalraju, J. and Safier, M. (1976) 'Growth centre strategies in less developed countries', in Gilbert, A. G. (ed.) (1976), 143-68.
Aradeon, D. (1978) 'Regional assessment of human settlements policies in Nigeria', Paper presented at the Symposium on National Human Settlements Policies and Theory held at the University of Sussex. February 1978.
Archer, D., Gartner, R., Akert, R., and Lockwood, T. (1978) 'Cities and homicide: a new look at an old paradox', *Comparative Studies in Sociology* 1. 73-95.
Arrighi, G. (1970) 'International corporations, labour aristocracies, and economic development in Tropical Africa', in Rhodes, R. I. (ed.) *Imperialism and underdevelopment: a reader*, Monthly Review Press, 220-67. Reprinted in Arrighi, G. and Saul, J. S. (1973) *Essays on the political economy of Africa*, Monthly Review Press.
Artle, R. (1971) 'Urbanization and economic growth in Venezuela', *Papers and Proceedings of the Regional Science Association* 27. 63-93.
Auerbach, F. (1913) 'Das Gesetz der Bevölkerungskonzentration', *Petermann's Mitteilungen* 59. 74-6.
Baer, W. (1964) 'Regional inequality and economic growth in Brazil', *Economic Development and Cultural Change* 12. 268-85.
Baerresen, D. W. (1971) *The border industrialization program of Mexico*, Heath Lexington.
Baker, P. H. (1974) *Urbanization and political change: the politics of Lagos, 1917-1967*, University of California Press.
Balán, J. (1976) 'Regional urbanization under primary-sector expansion in neo-colonial countries', in Portes, A. and Browning, H. L. (eds.) *Current perspectives in Latin American urban research*, University of Texas Press, 151-79.

Balassa, B. (1980) 'The process of industrial development and alternative development strategies', World Bank Staff Working Paper 438.

Banton, M. (1973) 'Urbanization and role analysis', in Southall, A. (ed.) *Urban anthropology: cross-cultural studies of urbanization*, Oxford University Press, 43–70.

—— (1965) 'Social alignment and identity in a West African city', in Kuper, H. (ed.) *Urbanization and migration in West Africa*, University of California Press, 131–47.

—— (1957) *West African city: a case study of tribal life in Freetown*, Oxford University Press.

Baran, P. A. (1957) *The political economy of growth*, Monthly Review Press.

Barratt-Brown, M. (1974) *The economics of imperialism*, Penguin.

Batley, R. (forthcoming) 'Urban renewal and expulsion in São Paulo', in Gilbert, A. G. Hardoy, J. E. and Ramírez, R. (eds.), 231–262.

Bauer, P. T. (1954) *West African trade*, Cambridge University Press.

Bedford, R. D. (1973) *New Hebridean mobility: a study of circular migration*, Department of Human Geography, Research School of Pacific Studies, Australian National University.

Bellwinkel, M. (1973) 'Rajasthani contract labour in Delhi: a case study of the relationship between company, middleman and worker', *Sociological Bulletin* 22. 78–97.

Berg, E. J. (1961) 'Backward-sloping labour supply functions in dual economies: the Africa case', *Quarterly Journal of Economics* 75. 468–92.

Bergsman, J. (1970) *Brazil: industrialization and trade policies*, Oxford University Press.

Berry, B. J. L. (ed.) (1976) *Urbanization and counter-urbanization*, Sage Publications.

—— (1972) 'Hierarchical diffusion: the basis of development filtering and spread in a system of growth centres', in Hansen, N. M. (ed.) (1972) *Growth centres in regional economic development*, Free Press, 108–38.

—— (1961) 'City-size distributions and economic development', *Economic Development and Cultural Change* 9. 573–87.

Berry, R. A. (1975) 'Open unemployment as a social problem in urban Colombia: myth and reality', *Economic Development and Cultural Change* 23. 276–91.

—— and Sabot, R. H. (1978) 'Labour market performance in developing countries: a survey', *World Development* 6. 1199–242.

Bhooshan, B. S. and Misra, R. P. (1980) *Habitat Asia: Issues and Responses*, vol. 1: *India*, Concept Publishing Company, New Delhi.

Bienefeld, M. (1979) 'Urban employment: a historical perspective', in Bromley, R. and Gerry, C. (eds.), 27–44.

Bill, J. A. (1978) 'Iran and the crisis of '78', *Foreign Affairs* 57. 323–342.

Birkbeck, C. (1979) 'Garbage industry and the "vultures" of Cali, Colombia', in Bromley and Gerry (eds.), 161–183.

Blake, G. H. and Lawless, R. I. (eds.) (1980) *The changing Middle Eastern city: processes and problems*, Croom Helm.

Boisier, S. (1979) 'La planificación del desarrollo regional en América Latina', Paper presented to the Seminario sobre Estategias Nacionales de Desarrollo Regional (Bogotá, 17–21 Sept. 1979).

—— (1973) 'Localización, tamaño urbano y productividad industrial: un caso de estudio de Brasil', *Revista Interamericana de Planificación* 6. 87–112.

Bonachea, R. L. and San Martín, M. (1974) *The Cuban insurrection 1952-1959*, Transaction Books.

Borukhov, E. (1975) 'On the urban agglomeration and economic efficiency: comment', *Economic Development and Cultural Change* 24. 199–205.

Bose, A. (1973) *Studies in India's urbanization 1901–1971*, Tata McGraw Hill.

Boserup, E. (1970) *Woman's role in economic development*, St. Martin's Press.

Brand, R. R. (1972) 'Migration and residential site selection in five low-income communities in Kumasi (Ghana)', *African Urban Notes* 7. 73–94.

Brandt, W. (1980) *North–South: a programme for survival. Report of the Independent Commission on International Development*, Pan Books.

Brazil (1976) *Amazonia*, Brazilian Embassy, London.

Breese, G. (ed.) (1969) *The city in newly developing countries: readings on urbanism and urbanization*, Prentice Hall.

Breman, J. (1976) 'A dualistic labour system? A critique of the "informal sector" concept', *Economic and Political Weekly* 11. 1870–6, 1905–8 and 1939–44.

Brett, S. (1974) 'Low income settlements in Latin America: the Turner model', in de Kadt and Williams (eds.) (1974) 171–96.

Bromley, R. (1978) 'Introduction – The urban informal sector: why is it worth discussing?', *World Development* 6. 1033–9.

—— (ed.) (1978) 'The urban informal sector: critical perspectives', *World Development* 6. 1031–198.

—— and Gerry, C. (eds.) (1979) *Casual work and poverty in Third World cities*, John Wiley & Sons.

Brookfield, H. C. (1979) 'Urban bias, rural bias, and the regional dimension: to the house of Tweedledee', in Rothko Chapel Symposium (1979), *Towards a new strategy of development*, Pergamon Press, 97–121.

—— (1978) 'Third World development', *Progress in Human Geography* 2. 121–32.

—— (1975) *Interdependent development*, Methuen.

—— (1973) 'On one geography and a third world', *Transactions of the Institute of British Geographers* 58. 1–20.

Browning, H. L. (1972) 'Primacy variation in Latin America during the twentieth century', in Instituto de Estudios Peruanos (ed.) *Integración y proceso social en América*, Lima.

Bruner, E. M. (1973) 'Kin and non-kin', in Southall, A. (ed.) *Urban anthropology: cross-cultural studies of urbanization*, Oxford University Press, 373–392.

—— (1972) 'Batak ethnic associations in three Indonesian cities', *Southwestern Journal of Anthropology* 28. 207–29.

Brush, J. E. (1962) 'The morphology of Indian cities', in Turner, R. (ed.) (1962), 57–70.

Bryant, C. (1980) 'Squatters, collective action, and participation: learning from Lusaka', *World Development* 8. 73–86.

Bryant, J. (1969) *Health and the developing world*, Cornell University Press.

Burgess, R. (1978) 'Petty commodity housing or dweller control? A critique of John Turner's views on housing policy', *World Development* 6. 1105–34.

Burland, C. A. (1967) *Peru under the Incas*, Evans Bros.

Burton, R. F. (1856) *First footsteps in East Africa*, Everyman.

Butterworth, D. (1980) *The people of Buena Ventura: relocation of slum dwellers in post-revolutionary Cuba*, University of Illinois Press.

—— (1977) 'Selectivity of out-migration from a Mixtec community', *Urban Anthropology* 6. 129–39.

—— (1972) 'Two small groups: a comparison of migrants and non-migrants in Mexico City', *Urban Anthropology* 1. 29–50.

Byres, T. J. (1974) 'Land reform, industrialization and the marketed surplus in

India: an essay on the power of rural bias', in Lehmann, D. (ed.) *Agrarian reform and agrarian reformism: studies of Peru, Chile, China and India*, Faber, 221–61.
Calder, N. (1974) *The weather machine*, BBC Publications.
Caldwell, J. C. (1969) *African rural–urban migration. The movement to Ghana's towns*, Columbia University Press.
Cardoso, F. H. (1977) 'Current theses on Latin American development and dependency: a critique', *Boletín de Estudios Latinoamericanos y del Caribe* 22. 53–64.
— (1972) 'Dependency and development in Latin America', *New Left Review* 84. 83–95.
— and Faletto, E. (1969) *Dependencia y desarrollo en América Latina*, Siglo XXI.
Castelain, C. (1975) 'Histoire du "Campamento Nueva Habana" (Chili)', *Espaces et Sociétés* 15. 117–31.
Castells, M. (1982) 'Squatters and politics in Latin America: a comparative analysis of urban social movements in Chile, Peru and Mexico', in Safa, H. I (ed.) *Towards a political economy of urbanization in Third World countries*, Oxford University Press, 249–82.
— (1977) *The urban question: a Marxist approach*, Edward Arnold. Original French edition 1972.
— (ed.) (1973) *Imperialismo y urbanización en América Latina*, Editorial Gustavo Gili.
Centro Latinoamericano de Demografía (1981) 'América Latina: Porcentajes de población urbana por países 1970, 1985 y 2000', *Boletín demográfico* 28.
CEU (Centro de Estudios Urbanos) (1977) *La intervención del estado y el problema de la vivienda: Ciudad Guayana*, CEU, Caracas.
Chamberlain, M. E. (1974) *Britain and India: the interaction of two peoples*, David & Charles.
Chandler, T. and Fox, G. (1974) *3000 Years of Urban Growth*, Academic Press.
Chandra, S. (1977) *Social participation in urban neighbourhoods*, National, New Delhi.
Chatterji, R. (1980) *Unions, politics and the state: a study of Indian labour politics*, South Asian Publishers.
Chaudhuri, S. (1962) 'Centralization and the alternative forms of decentralization: a key issue', in Turner, R. (ed.) (1962), 213–39.
Chavarría, R. E. (1982) 'The Nicaraguan insurrection: an appraisal of its originality', in Walker, T. W. (ed.) *Nicaragua in revolution*, Praeger, 25–40.
Chinchilla, N. S. (1977) 'Industrialization, monopoly capitalism, and women's work in Guatemala', *Signs* 3. 38–56.
Christaller, W. (1966) *Central places in Southern Germany*, Prentice Hall.
Clarke, C. G. (1974) 'Urbanization in the Caribbean', *Geography* 59. 223–32.
Cleaves, P. S. (1974) *Bureaucratic politics and administration in Chile*, California University Press.
Clinard, M. B. and Abbott, D. J. (1973) *Crime in developing countries: a comparative perspective*, John Wiley & Sons.
Cohen, A. (1969) *Custom and politics in urban Africa: a study of Hausa migrants in Yoruba towns*, University of California Press.
Cohen, J. A. (1968) *The criminal process in the People's Republic of China 1949–1963: an introduction*, Harvard Studies in East Asian Law 2, Harvard University Press.

Cohen, M. (1978) 'Regional development or regional location. A comparison of growth and equity approaches', Working Paper No. 6, Development Planning Unit, University College, London.

Cohen, M. A. (1974) *Urban policy and political conflict in Africa: a study of the Ivory Coast*, University of Chicago Press.

Collectif Chili (1972) 'Revendication urbaine, stratégie politique et mouvement social des "pobladores" au Chili', *Espaces et Sociétés* 6–7. 37–57.

Collier, D. (1976) *Squatters and oligarchs*, Johns Hopkins University Press.

—— and Collier, R. B. (1979) 'Labor, party, and regime in Latin America', Paper prepared for the 11th International Political Science Association World Congress, Moscow.

Coraggio, J. L. (1977) 'Cuestiones metodológicas relativas al análisis de los problemas regionales en América Latina', mimeo.

Corbridge, S. (1980) 'Urban bias, rural bias, and industrialization: an appraisal of the work of Michael Lipton and Terry Byres', Department of Geography, University of Cambridge, MS.

Cornelius, W. A. (1975a) *Politics and the migrant poor in Mexico City*, Stanford University Press.

—— (1975b) 'Introduction', *Latin American Urban Research* 5. 9–25.

—— (1973) 'The impact of governmental performance on political attitudes and behaviour: the case of the urban poor in Mexico', in Rabinovitz and Trueblood (eds.) (1973) *Latin American Urban Research* 3. 217–55.

Costello, V. F. (1977) *Urbanization in the Middle East*, Cambridge University Press.

Cross, M. (1979) *Urbanization and urban growth in the Caribbean*, Cambridge University Press.

Currie, L. L. (1965) *Una política urbana para los paises en desarrollo*, Tercer Mundo.

—— (1971) 'The exchange constraint of development: a partial solution to the problem', *Economic Journal* 81. 886–903.

da Camargo, C. P. et al. (1975) *São Paulo: crescimento e pobreza*, Ediçoes Loyola, São Paulo.

Dandekar, V. M. and Rath, N. (1971) *Poverty in India*, Ford Foundation.

DANE (Departamento Administrativo Nacional de Estadística) (1977) *La vivienda en Colombia*, Bogotá.

—— (1967) *Censo nacional de edificios y viviendas: 1964*, Bogotá.

Darwent, D. F. (1969) 'Growth poles and growth centres in regional planning – a review', *Environment and Planning* 1. 5–32.

Davenport, T. R. H. (1977) *South Africa: a modern history*, Macmillan.

Davis, K. (1962) 'Los causas y efectos del fenómeno de primacia urbana con referencia especial a América Latina', XIII Congreso Nacional de Sociología, Mexico.

—— (1969) *World urbanization 1950–1970*, 2 vols., University of California.

—— and Hertz, H. (1954) 'Urbanization and the development of pre-industrial areas', *Economic Development and Cultural Change* 4. 6–26.

Davis, S. H. (1977) *Victims of the miracle*, Cambridge University Press.

Daza Roa, A. (1967) 'La repartición de los ingresos', *Revista del Banco de la República*, 40, 880–889.

Debray, R. (1967) *Révolution dans la révolution?* Cahiers Libres 98. Paris: Maspero. English trans. 1967, *Revolution in the revolution? Armed struggle and political struggle in Latin America*, Monthly Review Press.

de Kadt, E. and Williams, E. (eds.) (1974) *Sociology and development*, Tavistock Publications.

Dewar, D. (1976) 'Metropolitan planning and income redistribution in Cape Town', University of Cape Town, Department of Urban and Regional Planning, Occasional Paper No. 1.

— and Ellis, G. (1979) *Low income housing policy in South Africa*, Citadel Press, Lansdowne.

Dietz, H. A. (1978) 'Metropolitan Lima: urban problem solving under military rule', in Cornelius, W. A. and Kemper, R. V. (eds.) (1978) *Metropolitan Latin America: the challenge and the response, Latin American Urban Research* 6. 205–26.

Dobbin, C. (1972) *Urban leadership in Western India: politics and communities in Bombay City 1840–1885*, Oxford University Press.

Doebele, W. A. (1975) 'The private market and low income urbanization in developing countries: the "pirate" subdivision of Bogota', Harvard University, Department of City and Regional Planning, Discussion Paper D75-11.

— (1978) 'Selected issues in urban land tenure', in World Bank (1978), 99–207.

— and Peattie, L. A. (1976) 'Some second thoughts on sites and services', mimeo.

Doeppers, D. F. (1976) 'The development of Philippine cities before 1900', in Yeung, Y. M. and Lo, C. P. (eds.) *Changing South-East Asian cities: readings on urbanization*, Oxford University Press, 28–44.

Domínguez, J. I. (1978) *Cuba: order and revolution*, Harvard University Press.

Dore, R. P. (1978) 'Learning from China: reflections on transferability', World Development 6. 715–17.

Doshi, H. (1974) *Traditional neighbourhood in a modern city*, Abhinav Publications.

Dos Santos, T. (1970) 'The structure of dependence', *American Economic Review* 60. 231–6.

Drakakis-Smith, D. W. (1981) *Urbanization, housing and the development process*, Croom Helm.

— (1976a) 'Some perspectives on slum and squatter settlements in Ankara', Paper presented to the Institute of British Geographers Annual Conference, 5 Jan. 1976, Lanchester Polytechnic.

— (1976b) 'Urban renewal in an Asian context: a case study in Hong Kong', *Urban Studies* 13. 295–305.

Dunham, D. (1979) 'What do regional theorists do after midnight?', Institute of Social Studies, The Hague, mimeo.

Dutt, R. C. (1968) *The economic history of India*, 2 vols.

Dwyer, D. J. (1975) *People and housing in Third World cities*, Longman.

— (ed.) (1972) *The city as a centre of change in Asia*, University of Hong Kong Press.

Eames, E. (1967) 'Urban migration and the joint family in a North Indian Village', *Journal of Developing Areas* 1. 163–78.

Eckstein, S. (1977a) *The poverty of revolution: the state and the urban poor in Mexico*, Princeton University Press.

— (1977b) 'The debourgeoisement of Cuban cities', in Horowitz, I. L. (ed.) *Cuban communism*, 3rd edition, Transaction Books, 443–74.

— (1976) 'The rise and demise of research on Latin American urban poverty', *Studies in Comparative International Development* 11. 107–26.

Edwards, M. (forthcoming) 'Cities of tenants: renting among the urban poor in Latin America', in Gilbert, A. G., Hardoy, J. E., and Ramírez, R. (eds.), 129–58.

Ellis, G. et al. (1977) *The squatter problem in the Western Cape: some causes and remedies*, South African Institute of Race Relations.

Elizaga, J. C. (1979) 'The participation of women in the labour force of Latin America: fertility and other factors', *International Labour Review* 109. 519–38.

El-Shakhs, S. (1972) 'Development, primacy and systems of cities', *Journal of Developing Areas* 7. 11–36.

—— (1965) 'Development, primacy and the structure of cities', Harvard University Doctoral Dissertation.

Emmanuel, A. (1972) *Unequal exchange: a study of imperialism of trade*, New Left Books.

Epstein, A. L. (1958) *Politics in an urban African community*, Manchester University Press.

Epstein, D. G. (1973) *Brasília – plan and reality: a study of planned and spontaneous settlement*, University of California Press.

Evers, H.-D. (1977) 'Urban expansion and land ownership in underdeveloped societies', in Walton and Masotti (eds.) (1977), 67–79.

—— (1975) 'Urbanization and urban conflict in Southeast Asia', *Asian Survey* 15. 775–85.

Eyre, L. A. (1972) 'The shanty towns of Montego Bay, Jamaica', *Geographical Review* 62. 394–413.

Fair, T. J. D. and Davies, R. J. (1976) 'Constrained urbanization: white South Africa and Black Africa compared', in Berry, B. J. L. (ed.) (1976), 145–68.

Feindt, W. and Browning, H. L. (1972) 'Return migration: its significance in an industrial metropolis and an agricultural town in Mexico', *International Migration Review* 6. 158–65.

Feldman, K. (1975) 'Squatter migration dynamics in Davao City, Philippines', *Urban Anthropology* 4. 123–44.

Fischer, C. A. (1976) 'The ecology of modernization with special reference to Asia', in Lim Teck Ghee and Lowe, V. (eds.) *Towards modern Asia: aims, resources and strategies*, Heinemann, 108–21.

Fischer, C. S. (1976) *The urban experience*, Harcourt Brace Jovanovich.

Fitzgerald, E. V. K. (1976) *The state and economic development: Peru since 1968*, Cambridge University Press.

Flanagan, W. G. (1978) 'The extended family as an agent of social change: family process, urbanization, and economic development', Paper presented at the 9th World Congress of Sociology, Uppsala, August 1978.

—— (1977) 'The extended family as an agent in urbanization: a survey of men and women working in Dar es Salaam, Tanzania', PhD dissertation, University of Connecticut.

Ford Foundation (1972) *International urbanization survey: findings and recommendations*, Ford Foundation.

Foster-Carter, A. (1978) 'The modes of production controversy', *New Left Review* 107. 47–77.

—— (1976) 'From Rostow to Gunder Frank: conflicting paradigms in the analysis of underdevelopment', *World Development* 4. 167–80.

Fox, R. (1975) *Urban population growth trends in Latin America*, Inter-American Development Bank.

Frank, A. G. (1969) *Latin America: underdevelopment or revolution*, Monthly Review Press.
— — (1967) *Capitalism and underdevelopment in Latin America: historical studies of Chile and Brazil*, Monthly Review Press.
French, R. A. and Hamilton, F. E. I. (eds.) (1979) *The socialist city: spatial structure and urban policy*, John Wiley.
Friedmann, J. P. (1972-3) 'The spatial organization of power in the development of urban systems', *Development and Change* 4. 12-50.
— — (1968) 'The strategy of deliberate urbanization', *Journal of the American Institute of Planners* 34. 364-73.
— — (1966) *Regional development policy: a case study of Venezuela*, MIT Press.
— — (1961) 'Cities in social transformation', *Comparative Studies in Society and History* 4. 86-103.
— — and Douglass, M. (1976) 'Agropolitan development: towards a new strategy for regional planning in Asia', in UNCRD (1976), 333-87.
— — and Weaver, C. (1979) *Territory and function: the evolution of regional planning*, Edward Arnold.
— — and Wulff, R. (1976) *The urban tradition: comparative studies of newly industrializing societies*, Edward Arnold.
Frisbie, W. (1976) *The scale and growth of world urbanization*, University of Texas Population Research Center.
Frolic, B. M. (1976) 'Noncomparative communism: Chinese and Soviet urbanization', in Field, M. (ed.) (1976) *Social consequences of modernization in communist societies*, Johns Hopkins.
Fuchs, R. J. and Demko, G. J. (1979) 'Geographic inequality under socialism', *Annals of the American Association of Geographers* 69. 304-18.
Funnell, D. (1976) 'The role of small service centres in regional and rural development: with special reference to Eastern Africa', in Gilbert, A. G. (ed.), 77-112.
Furtado, C. (1971) *Economic development of Latin America: a survey from colonial times to the Cuban revolution*, Cambridge University Press.
Gans, H. J. (1962a) *The urban villagers: group and class in the life of Italian-Americans*, Free Press of Glencoe.
— — (1962b) 'Urbanism and suburbanism as ways of life: a re-evaluation of definitions', in Rose, A. H. (ed.) *Human behaviour and social processes*, Houghton Mifflin, 625-48.
Geisse, G. and Coraggio, J. L. (1972) 'Metropolitan areas and national development', *Latin American Urban Research* 2. 45-60.
Gellner, E. (1977) 'Patrons and clients', in Gellner, E. and Waterburgy, J. (eds.) *Patrons and clients in Mediterranean societies*, Duckworth, 1-6.
Gilbert, A. G. (1981a) 'Bogotá: an analysis of power in an urban setting', in Pacione, M. (ed.) *Problems and planning in third world cities*, Croom Helm, 65-93.
— — (1981b) Pirates and invaders: land acquisition in urban Colombia and Venezuela, *World Development* 9. 657-78.
— — (1978) 'The state and regional income disparity in Latin America', *Bulletin of the Society for Latin American Studies* 29. 5-30.
— — (ed.) (1976a) *Development planning and spatial structure*, John Wiley.
— — (1976b) 'The arguments for very large cities reconsidered', *Urban Studies* 13. 27-34.
— — (1975) 'A note on the incidence of development in the vicinity of a growth

centre', *Regional Studies* 9. 325-33.
—— (1974a) *Latin American Development: a geographical perspective*, Penguin Books.
—— (1974b) 'Industrial location theory: its relevance to an industrializing nation', in Hoyle, B. S. (ed.) *Spatial aspects of development*, Wiley, 271-90.
—— (1974c) 'The spatial allocation of education and health facilities in a less developed nation', in Helleiner, F. M. and Stöhr, W. B. (eds.) (1972) *Proceedings of the Commission on Regional Aspects of Development of the International Geographical Union, II: Spatial aspects of the development process*, Allister, Toronto, 307-44.
—— (1970) 'Industrial growth in the spatial development of the Colombian economy, 1951-1964', University of London Doctoral Dissertation.
—— and Goodman, D. E. (1976) 'Regional income disparities and economic development: a critique', in Gilbert (ed.) (1976), 113-42.
—— Hardoy, J. E., and Ramírez, R. (eds.) (forthcoming) *Urbanization in contemporary Latin America*, John Wiley.
—— and Ward, P. M. (1978) 'Housing in Latin American cities', in Herbert, D. T. and Johnston, R. J. (eds.) *Geography and the urban environment*, vol. 1, John Wiley, 285-318.
Ginsburg, N. (1973) 'From colonialism to national development: geographical perspectives on patterns and policies', *Annals of the Association of American Geographers* 63. 1-21.
Gish, O. (1971) *Doctor migration and world health*, Bell.
Gluckman, M. (1960) 'Tribalism in modern British Central Africa', *Cahiers d'Etudes Africaines* 1. 55-70.
Goldstein, S. (1978) *Circulation in the context of total mobility in Southeast Asia*, Papers of the East-West Population Institute 53, Honolulu: East-West Center.
Gonzalez, S. G. (1976) 'Participation of women in the Mexican labor force', in Nash, J. and Safa, H. I. (eds.) *Sex and class in Latin America*, Praeger, 183-201.
Goodland, R. J. A. and Irwin, H. S. (1975) *Amazonian jungle: green hell to red desert*, Elsevier.
Goodman, D. E. (1972) 'Industrial development in the Brazilian northeast: an interim assessment of the tax credit scheme of article 34/18', in Roett, R. J. A. (ed.) (1972) *Brazil in the sixties*, Vanderbilt University Press, 231-74.
Gore, M. S. (1971) *Immigrants and neighbourhoods: two aspects of life in a metropolitan city*, Tata Institute of Social Sciences, Bombay.
Gott, R. (1971) *Guerrilla movements in Latin America*, Doubleday.
Graham, R. (1979) *Iran: the illusion of power*, St. Martin's Press.
Graves, T. D. and Graves, N. B. (1980) 'Kinship ties and the preferred adaptive strategies of urban migrants', in Cordell, L. S. and Beckerman, S. (eds.) *The versatility of kinship: essays presented to Harry W. Basehart*, Academic Press, 195-217.
Green, R. H. (1978) 'Transferability, exotism and other forms of dogmatic revisionism', *World Development* 6. 709-14.
Greenwood, W. (1933) *Love on the dole*, Jonathan Cape.
Grennel, P. (1972) 'Planning for invisible people: some consequences of bureaucratic values and practices', in Turner, J. F. C. and Fichter, R. (eds.) (1972), 95-121.

Griffin, K. (1978) Review of 'Why poor people stay poor', *Journal of Development Studies* 15. 108–9.
— and Ghose, A. K. (1979) 'Growth and impoverishment in the rural areas of Asia', *World Development* 7. 361–84.
— and Khan, A. R. (1978) 'Poverty in the Third World: ugly facts and fancy models', *World Development* 6. 295–304.
Griffith-Jones, S. (1978) 'A critical evaluation of Popular Unity's short-term and financial policy', *World Development* 6. 1019–29.
Grimes, O. F. (1976) *Housing for low income urban families*, Johns Hopkins University Press.
Grindal, B. T. (1973) 'Islamic affiliations and urban adaptations: the Sisala migrant in Accra, Ghana', *Africa* 43. 333–46.
Guevara, E. (1968) *The diary of Che Guevara. Bolivia: November 7, 1966– October 7, 1967. The authorized text in English and Spanish*. Bantam Books.
— (1960) *La guerra de guerrillas*, Departmento del Minfar, Havana. English trans. (1961) *Guerrilla warfare*, Monthly Review Press.
Gugler, J. (1982) 'Overurbanization reconsidered', *Economic Development and Cultural Change* 30. 173–89.
— (1980) '"A minimum of urbanism and a maximum of ruralism": the Cuban experience', *International Journal of Urban and Regional Research* 4. 516–534.
— (1976) 'Migrating to urban centres of unemployment in tropical Africa', in Richmond, A. H. and Kubat, D. (eds.) *Internal migration: The New and the Third World*, Sage Publications, 184–204.
— (1975a) 'Particularism in Subsaharan Africa: "Tribalism" in town', *Canadian Review of Sociology and Anthropology* 12. 303–15.
— (1975b) 'Part-time farmers: the peri-urban holdings of urban workers in Kampala', *Journal of Eastern African Research and Developments* 5. 219–24.
— (1971) 'Life in a dual system: Eastern Nigerians in town, 1961', *Cahiers d'Etudes Africaines* 11. 400–21.
— (1969) 'On the theory of rural-urban migration: the case of Subsaharan Africa', in Jackson, J. A. (ed.) *Migration*, Cambridge University Press, 134–155.
— and Flanagan, W. G. (1978a) *Urbanization and social change in West Africa*, Cambridge University Press.
— and Flanagan, W. G. (1978b) 'Urban–rural ties in West Africa: extent, interpretation, prospects and implications', *African Perspectives* 1. 68–78.
— and Flanagan, W. G. (1977) 'On the political economy of urbanization in the Third World: the case of West Africa', *International Journal of Urban and Regional Research* 1. 272–92.
Guillén, A. (1966) *Estrategia de la guerrilla urbana: principios básicos de guerra revolucionaria, Ediciones Liberación, Montevideo. English trans.: Donald Hodges (ed.) (1973) Philosophy of the urban guerrilla: the revolutionary writings of Abraham Guillén*, William Morrow.
Guillet, D. (1976) 'Migration, agrarian reform, and structural change in rural Peru', *Human Organization* 35. 295–302.
Gwynne, R. N. (1978) 'Government planning and the location of the motor vehicle industry in Chile', *Tijdschrift voor Economische en Sociale Geografie* 69. 130–40.
Haley, A. (1977) *Roots*, Pan Books.
Handelman, H. (1975) 'The political mobilization of urban squatter settlements:

Santiago's recent experience and its implications for urban research', *Latin American Research Review* 10 (2). 35–72.

Hannerz, U. (1980) *Exploring the city: inquiries toward an urban anthropology*, Columbia University Press.

—— (1969) *Soulside: inquiries into ghetto culture and community*, Columbia University Press.

Hardoy, J. E. (1975) 'Two thousand years of Latin American urbanization', in Hardoy, J. E. (ed.) (1975), 3–56.

—— (ed.) (1975) *Urbanization in Latin America: approaches and issues*, Anchor/ Doubleday.

Harris, J. R. and Sabot, R. H. (1982) 'Urban unemployment in LDCs: towards a more general search model', in Sabot, R. H. (ed.) *Migration and the labor market in developing countries*, Westview Press, 65–89.

—— and Todaro, M. P. (1970) 'Migration, unemployment and development: a two-sector analysis', *American Economic Review* 60. 126–42.

—— and Todaro, M. P. (1968) 'Urban unemployment in East Africa: an economic analysis of policy alternatives', *East African Economic Review* 4. 17–36.

Hart, K. (1973) 'Informal income opportunities and urban employment in Ghana', *Journal of Modern African Studies* 11. 61–89.

Harvey, D. (1973) *Social justice and the city*, Arnold.

Hellman, J. A. (1978) *Mexico in crisis*, Holmes and Meier.

Henfrey, C. and Sorj, B. (1977) *Chilean voices: activists describe their experiences of the Popular Unity period*, Harvester Press.

Herrick, B. H. (1965) *Urban migration and economic development in Chile*, MIT Press.

Hinderink, J. and Sterkenburg, J. (1975) *Anatomy of an African town*, State University of Utrecht.

Hindess, B. and Hirst, P. (1975) *Precapitalist modes of production*, Routledge & Kegan Paul.

Hirschman, A. O. (1958) *The strategy of economic development*, Yale University Press.

Hoch, I. (1972) 'Income and city size', *Urban Studies* 9. 299–328.

Hodges, D. C. (1973) 'Introduction: the social and political philosophy of Abraham Guillén', in Hodges, D. C. (ed.) *Philosophy of the urban guerrilla: the revolutionary writings of Abraham Guillén*, William Morrow, 1–55.

Holland, S. (1976) *Capital and the regions*, Macmillan.

Hollnsteiner, M. R. (1974) 'The case of "the people versus Mr. Urbano Planner y Administrador"', in Abu-Lughod and Hay (eds.) (1977), 307–20.

—— (1972) 'Becoming an urbanite: the neighbourhood as a learning environment', in Dwyer, D. J. (ed.), 29–40.

Hopkins, A. G. (1973) *An economic history of West Africa*, Longman.

Hopkins, N. S. (1972) *Popular government in an African town; Kita, Mali*, University of Chicago Press.

Horvath, R. J. (1972) 'A definition of colonialism', *Current Anthropology* 13. 45–51.

Hoselitz, B. F. (1957) 'Generative and parasitic cities', *Economic Development and Cultural Change* 3. 278–94.

—— (1953) 'The role of cities in the economic growth of underdeveloped countries', *Journal of Political Economy* 61. 195–208.

Howe, C. (1978) *China's economy: a basic guide*, Basic Books.

Hugo, G. J. (1977) 'Circular migration', *Bulletin of Indonesian Economic Studies* 13. 57–66.

Hutton, C. (1973) *Reluctant farmers? A study of unemployment and planned rural development in Uganda*, East African Publishing House.

IBGE (Instituto Brasileiro de Estatística) (1970) Anuario Estatístico do Brasil, 1970.

Inkeles, A. and Smith, D. H. (1970) 'The fate of personal adjustment in the process of modernization', *International Journal of Comparative Sociology* 11. 81–114.

International Labour Office (1972) *Employment, incomes and equality: a strategy for increasing productive employment in Kenya*, ILO.

Isard, W. (1960) *Methods of regional analysis*, MIT Press.

Izaguirre, M. (1977) *Ciudad Guayana; la estrategia del desarrollo polarizado*, Ediciones SIAP-Planteos, Buenos Aires.

Jakobson, L. and Prakash, V. (1974) 'Urban planning in the context of a "new urbanization"', in Jakobson and Prakash (eds.) (1974), 259–86.

—— —— (eds.) (1974) *Metropolitan growth: public policy for South and Southeast Asia*, Halsted Press.

Jeffersen, M. (1939) 'The law of the primate city', *Geographical Review* 29. 226–82.

Jeffries, R. D. (1978) *Class, power and ideology in Ghana: the railwaymen of Sekondi*, African Studies Series, Cambridge University Press.

Jellinek, L. (1978) 'Circular migration and the *pondok* dwelling system: a case study of ice-cream traders in Jakarta', in Rimmer, P. J., Drakakis-Smith, D. W., and McGee, T. G. (eds.) *Food, shelter and transport in Southeast Asia and the Pacific*, Research School of Pacific Studies, Department of Human Geography HG/12, Australian National University, 135–54.

—— (1977) 'The life of a Jakarta street trader', in Abu-Lughod, J. and Hay, R. Jr. (eds.), 244–56.

—— (1976) 'The life of a Jakarta street trader – two years later', Working Paper 13, Centre of Southeast Asian Studies, Monash University.

Jesus, C. M. de (1960) *Quarto de despejo: diario de uma favelada*, São Paulo: Francisco Alves. English trans. (1962) *Child of the dark: the diary of Carolina Maria de Jesus*, Souvenir Press/Dutton.

Jocano, F. L. (1975) *Slum as a way of life: a study of coping behaviour in an urban environment*, University of the Philippines Press.

Johnson, E. A. J. (1970) *The organization of space in developing countries*, Harvard University Press.

Johnson, L. L. (1967) 'Problems of import substitution: the Chilean automobile industry', *Economic Development and Cultural Change* 15. 202–16.

Johnson, M. (1977) 'Political bosses and their gangs: Zu'ama and qabadayat in the Sunni Muslim quarters of Beirut', in Gellner, E. and Waterbury, J. (eds.) *Patrons and clients in Mediterranean societies*, Duckworth, 207–24.

Johnson, R. E. (1979) *Peasant and proletarian: the working class of Moscow in the late nineteenth century*, Rutgers University Press/Leicester University Press.

Johnston, B. F. and Mellor, J. W. (1961) 'The role of agriculture in economic development', *American Economic Review* 51. 566–92.

Johnston, R. J. (1976) 'Observations on accounting procedures and urban-size policies', *Environment and Planning* A 8. 327–39.

Joseph, S. (1982) 'Family as security and bondage: a political strategy of the Lebanese working class', in Safa, H. I. (ed.) *Towards a political economy of urbanization in Third World countries*, Oxford University Press, 151–71.

Joshi, H. and Joshi, V. (1976) *Surplus labour and the city: a study of Bombay*, Oxford University Press.

Kalmanovitz, S. (1977) *Ensayos sobre el desarrollo del capitalismo dependiente*, Editorial Pluma, Bogotá.

Kang, G. E. and Kang, T. S. (1978) 'The Korean urban shoeshine gang: a minority community', *Urban Anthropology* 7. 171–83.

Karol, K. S. (1970) *Les guérilleros au pouvoir: l'itinéraire politique de la révolution cubaine*. L'histoire que nous vivons, Robert Laffont, Paris. English trans. (1970) *Guerrillas in power: the course of the Cuban revolution*, Hill & Wang.

Katzenstein, M. F. (1979) *Ethnicity and equality: the Shiv Sena party and preferential policies in Bombay*, Cornell University Press.

Katzman, M. T. (1977) *Cities and frontiers in Brazil: regional dimensions of economic development*, Harvard University Press.

Keles, R. (1973) *Urbanization in Turkey*, Ford Foundation.

Khalaf, S. (1977) 'Changing forms of political patronage in Lebanon', in Gellner, E. and Waterbury, J. (eds.) *Patrons and clients in Mediterranean societies*, Duckworth, 185–205.

Kiernan, V. G. (1972) *The lords of human kind: European attitudes to the outside world in the Imperial age*, Penguin.

King, A. D. (1976) *Colonial urban development: culture, social power and environment*, Routledge & Kegan Paul.

King, T. (1970) *Mexico: industrialization and trade policies since 1940*, Oxford University Press.

Klare, M. T. (1972) *War without end: American planning for the next Vietnams*, Alfred A. Knopf.

Kleinpenning, J. M. G. (1978) 'A further evaluation of the policy for the integration of the Amazon region (1974–1976)', *Tijdschrift voor Economische en Sociale Geografie* 69. 78–85.

Kohl, J. and Litt, J. (1974) *Urban guerrilla warfare in Latin America*, MIT Press.

Krishnamurty, J. (1975) 'Some aspects of unemployment in urban India', *Journal of Development Studies* 11. 11–19.

Kubler, G. (1964) 'Cities and culture in the colonial period in Latin America', *Diogenes* 47. 53–62.

Kuklinski, A. (ed.) (1972) *Growth poles and growth centres in regional planning*, Mouton.

Kusnetzoff, F. (1975) 'Housing policies or housing politics: an evaluation of the Chilean experience', *Journal of Interamerican Studies and World Affairs*, 17. 281–310.

Kuznets, S. (1966) *Modern economic growth: rate, structure and spread*, Yale University Press.

Laclau, E. (1971) 'Feudalism and capitalism in Latin America', *New Left Review* 67. 19–38.

Lahiri, T. B. (1978) 'Calcutta: a million city with a million problems', in Misra R. P. (ed.) (1978), 43–72.

Laite, J. (1981) *Industrial development and migrant labour in Latin America*, Manchester University Press.

Landé, C. H. (1977) 'Introduction: the dyadic basis of clientelism', in Schmidt, S. W., Guasti, L., Landé, C. H. and Scott, J. C. (eds.) *Friends, followers, and factions: a reader in political clientelism*, University of California Press, xiii-xxxvii.

Lander, L. and Funes, J. C. (1965) 'Urbanization and Development', reprinted in Hardoy, J. E. (ed.) (1975), 287-337.

Laquian, A. A. (1977) 'Whither site and services?' *Habitat* 2. 291-301.

—— (ed.) (1971) *Rural-urban migrants and metropolitan development*, Intermet, Toronto.

Lardy, N. R. (1978) *Economic growth and distribution in China*, Cambridge University Press.

Lartéguy, J. (1976) *Les guérilleros*, Raoul Solar. English translation (1970) *The guerrillas*, New American Library.

Laun, J. I. (1976) 'El estado y la vivienda en Colombia: análisis de urbanizaciones del Instituto de Crédito Territorial en Bogotá', in Castillo, C. (ed.) *Vida urbana y urbanismo*, Instituto Colombiano de Cultura.

Lavell, A. M. (1971) 'Industrial development and the regional problem: a case study of Central Mexico', Unpublished doctoral thesis, University of London.

Leeds, A. (1973) 'Locality power in relation to supralocal power institutions', in Southall, A. (ed.) *Urban anthropology: cross-cultural studies of urbanization*, Oxford University Press, 15-41.

—— (1971) 'The concept of the "culture of poverty": conceptual, logical, and empirical problems, with perspectives from Brazil and Peru', in Leacock, E. B. (ed.) *The culture of poverty: a critique*, Simon & Schuster, 226-284.

—— (1969) 'The significant variables determining the character of squatter settlements', *América Latina* 12. 44-86.

—— and Leeds, E. (1976) 'Accounting for behavioral differences: three political systems and the responses of squatters in Brazil, Peru, and Chile', in Walton, J. and Masotti, L. H. (eds.), 193-248.

—— —— (1970) 'Brazil and the myth of urban rurality: urban experience, work, and values in the "squatments" of Rio de Janeiro and Lima', in Field, A. (ed.) *City and country in the Third World: issues in the modernization of Latin America*, Schenkman Publishing, 229-85.

Lefeber, L. (1978) 'Spatial population distribution: urban and rural development', Paper presented to the ECLA/CELADE Seminar on Population Redistribution, August 1978.

Lefebvre, H. (1970) *La révolution urbaine*, Paris.

Leiserson, A. (1979) 'Child labour in developing countries', *Internationale Entwicklung* 4. 3-13.

Lewis, J. P. (1962) *Quiet crisis in India: economic development and American policy*, The Brookings Institution, Washington DC.

Lewis, O. (1970) 'The culture of poverty', in Lewis, O., *Anthropological essays*, Random House, 67-80. First published in 1966.

—— (1959) *Five families: Mexican case studies in the culture of poverty*, Basic Books.

—— Lewis, R. M. and Rigdon, S. M. (1978) *Neighbors: living the Revolution. An oral history of contemporary Cuba*, University of Illinois Press.

Lieuwen, E. (1961) *Venezuela*, Oxford University Press.

Linsky, A. S. (1965) 'Some generalizations concerning primate cities', *Annals of the American Association of Geographers* 55. 506-13.

Lipton, M. (1977) *Why poor people stay poor: a study of urban bias in world development*, Temple Smith/Harvard University Press.

Little, K. (1974) *Urbanization as a social process*, Routledge & Kegan Paul.

Lloyd, P. (1979) *Slums of hope? Shanty towns of the Third World*, Penguin.

Lofman, B. G. (1979) 'Third World urbanization: regional patterns and significant variables', University of Connecticut, Undergraduate dissertation.
Lomnitz, L. (1978) 'Mechanisms of articulation between shantytown settlers and the urban system', *Urban Anthropology* 7. 185–205.
—— (1977) *Networks and marginality: life in a Mexican shantytown*, Academic Press.
—— (1974) 'The social and economic organization of a Mexican shantytown', in Cornelius, W. A. and Trueblood, F. M. (eds.) *Anthropological perspectives on Latin American urbanization*, *Latin American Urban Research* 4, Sage, 135–155.
Losada, R. and Gómez, H. (1976) *La tierra en el mercado pirata de Bogotá*, Fedesarrollo.
Lowder, S. (1978) 'The context of Latin American labor migration: a review of the literature post-1970', *Sage Race Relations Abstracts* 6. 1–49.
Lozano, E. E. (1975) 'Housing the urban poor in Chile: contrasting experiences under "Christian Democracy" and "Unidad Popular"', in Cornelius, W. A. and Trueblood, F. M. (eds.) (1975) *Latin American Urban Research* 5. 177–96.
Lubeck, P. M. (1981) 'Class formation at the periphery: class consciousness and Islamic nationalism among Nigerian workers', *Research in the Sociology of Work* 1. 37–70.
Mabogunje, A. L. (1962) *Yoruba towns*, Ibadan University Press.
—— Hardoy, J. E. and Misra, R. P. (1978) *Shelter provision in developing countries*, John Wiley.
McGee, T. G. (1976) 'The persistence of the proto-proletariat: occupational structures and planning for the future of Third World cities', *Progress in Geography* 9. 3–38.
—— (1971) *The urbanization process in the Third World: explorations in search of a theory*, Bell.
—— (1967) *The Southeast Asian city*, Bell.
McGreevey, W. P. (1971a) 'A statistical analysis of primacy and normality in the size distribution of Latin American cities, 1750–1960', in Morse, R. M. (ed.) *The urban development of Latin America 1750–1920*, Stanford University, 116–29.
—— (1971b) *An economic history of Colombia, 1845–1930*, Cambridge University Press.
Maddison, A. (1971) *Class structure and economic growth: India and Pakistan since the Moghuls*, W. W. Norton.
Majumdar, M. (1977) 'Regional income disparities, regional income change and federal policy in India, 1950–51 to 1967–68: an empirical evaluation', Dundee University, Department of Economics Occasional Paper No. 7.
Majumdar, T. K. (1978) 'The urban poor and social change: a study of squatter settlements in Delhi', in de Souza, A. (ed.) *The Indian City: poverty, ecology and urban development*, Manohar, New Delhi, 29–60.
Malloy, J. M. (1979) *The politics of social security in Brazil*, Pitt Latin American Series, University of Pittsburgh Press.
—— (1970) *Bolivia: the uncompleted revolution*, University of Pittsburgh Press.
Mangin, W. (1967) 'Latin American squatter settlements: a problem and a solution', *Latin American Research Review* 2. 65–98.
Marris, P. (1979) 'The meaning of slums and patterns of change', *International Journal of Urban and Regional Research* 3. 419–41.
Marx, K. (1967) *Capital*, three vols. International Publishers Edition.

—— (1853) 'The results of British rule in India', *New York Daily Tribune*, 11 July 1853. Reprinted in *On Colonialism*, Lawrence & Wishart, 1950.

Mason, E. et al. (1980) *The economic and social modernization of the Republic of Korea*, MIT Press.

Mason, M. (1978) 'Contemporary colonization processes in the northeast Mato Grosso', Unpublished doctoral dissertation, University of London.

Mathur, O. P. (1977) 'The problem of regional disparities: an analysis of Indian policies and programmes', *Habitat International* 2. 427-53.

Mattelart, M. (1976) 'Chile: the feminine version of the coup d'état', in Nash, J. and Safa, H. I. (eds.) *Sex and class in Latin America*, Praeger, 279-301.

Mayans, E. (ed.) (1971) *Tupamaros: antología documental*, CIDOC Cuaderno 60, Centro Intercultural de Documentación, Cuernavaca.

Mayer, P. (1971) *Townsmen or tribesmen: conservatism and the process of urbanization in a South African city*, 2nd edition, Oxford University Press. First published in 1961.

Maxwell, N. (ed.) (1979) *China's road to development*, 2nd edition, Pergamon.

Mazumdar, D. (1979) 'Paradigms in the study of urban labour markets in LDCs: a reassessment in the light of an empirical survey in Bombay City', World Bank Staff Working Paper 366.

—— (1976) 'The urban informal sector', *World Development* 4. 655-79.

Mehta, S. K. (1964) 'Some demographic and economic correlates of primate cities: a case for re-evaluation', *Demography* 1. 136-47.

Mera, K. (1976) 'The changing pattern of population distribution in Japan and its implications for developing countries', in UNCRD (1976) 247-77.

—— (1973) 'On the urban agglomeration and economic efficiency', *Economic Development and Cultural Change* 22. 309-24.

Merrick, T. W. (1976) 'Employment earnings in the informal sector in Brazil: The case of Belo Horizonte', *Journal of Developing Areas* 10. 337-53.

Mesa-Lago, C. (1978) *Social security in Latin America: pressure groups, stratification, and inequality*, Pitt Latin American Series, University of Pittsburgh Press.

Meunier, C. (1976) 'Revendications urbaines, stratégie politique et transformation idéologique: le campamento "Nueva Habana" (Santiago) 1970-73', Doctoral Dissertation, Ecole des Hautes Etudes en Sciences Sociales, Paris.

Michaelson, K. L. (1979) 'Power, patrons, and political economy: Bombay', in Leons, M. B. and Rothstein, F. (eds.) *New directions in political economy: an approach from anthropology*. Contributions in Economics and Economic History 22, Greenwood Press, 235-48.

—— (1976) 'Patronage, mediators, and the historical context of social organization in Bombay', *American Ethnologist* 3. 281-95.

Miliband, R. (1977) *Marxism and politics*, Oxford University Press.

—— (1969) *The state in capitalist society*, Quartet Books, 1st edition 1967.

Miller, J. C. (1974) *Regional development: a review of the state of the art*, USAID, Washington DC.

Mills, E. S. (1972) 'Welfare aspects of national policy towards city sizes', *Urban Studies* 9. 117-24.

Misra, R. P. (ed.) (1978) *Million cities of India*, Vikas Publishing House.

Mitra, Ashok (1977) *Terms of trade and class relations*, Frank Cass.

Mitra, Asok, Mukherji, S. and Bose, R. (1980) *Indian cities: their industrial structure, immigration and capital investment 1961-1971*, Abhinav Publications.

Moore, B. Jr. (1966) *Social origins of dictatorship and democracy: lord and peasant in the making of the modern world*, Beacon Press.

Moorsom, R. (1979) 'Labour consciousness and the 1971-72 contract workers strike in Namibia', *Development and Change* 10. 205-31.

Morawetz, D. (1979) 'Walking on two legs: reflections on a China visit', *World Development* 7. 877-92.

Morse, R. M. (1975) 'The development of urban systems in the Americas in the nineteenth century', *Journal of Inter-American Studies and World Affairs*, 17. 4-26.

—— (1971) 'Trends and issues in Latin American urban research, 1965-1970', *Latin American Research Review* 7. 3-52 and 19-76.

Moseley, M. J. (1975) *Growth centres in spatial planning*, Pergamon Press.

Moser, C. O. N. (forthcoming) 'A home of one's own: squatter housing strategies in Guayaquil, Ecuador', in Gilbert, A. G., Hardoy, J. E., and Ramírez, R. (eds.), 159-90.

—— (1978) 'Informal sector or petty commodity production: dualism or dependence in urban development?', *World Development* 6. 1041-64.

Muench, L. H. (1978) 'The private burden of urban social overhead: a study of the informal housing market of Kampala, Uganda', University of Pennsylvania, Doctoral Dissertation.

Mumford, L. (1975) *The city in history*, Penguin, 1st edition 1961.

—— (1938) *The culture of cities*, Harcourt Brace.

Murphey, R. (1980) *The fading of the Maoist vision: city and country in China's development*, Methuen.

—— (1976) 'Chinese urbanization under Mao', in Berry, B. J. L. (ed.) (1976) 311-30.

—— (1972) 'City and countryside as ideological issues: India and China', *Comparative Studies in History and Society* 14. 250-67.

—— (1969) 'Traditionalism and colonialism: changing urban roles in Asia', *Journal of Asian Studies* 29. 67-84.

Myers, D. (1978) 'Caracas: the politics of intensifying primacy', *Latin American Urban Research* 5. 227-58.

Myrdal, G. (1970) *The challenge of world poverty: a world anti-poverty program in outline*, Pantheon.

—— (1957) *Economic theory and underdeveloped regions*, Duckworth.

Naipaul, V. S. (1977) *India: a wounded civilization*, André Deutsch.

—— (1969) *The mimic men*, Penguin, 1st edition 1967.

Nelson, J. M. (1979) *Access to power: politics and the urban poor in developing nations*, Princeton University Press.

Nelson, N. (1979) 'How women and men get by: the sexual division of labour in the informal sector of a Nairobi squatter settlement', in Bromley, R. and Gerry, C. (eds.) (1979) 283-302.

Nurkse, R. (1952) 'Some international aspects of the problem of economic development', *American Economic Review* 42. 571-83.

O'Connor, A. M. (1976) '"Third World" or one world?' *Area* 8. 269-71.

—— (1971) *A geography of tropical African development*, Pergamon.

Odell, P. R. and Preston, D. A. (1973) *Economies and societies in Latin America: a geographical interpretation*, John Wiley.

Odongo, J. and Lea, J. P. (1977) 'Home ownership and rural-urban links in Uganda', *Journal of Modern African Studies* 15. 59-73.

OHE (Office of Health Economics) (1972) *Medical care in developing countries*, Office of Health Economics.

Ojo, G. J. A. (1966) *Yoruba palaces: a study of afins of Yorubaland*, University of London Press.

Oliver, P. (1973) *Urbanization in Indonesia*, Ford Foundation.

Oram, N. D. (1976) *Colonial town to Melanesian city: Port Moresby 1884-1974*, Australian National University.

Orwell, G. (1937) *The road to Wigan Pier*, Victor Gollancz.

Oxaal, I., Barnett, T., and Booth, D. (eds.) (1975) *Beyond the sociology of development: economy and society in Latin America and Africa*, Routledge & Kegan Paul.

Paden, J. N. (1973) *Religion and political culture in Kano*, University of California Press.

Pahl, R. (1977) 'Managers, technical experts and the state: forms of mediation, manipulation and dominance in urban and regional development', in Harloe, M. (ed.) *Captive cities*, John Wiley, 49–60.

Palma, G. (1978) 'Dependency: a formal theory of underdevelopment or a methodology for the analysis of concrete situations of underdevelopment?', *World Development* 6. 881-924.

Pandhe, M. K. (ed.) (1979) *Child labour in India: based on official reports*, India Book Exchange, Calcutta.

Papanek, G. (1975) 'The poor of Jakarta', *Economic Development and Cultural Change* 24. 1-27.

—— (1954) 'Development problems relevant to agricultural tax policy', Papers and Proceedings of the Conference on Agricultural Taxation and Economic Development, Harvard.

Parr, J. B. (1974) 'Regional differences within a nation: a comment', *Papers and Proceedings of the Regional Science Association* 32. 83-91.

—— (1970) 'Models of city size in an urban system', *Papers and Proceedings of the Regional Science Association* 25. 221-53.

Payne, G. K. (forthcoming) 'Self-help housing: a critique: The gecekondus of Ankara', in Ward, P. M. (ed.), 117-40.

—— (1977) *Urban housing in the Third World*, Leonard Hill.

Peace, A. (1975) 'The Lagos proletariat: labour aristocrats or populist militants?', in Sandbrook, R. and Cohen, R. (eds.) *The development of an African working class: studies in class formation and action*, Longman, 281-302.

Pearse, A. (1975) *The Latin American peasant*, Frank Cass.

—— (1970) 'Urbanization and the incorporation of the peasant', in Field, A. J. (ed.) *City and country in the Third World: issues in the modernization of Latin America*, Schenkman, 201-12.

Pearson, L. B. (ed.) (1969) *Partners in development: report of the Commission on International Development*, Pall Mall Press.

Peattie, L. R. (1979) 'Housing policy in developing countries: two puzzles', *World Development* 7. 1017-22.

—— (1975) '"Tertiarization" and urban poverty in Latin America', in Cornelius, W. A. and Trueblood, F. M. (eds.) *Urbanization and inequality: the political economy of urban and rural development in Latin America*, Latin American Urban Research 5, Sage, 109-23.

Peil, M. (1981) *Cities and suburbs: urban life in West Africa*, Africana Publishing.

—— (1976) 'African squatter settlements: a comparative study', *Urban Studies* 13. 155-66.

Pérez Perdomo, R. and Nikken, P. (1979) *Derecho y propiedad de la vivienda en los barrios de Caracas*, Universidad Central de Venezuela, Fondo de Cultura Económica. Forthcoming in English in Gilbert, A. G., Hardoy, J. E., and Ramírez, R. (eds.), 205-30.

Perlman, J. (1976) *The myth of marginality: urban poverty and politics in Rio de Janeiro*, University of California Press.

Perrings, C. (1979) *Black mineworkers in Central Africa: industrial strategies and the evolution of an African proletariat in the Copperbelt 1911-41*, Heinemann/Africana Publishing.

Petras, E. M. (1973) *Social organization of the urban housing movement in Chile*, Council on International Studies, Special Studies 39, State University of New York.

Pirenne, H. (1925) *Medieval cities*, Princeton University Press.

Polanyi, K. (1945) *Origins of our time: the great transformation*, Gollancz.

Pollak-Eltz, A. (1979) 'Migration from Barlovento to Caracas', in Margolies, L. (ed.) *The Venezuelan peasant in country and city*, Antropología Social 1. Ediciones Venezolanas de Antropología, Caracas, 29-40.

Portes, A. (1979) 'Housing policy, urban poverty, and the state: the favelas of Rio de Janeiro, 1972-76', *Latin American Research Review* 14. 3-24.

—— (1972) 'Rationality in the slum: an essay on interpretative sociology', *Comparative Studies on History and Society* 14. 268-86.

—— and Walton, J. (1981) *Labor, class, and the international system*, Academic Press.

—— —— (1976) *Urban Latin America: the political condition from above and below*, University of Texas Press.

Poulantzas, N. (1976) 'The capitalist state: a reply to Miliband and Laclau', *New Left Review* 95. 63-83.

—— (1973) *Political power and social classes*, New Left Books.

—— (1969) 'The problem of the capitalist state', *New Left Review* 58. 67-78.

Powell, J. D. (1980) 'Electoral behavior among peasants', in Volgyes, I., Lonsdale, R. E., and Avery, W. P. (eds.) *The process of rural transformation: Eastern Europe, Latin America and Australia*, Comparative Rural Transformation Series, Pergamon Press, 193-241.

Pradilla, E. (1976) 'Notas acerca del "problema de la vivienda"', *Ideología y Sociedad* 16. 70-107.

Prebisch, R. (1950) *The economic development of Latin America and its principal problems*, United Nations.

Qadeer, M. A. (1974) 'Do cities modernize the developing countries? An examination of South Asian experience', *Comparative Studies in Society and History* 16. 266-83.

Quijano, A. (1974) 'The marginal pole of the economy and the marginalised labour force', *Economy and Society* 3. 393-428.

—— (1971) 'La formación de un universo marginal en las ciudades de América Latina', in Castells, M. (ed.), 141-66.

Ramachandran, P. (1974) *Pavement dwellers in Bombay City*, Tata Institute of Social Sciences, Bombay.

Ramaswamy, E. A. (1973) 'Politics and organized labour in India', *Asian Survey* 13, 914-28. Reprinted in Cohen, R., Gutkind, P. C. W., and Brazier, P. (eds.) (1979) *Peasants and proletarians: the struggle of Third World workers*, Monthly Review Press.

Ramaswamy, U. (1979) 'Tradition and change among industrial workers', *Economic and Political Weekly* 14. 367-76.

Rawski, T. G. (1979) *Economic growth and employment in China*, Oxford University Press.

Ray, T. (1969) *The politics of the barrios of Venezuela*, University of California Press.

Redclift, M. R. (1973) 'Squatter settlements in Latin American cities: the response from government', *Journal of Development Studies* 10. 92–109.

Reed, R. R. (1976) 'Indigenous urbanism in South-East Asia', in Yeung, Y. M. and Lo, C. P. (eds.) *Changing South-East Asian cities: readings on urbanization*, Oxford University Press, 14–27.

Rempel, H. (1979) 'Rural–urban labour migration and urban unemployment in Kenya', mimeo.

Richardson, H. W. (1977) 'City size and national spatial strategies in developing countries', World Bank Staff Working Paper 252.

— (1976) 'The argument for very large cities reconsidered: a comment', *Urban Studies* 13. 307–10.

— (1973) *Economics of urban size*, Saxon House.

Roberts, B. R. (1978) *Cities of peasants: the political economy of urbanization in the Third World*, Edward Arnold/Sage.

— (1976) 'The provincial urban system and the process of dependency', in Portes, A. and Browning, H. L. (eds.) *Current perspectives in Latin American urban research*, University of Texas Press, 99–131.

Robinson, G. and Salih, K. B. (1971) 'The spread of development around Kuala Lumpur', *Regional Studies* 5. 303–14.

Rocca, C. A. (1970) 'Productivity in Brazilian manufacturing', in Bergsmann (ed.) *Brazil: industrialization and trade policies*, Oxford University Press, 22–41.

Rodwin, L. L. (1973) 'Choosing regions for development', in Friedrich, C. J. and Harris, S. E. (eds.) *Public policy*, Harvard University Graduate School of Public Administration, Cambridge, Mass., 141–62.

— (1961) 'Metropolitan policy for developing areas', in Isard, W. and Cumberland, J. H. (eds.) *Regional economic planning*, OECD.

— and Associates (1969) *Planning urban growth and regional development: the experience of the Guayana program in Venezuela*, MIT Press.

Rofman, A. B. (1974) *Dependencia, estructura de poder y formación regional en América Latina*, Ed. Suramericana, Buenos Aires.

Rollwagen, J. R. (1971) 'Region of origin and rural–urban migration in Mexico: some general comments and a case study of entrepreneurial migration from the West', *International Migration Review* 5. 277–338.

Romero, E. (1949) *Historia económica del Perú*, Editorial Suramericana, Buenos Aires.

Romm, J. (1973) *Urbanization in Thailand*, Ford Foundation.

Rondinelli, D. A. and Ruddle, K. (1976) *Urban functions in rural development: an analysis of integrated spatial development policy*, USAID.

Rosenberg, M. B. and Malloy, J. M. (1978) 'Indirect pariciption versus social equity in the evolution of Latin American social security policy', in Booth, J. A. and Seligson, M. A. (eds.) *Political participation in Latin America*, vol. 1: *Citizen and State*, Holmes & Meier, 157–71.

Rosenstein-Rodan, P. N. (1943) 'Problems of industrialization of eastern and south-eastern Europe', *Economic Journal* 53. 202–11.

Rosing, K. E. (1966) 'A rejection of the Zipf model (rank-size rule) in relation to city size', *Professional Geographer* 18. 75–81.

Rosser, C. (1972) 'Housing and planned urban change: the Calcutta experience', in Dwyer (ed.) (1972), 179–90.

Rostow, W. W. (1960) *The stages of economic growth: a non-communist manifesto*, Cambridge University Press.

Rouch, J. (1956) 'Migrations au Ghana (Gold Coast): enquête 1953-1955',

Journal de la Société des Africanistes 26. 33–196.

Roxborough, I. (1979) *Theories of underdevelopment*, Macmillan.

Russell, C. A., Miller, J. A. and Hildner, R. E. (1974) 'The urban guerrilla in Latin America: a select bibliography', *Latin American Research Review* 9 (1). 37–79.

Ryan, W. (1971) *Blaming the victim*, Pantheon.

Saberwal, S. (1981) 'Elements of communalism', *Mainstream* 19 (29). 27–30 and (30). 15–19.

Sabot, R. H. (1979) *Economic development and urban migration: Tanzania 1900–1971*, Clarendon Press.

Sada, P. O. (1972) 'Residential land-use in Lagos: an inquiry into the relevance of traditional models', *African Urban Notes* 7. 3–25.

Salisbury, R. F. (1970) *Vunamami: economic transformation in a traditional society*, University of California Press.

Sandbrook, R. and Arn, J. (1977) *The labouring poor and urban class formation: the case of Greater Accra*, Occasional Monograph, Center for Developing-Area Studies, McGill University.

Santos, M. (1979) *The shared space: the two circuits of the urban economy in underdeveloped countries*, Methuen.

Sargent Jr., C. S. (1972) 'Toward a dynamic model of urban morphology', *Economic Geography* 48. 357–74.

Sarin, M. (1979) 'Urban planning, petty trading, and squatter settlements in Chandigarh, India', in Bromley, R. and Gerry, C. (eds.) (1979), 133–60.

Saul, J. S. (1975) 'The "labour aristocracy" thesis reconsidered', in Sandbrook, R. and Cohen, R. (eds.) *The development of an African working class: studies in class formation and action*, Longman, 303–310.

Saunders, P. (1980) *Urban politics: a sociological interpretation*, Penguin. First published 1979.

Saxena, D. P. (1977) *Rururban migration in India: causes and consequences*, Popular Prakashan, Bombay.

Schnore, L. F. (1965) 'On the spatial structure in the two Americas', in Hauser, P. and Schnore, L. F. (eds.) *The study of urbanization*, John Wiley, 347–98.

Schwerdtfeger, F. (1972) 'Urban settlement patterns in northern Nigeria', in Ucko, P. J. et al. (eds.) (1972), 547–56.

Scobie, J. R. (1964) *Argentina: a city and a nation*, Oxford University Press.

Seers, D. et al. (eds.) (1979) *Underdeveloped Europe: studies in core-periphery relations*, Harvester Press.

Sen Dou Chang (1968) 'The million city of mainland China', *Pacific Viewpoint* 9. 128–53.

Sengupta, A. K. (1977) 'Trade unions, politics and the state: a case from West Bengal', *Contributions to Indian Sociology*, NS 11. 45–68.

Shaheed, Z. A. (1979) 'Union leaders, worker organization and strikes: Karachi 1969–72', *Development and Change* 10. 181–204.

Sharpston, M. J. (1972) 'Uneven geographical distribution of medical care: a Ghanaian case study', *Journal of Development Studies* 9. 205–22.

Shaw, R. P. (1976) *Land tenure and the rural exodus in Chile, Colombia, Costa Rica and Peru*, Latin American Monographs, 2nd Series 19, The University Presses of Florida.

—— (1975) *Migration theory and fact: a review and bibliography of current literature*, Bibliography Series 5, Regional Science Research Institute, Philadelphia.

Shawcross, W. (1979) *Sideshow: Kissinger, Nixon and the destruction of Cambodia*, André Deutsch.
Shibli, K. (1974) 'Metropolitan planning in Karachi: a case study', in Jakobson and Prakash (eds.) (1974), 109–29.
Simmie, J. M. (1974) *Citizens in conflict: the sociology of town planning*, Hutchinson.
Simmons, A. B. (1978) 'Slowing metropolitan city growth in Asia; a review of policies, programmes and results', Paper presented to the ECLA/CELADE Seminar on Population Redistribution, August 1978.
—— Diaz-Briquets, S. and Laquian, A. A. (1977) *Social change and internal migration: a review of research findings from Africa, Asia, and Latin America*, International Development Research Centre, Ottawa.
—— and Cardona, R. (1972) 'Rural-urban migration: who comes, who stays, who returns? The case of Bogotá, Colombia, 1929–1968', *International Migration Review* 6. 166–81.
Sinclair, S. W. (1978) *Bibliography on the 'informal' sector*, Bibliography Series 10, Center for Developing-Area Studies, McGill University.
Sinclair, U. (1906) *The jungle*, Heinemann.
Singer, P. (1975) 'Urbanization and development: the case of São Paulo', in Hardoy, J. E. (ed.), 435–56.
—— (1973) 'Urbanización, dependencia y marginalidad en América Latina', in Castells, M. (ed.) (1973), 287–312.
Singh, A. M. (1976) *Neighbourhood and social networks in urban India*, Marwah, New Delhi.
Sjoberg, G. (1963) 'The rise and fall of cities: a theoretical perspective', *International Journal of Comparative Sociology* 4. 107–20.
—— (1960) *The pre-industrial city*, Free Press.
Skeldon, R. (1977) 'The evolution of migration patterns during urbanization in Peru', *Geographical Review* 67. 394–411.
Skinner, E. P. (1965) 'Labor migration among the Mossi of Upper Volta', in Kuper, H. (ed.) *Urbanization and migration in West Africa*, University of California Press, 60–84.
Skinner, R. (forthcoming) 'Self help, community organization and politics: Villa El Salvador, Lima', in Ward, P. M. (ed.), 209–29.
Sklar, R. L. (1963) *Nigerian political parties: power in an emergent African nation*, Princeton University Press.
Skocpol, T. (1979) *States and social revolutions: a comparative analysis of France, Russia, and China*, Cambridge University Press.
Songre, A., Sawadogo, J.-M., and Sanagoh, G. (1974) 'Réalités et effets de l'émigration massive des Voltaïques dans le contexte de l'Afrique Occidentale', in Amin, S. (ed.) *Modern migrations in Western Africa*, Oxford University Press, 384–402.
Souza, P. R. and Tokman, V. (1976) 'The informal urban sector in Latin America', *International Labour Review* 114. 355–65.
Sovani, N. V. (1964) 'The analysis of "over-urbanization"', *Economic Development and Cultural Change* 2. 113–22.
Spence, J. (1979) *Search for justice: neighborhood courts in Allende's Chile*, Westview Press.
Squire, L. (1981) *Employment policy in developing countries: a survey of issues and evidence*, Oxford University Press.
Srole, L. (1978) 'The city versus town and country: new evidence on an ancient

bias, 1975', in Srole, L. and Kassen Fischer, A. (eds.) *Mental health in the metropolis: the midtown Manhattan study*, revised edition, New York University Press, 433-59.

Steel, W. F. (1977) *Small-scale employment and production in developing countries: evidence from Ghana*, Praeger.

Stein, S. J. and Stein, B. H. (1970) *The colonial heritage in Latin America*, Oxford University Press.

Stewart, C. T. (1958) 'The size and spacing of cities', *Geographical Review* 48. 222-45.

Stöhr, W. B. (1975) *Regional development in Latin America: experience and prospects*, Mouton.

— and Fraser, D. R. F. (eds.) (1981) *Development from above or below? The dialectics of regional planning in developing countries*, John Wiley.

— and Tödtling, F. (1979) 'Spatial equity: some anti-theses to current regional development doctrine', in Folmer, H. and Oosterhaven, J. (eds.) *Spatial inequalities and regional development*, Martinus Nijhoff Publishing, 133-60.

Stren, R. (1975) 'Urban policy and performance in Kenya and Tanzania', *Journal of Modern African Studies* 13. 267-94.

Stretton, A. (1979) 'Instability of employment among building industry labourers in Manila', in Bromley, R. and Gerry, C. (eds.), 267-82.

Stuckey, B. (1975) 'Spatial analysis and economic development', *Development and Change* 6. 98-101.

Svenson, G. (1977) *El desarrollo económico departamental 1960-1975*, Inandes, Bogotá.

Ternent, J. A. S. (1976) 'Urban concentration and dispersal: urban policies in Latin America', in Gilbert, A. G. (ed.), 169-96.

Thomas, H. (1977) *The Cuban Revolution*, Harper & Row. First published in 1971 as part of *Cuba: the pursuit of freedom*, Harper & Row.

Thompson, R. (1979) 'City planning in China', in Maxwell, N. (ed.) (1979) 299-312.

Tipple, A. G. (1976) 'Self-help housing policies in a Zambian mining town', *Urban Studies* 13. 167-9.

Todaro, M. P. (1976) *Internal migration in developing countries: a review of theory, evidence, methodology and research priorities*, International Labour Office.

Tokman, V. E. (1978) 'An exploration into the nature of informal-formal sector relationships', *World Development* 6. 1065-75.

Townroe, P. M. (1979) 'Employment decentralization: policy instruments for large cities in less developed countries', *Progress in Planning* 10. 85-154.

Travieso, F. (1972) *Ciudad, región y subdesarrollo*, Fondo Editorial Común, Caracas.

Trowbridge, J. W. (1973) *Urbanization in Jamaica*, The Ford Foundation International Urbanization Survey, New York.

Turner, J. F. C. (1976) *Housing by people*, Marion Boyars.

— (1972) 'Housing as a verb', in Turner and Fichter (eds.), 148-75.

— (1969) 'Uncontrolled urban settlements: problems and policies', in Breese (ed.) (1969), 507-31.

— (1968) 'Housing priorities, settlement patterns and urban development in modernizing countries', *Journal of the American Institute of Planners* 34. 354-63.

— (1967) 'Barriers and channels for housing development in modernizing countries', *Journal of the American Institute of Planners*, 33. 167-81.

–– and Fichter, R. (eds.) (1972) *Freedom to Build*, Collier MacMillan.
Turner, R. (ed.) (1962) *India's urban future*, University of California Press.
Turnham, D. (1970) *The employment problem in less developed countries: a review of evidence*, OECD Development Centre.
Turok, B. and Maxey, K. (1976) 'Southern Africa: white power in crisis', in Gutkind, P. C. W. and Wallerstein, I. (eds.) *The political economy of contemporary Africa*, Sage Series on African Modernization and Development 1, Sage, 232–60.
Unikel, L. (1976) *El desarrollo urbano de México: diagóstico e implicaciones futuras*, El Colegio de México.
UNCRD (United Nations Centre for Regional Development) (1976) *Growth pole strategy and regional development planning in Asia*, UNCRD.
UNECLA (United Nations Economic Commission for Latin America) (1971) *Income Distribution in Latin America*, New York.
UNESCO (1957) *Urbanization in Asia and the Far East*, UNESCO.
United Nations (1980) *Patterns of urban and rural population growth*, Population Studies 68, United Nations.
–– (1969) *Growth of the world's urban and rural population 1920–2000*, United Nations.
UNRISD (United Nations Research Institute for Social Development) (1971) *Regional Development: experiences and prospects*, Vol. 1: *South and Southeast Asia*, Mouton.
Utría, R. (1972) 'Regional structure in Latin American development', *Latin American Urban Research* 2. 61–84.
Valentine, C. A. (1968) *Culture and poverty: critique and counter-proposals*, University of Chicago Press.
–– et al. (1969) 'Culture and poverty: critique and counter-proposals', *Current Anthropology* 10. 181–201.
Valenzuela, J. and Vernez, G. (1974) 'Construcción popular y estructura del mercado de vivienda: el caso de Bogotá', *Revista Interamericana de Planificación* 8. 88–104.
Valladares, L. do P. (1978a) *Passa-se uma casa: análise do programa de remoção de favelas do Rio de Janeiro*, Biblioteca de Ciencias Sociais, Zahar Editores.
–– (1978b) 'Working the system: squatter response to resettlement in Rio de Janeiro', *International Journal of Urban and Regional Research* 2. 12–25.
Van Huyck, A. P. (1968) 'The housing threshold for lowest income groups: the case of India', in Herbert, J. D. and Van Huyck, A. P. (1968) *Urban planning in the developing countries*, Praeger.
Vapñarsky, C. A. (1969) 'On rank-size distribution of cities: an ecological approach', *Economic Development and Cultural Change* 17. 584–95.
Vatuk, S. (1972) *Kinship and urbanization: white collar migrants in North India*, University of California Press.
Vernez, G. (1973) *The residential movements of low-income families: the case of Bogotá, Colombia*, Rand Institute.
Violich, F. (1944) *Cities of Latin America*, Reinhold.
Wallerstein, I. (1980) *The modern world-system II: mercantilism and the consolidation of the European world-economy, 1600–1750*, Academic Press.
–– (1974) *The modern world-system: capitalist agriculture and the origins of the European world economy in the sixteenth century*, Academic Press.
Walters, A. A. (1978) 'The value of urban land', in World Bank (1978) 65–98.
Walton, J. and Masotti, L. H. (eds.) (1976) *The city in comparative perspective*, Halsted Press.

Ward, B. (1964) 'Creating man's future: goals for a world of plenty', *Saturday Review*, 9 August, 27–29 and 191–3.
Ward, P. M. (ed.) (forthcoming) *Self-help housing: a critique*, Alexandrine Press.
—— (1978) 'Self-help housing in Mexico City: social and economic determinants of success', *Town Planning Review* 49. 38–50.
—— (1976a) 'The squatter settlement as slum or housing solution: the evidence from Mexico City', *Land Economics* 52. 330–46.
—— (1976b) 'Intra-city migration to squatter settlements in Mexico City', *Geoforum* 7. 369–83.
Warren, B. (1973) 'Imperialism and capitalist industrialization', *New Left Review* 81.
Webb, R. C. (1977) 'Wage policy and income distribution in developing countries', in Frank, Jr., C. R. and Webb, R. C. (eds.) *Income distribution and growth in less-developed countries*, Brookings Institution, 215–258.
Wee, A. (1972) 'Some social implications of rehousing programmes in Singapore', in Dwyer, D. J. (ed.) (1972), 216–30.
Wegelin, E. A. (1977) *Urban low-income housing and development*, Martinus Nijhoff.
Weiner, M. (1978) *Sons of the soil: migration and ethnic conflict in India*, Princeton University Press.
Weisner, T. S. (1976) 'Kariobangi: the case history of a squatter resettlement scheme in Kenya', in Arens, W. (ed.) (1976) *A century of change in East and Central Africa*, Mouton, 77–97.
—— (1973) 'One family, two households: rural-urban ties in Kenya', PhD dissertation, Harvard University.
—— and Abbott, S. (1977) 'Women, modernity, and stress: three contrasting contexts for change in East Africa', *Journal of Anthropological Research* 33. 421–51.
Welch, C. E. (1977) 'Obstacles to "peasant war" in Africa', *African Studies Review* 20. 121–30.
Wheatley, P. (1970) 'The significance of traditional Yoruba urbanism', *Comparative Studies in Society and History* 12. 393–423.
—— (1967) *City as symbol*, University College London, Inaugural Lecture.
White, A. (1975) 'Squatter settlements, politics and class conflict', University of Glasgow, Institute of Latin American Studies Occasional Papers No. 17.
Whyte, M. K. (n.d.a) 'Social control and rehabilitation in urban China', mimeo.
—— (n.d.b) 'Urban administration and distribution', mimeo.
Whyte, W. F. (1981) *Street corner society: the social structure of an Italian slum*, third edition, University of Chicago Press.
Williamson, J. G. (1965) 'Regional inequality and the process of national development: a description of the patterns', *Economic Development and Cultural Change* 13. 3–45.
Wilsher, P. and Righter, R. (1975) *The exploding cities*, Deutsch.
Wilson, F. (1972a) *Labour in the South African gold mines, 1911–1969*, African Studies 6, Cambridge University Press.
—— (1972b) *Migrant labour in South Africa*, Johannesburg, South African Council of Churches and Spro-cas.
Wilson, P. A. (1975) 'From mode· of production to spatial formation: the regional consequences of dependent industrialization in Peru', Cornell University Doctoral Dissertation.

Winston, G. (1979) 'The appeal of inappropriate technologies: self-inflicted wages, ethnic pride and corruption', *World Development* 7. 835–45.

Wirsing, R. G. (1976) 'Strategies of political bargaining in Indian city politics', in Rosenthal, D. B. (ed.) *The city in Indian politics*, Thomson Press (India), 192–212.

—— (1973) 'Associational "micro-arenas" in Indian urban politics', *Asian Survey* 13. 408–20.

Wirth, L. (1938) 'Urbanism as a way of life', *American Journal of Sociology* 44. 1–24.

Wolf, E. R. and Mintz, S. W. (1957) 'Haciendas and plantations in middle America and the Antilles', *Social and Economic Studies* 6. 380–412.

Wolf-Phillips, L. (1979) 'Why Third World?', *Third World Quarterly* 1. 105–16.

Womack, J. (1969) *Zapata and the Mexican Revolution*, Thames & Hudson.

World Bank (1981) *China: socialist economic development*, the main report, World Bank East Asia and Pacific Regional Office.

—— (1980) *World Development Report 1980*, The World Bank.

—— (1979) *World Development Report 1979*, The World Bank.

—— (1978) 'Urban land policy issues and opportunities, Vol. 1'. World Bank Staff Working Paper No. 283.

Yap, L. Y. L. (1977) 'The attraction of cities: a review of the migration literature', *Journal of Development Economics* 4. 239–64.

Yeung, Y. M. and Lo, C. P. (eds.) (1977) *Changing South-East Asian cities*, Oxford University Press.

Young, C. (1976) *The politics of cultural pluralism*, University of Wisconsin Press.

Zapata, F. S. (1979) 'Trade-union action and political behavior of the Chilean miners of Chuquicamata', in Cohen, R., Gutkind, P. C. W., and Brazier, P. (eds.) *Peasants and proletarians: the struggles of Third World workers*, Monthly Review Press, 460–81. First published in 1975 as 'Action syndicale et comportement politique des mineurs chiliens de Chuquicamata', *Sociologie du Travail* 17. 225–42.

Zipf, G. K. (1941) *National unity and disunity*, Principia Press.

Zola, E. (1877) *L'assommoir*, Bibliothèque Charpentier.

NAME INDEX

SUBJECT INDEX

elections, 134-5
El Salvador, 53
  San Salvador, 88, 101
environmental concerns, 184, 196
Ethiopia, 6, 28
ethnic identity:
  and formal organizations, 120, 143-5
  and political conflict, 142-5
  and social ties, 119-21
export orientation and urban structure,
  39-44

Gabon, 53
  Libreville, 116
Gambia:
  Banjul, 170
Ghana, 6, 29, 53, 55, 63, 204 n27
  Accra, 55, 72, 78, 81, 153
  Cape Coast, 81
  Kumasi, 81
  Takoradi, 81
growth centres, 33, 173-5, 189-90
Guatemala, 7, 53, 121, 154, 203 n18, 209
  n28
  Guatemala City, 30
  Quezaltenango, 30
Guayana programme, 190, 191, 192
guerrilla:
  rural, 155, 156-7, 159, 161
  urban, 157, 158, 159, 160-1
Guinea, 6
Guinea-Bissau, 156
Guyana, 53, 126
  Georgetown, 126

Haiti, 209 n28
Honduras, 10, 53
Hong Kong, 66, 102, 204 n29
housing, 81-115
  and economic policy, 97-8, 102-3
  conditions, 81-3, 85-7, 94-6
  politics of, 107-15
  public, 101-3
  rental, 82-3, 86-7, 88-9, 93-4, 103
  see also spontaneous housing

India, 6, 10, 18, 19, 28, 29, 30, 42, 45, 53,
  54, 56, 59, 62, 65, 66, 67, 72, 81, 95,
  97, 104, 108, 110, 125, 126, 140-1,
  142, 144-5, 153, 155, 165, 174, 175,
  177, 189, 200 n10, n13, 201 n25,
  202 n4, n5, n7, 203 n12, 207 n9
  Ahmedabad, 205 n8
  Bombay, 14, 40, 54, 81, 126, 144-5,
    204 n20
  Calcutta, 14, 39, 40, 81, 94, 95, 102,
    116, 171

Chandigarh, 191
Delhi, 14, 20, 40, 50-1, 88, 98, 204 n20
Hyderabad, 14
Kanpur, 121
Madras, 14, 40
Meerut, 118
Nagpur, 135, 141
Indonesia, 6, 28, 42, 53, 56, 61, 66, 78, 79,
  118, 156
  Djakarta (Batavia), 39, 50, 76, 81, 94, 98,
    118, 188, 203 n15, n17, n18, 204 n30
  Medan, 118
industrialization, 44-7
  and foreign interests, 46-7
  capital-intensive, 65-6
  export-oriented, 44
  import substitution, 44-5
  rural, 184
inequality, 8, 10, 24-6, 70, 137
  in rural areas, 49-50, 51
  see also regional disparities; rural-urban
    disparities
infant mortality, 52-3
informal sector, 72-6
  incomes, 75
  linkages with formal sector, 75-6
  size of, 74
Iran, 7, 53, 136, 158-61
  Qom, 158
  Tabriz, 158
Iraq, 7, 53, 104
  Baghdad, 20
irregular settlements, see spontaneous
  housing
Ivory Coast, 6, 134

Jamaica, 53, 179
  Kingston, 30
  Montego Bay, 30, 90
Jordan, 53

Kampuchea, see Cambodia
Kenya, 6, 29, 39, 53, 73, 74, 126, 202 n7,
  203 n23
  Nairobi, 14, 71, 100, 104, 112, 125, 126,
    201 n26, 204 n23
Khmer Republic, see Cambodia
kinship
  in migration, 54-5, 60, 78
  networks, 121, 132

labour aristocracy, see protected labour
  force
labour market
  brokers, 78
  fragmentation, 77-80
  segmentation, 77-9